The Keystone Kid

Tales of Early Hollywood

Coy Watson, Jr.

SANTA MONICA PRESS

Published by:
Santa Monica Press LLC
P.O. Box 1076
Santa Monica, CA 90406-1076
1-800-784-9553
www.santamonicapress.com
books@santamonicapress.com

S A N T A
M O N I C A
P R E S S

Printed in the United States

Book design by Ohm on the Range Design

Santa Monica Press books are available at special quantity discounts when purchased in bulk by corporations, organizations, or groups. Please call our Special Sales department at 1-800-784-9553.

This book is intended to provide general information. The publisher, author, distributor, and copyright owner are not engaged in rendering health, medical, legal, financial, or other professional advice or services. The publisher, author, distributor, and copyright owner are not liable or responsible to any person or group with respect to any loss, illness, or injury caused or alleged to be caused by the information found in this book.

ISBN 1-891661-21-3

Library of Congress Cataloging-in-Publication Data

Watson, Coy, 1912-
       The Keystone kid : tales of early Hollywood / by Coy Watson, Jr.
       p.   cm.
       ISBN 1-891661-21-3
         1. Watson, Coy, 1912- 2. Motion picture actors and actresses—United States—Biography.
         3. Child actors—United States—Biography. I. Title.

PN2287.W358 A3 2001
791.43'028'092—dc21   [B]   2001040024

On the cover: Coy Watson, Sr. (as a Keystone Cop) and Coy Watson, Jr. share a scene in A Nick-of-Time Hero *(1921).*

TABLE OF CONTENTS

*Dedicated with love and gratitude to Mom and Dad and to the pioneers
who made the first silent moving pictures in California*

J N F

The five generations of James Coy Watson

ACKNOWLEDGMENTS

I am indebted to:

"Willie" Watson, my wife, who has always been my thoughtful partner and helpmate.

Pattie and Mark Price, my daughter and son-in-law, who encouraged me and labored to organize and ready the stories and caption the pictures for publication.

Dr. Jack E. Hoes, my cousin, and his wife Lorinda, who edited many of the stories.

Delmar Watson, my brother, who helped me select the photos.

Eileen Pacello, my neighbor and friend who typed the manuscript.

And to all those who, through the years, encouraged me to write my stories.

ABOUT THE PICTURES

The pictures seen with my stories are a part of our Watson Family Collection of over a million photographs. Some were enlarged from a single frame of motion picture film.

The collection was begun in Los Angeles County, at the turn of the century, when our Grandpa James Watson started taking pictures. During the following one hundred years, ten Watsons became professional news photographers.

To date, the collection includes photographs from old friends, fellow news photographers, news picture syndicates, motion picture studios, directors, stars, and other collectors of Hollywood history.

Thanks to Will Fowler, Marc Wanamaker and Art Worden for photos added to our Watson collection.

INTRODUCTION

Entertainment in America began long before there were moving pictures. During the first unsettled years in the West, early pioneer families gathered around campfires, in barns and taverns to tell stories, sing songs and dance to entertain and encourage each other. In cities, both large and small, meeting halls and show houses were built to amuse and help tired citizens forget their troubles for awhile.

In time, entertainment boomed as audiences crowded into theaters to see stage plays, operas, musical shows and melodramas. From grandstands, entertainment-hungry crowds cheered horse races, circuses, and were on their feet when cowboys and Indians chased each other in Wild West shows.

Douglas Fairbanks and Dad, early moviemakers

In 1885, the country's show-goers saw vaudeville, a new type of variety show that presented six to eight surprisingly different acts. Performers from all parts of the country included singers, dancers, tumblers, mind readers, jugglers, magicians, animal acts, music of all kinds and stand-up comedians. To guarantee fresh entertainment, the bill was changed each week. By 1888, stage plays and vaudeville were America's number one choice for entertainment. That was it. There was nothing better and nothing more was expected.

By 1889, just a year before my Dad was born, two American inventors in the state of New Jersey created a machine with a lens on a large three-by-three-foot box that photographed the movements of dancers, tumblers and animal acts on long, thin, one-inch strips of sensitized celluloid. When the chemically coated strips were processed and rolled through the same machine, the bright light of a newly invented electric light bulb enlarged and projected the tiny, flickering, moving images to many times their size onto a large, white screen. Those flickering pictures on that screen gave birth to an industry that would, in time, become the world's most popular form of entertainment.

Twenty years passed before the "flicker makers" reduced the box to a handy size and improved their machine enough to produce acceptable moving pictures. By 1909, movie producers came to realize they needed better weather and more reliable sunlight to make good movies. With their cameras and actors they followed the sun west to a peaceful town called Edendale in a sunny canyon near Los Angeles, California.

It was in Edendale that the first movie colony in the West was established, and for five prosperous years made moving-picture history. Production success realized in Edendale called for growth and expansion but the canyon was too small. Ten miles west of Edendale lay an aggressive agricultural community called Hollywood. All the producers, except Mack Sennett, who remained until 1926, left Edendale, bought acres of land in Hollywood, built larger studios and made bigger pictures. With the colony gone, Edendale faded and became known only as what had been "Hollywood's Garden of Edendale," where the first movies were made.

Mom and Mary Pickford, lovely movie pioneers

For years, hand-cranked cameras continued to turn out good, flickering, silent, black and white movies until improved cameras with electric motors produced better pictures. Actors, stars and directors came to Hollywood from other moviemaking countries to work for the industry's best producers. Then came sound; moving pictures learned to talk and sing. Finally, in beautiful color, American motion pictures were seen on silver screens around the world! Hollywood became known as "The Motion Picture Capital of the World."

Today, moviemaking in Edendale is long gone but it will never be forgotten. My stories about growing up in Edendale are reminders of those first interesting days when the motion picture business—and Hollywood—got their start.

❖   ❖   ❖   ❖   ❖

Famous early silent film star and specially honored Academy Award winner, Lillian Gish, once said: "I've lived long enough to know that the whole truth is never told in history texts. Only the people who have lived through an era and who are the participants in the drama, as it occurred, know the truth. The people of each generation are the accurate historians of their time."

Lillian Gish

I've taken the words of Miss Gish to heart; not as an historian but as one born to live and grow with the first 20 years of the motion picture business in California. With a good memory and the help of two *real* motion picture pioneers (Mom and Dad), I have labored to write some true, simple, everyday stories of my boyhood. In addition to being a remembrance of the early days of filmmaking, this is also a remembrance of a time in America. It was a slower, less complicated time that no longer exists, and that many people miss deeply.

I was born in little Edendale in 1912, next door to Mack Sennett's studio. This was the same year that Mr. Sennett, the "King of Comedy," gave birth to his world famous "Keystone Cops."

I appeared in my first motion picture when I was nine months old. Before I could walk or talk, I appeared in many of the first "Keystone Comedies." I heard stories about the early days of West Coast moviemaking and pioneering the industry from my dad and mom from as far back as I can remember. I was "Little Coy" or "The Keystone Kid"!

As I grew up, Sennett's movie sets were my playground and his family of early moviemakers and stars were my friends and playmates. They were the creative pioneers that started the motion picture industry in Edendale and on into Hollywood. I acted in over 60 movies over an 18 year period, from 1913 to 1930. Then I went on to be a Los Angeles newspaper photographer and often covered stories about Hollywood, her people and the movie industry. Eventually I pioneered television film production and put some of Hollywood's biggest stars on television for the first time. But those childhood days in Edendale and the fun of the movie lots are the times and memories that are closest to my heart.

Here's how Dad, Mom and I remember those years . . . . My stories are like the days of your life, some are better than others.

— Coy Watson, Jr.

EDENDALE

1905

Edendale was a typical little western town a few blocks north of the Echo Park Lake in the northwest district of Los Angeles. Its earliest settlers, who thought it resembled an idyllic paradise where our ancestors' history began, probably named the beautiful place.

As early as 1905, a seven-mile-long electric railroad ran from downtown Los Angeles to-and-through the center of Edendale, along the bottom of the dale on Allesandro Avenue.

Allesandro Street (later Glendale Boulevard) in Edendale, circa 1905

The town's dusty main street was later paved and became known as Glendale Boulevard. Both sides of the street were studded with wooden buildings, housing a grocery store, a bakery, a pool hall, a barber shop, a small cafe, a drugstore and the brick Clifford Street School on the side of the hill. The residents were hard-working pioneer families of ranchers, farmers, cowboys, storekeepers, carpenters and some business folks who worked in Los Angeles. Here, also, were men and women who traveled and performed with circuses, rodeos and tent shows around the country.

My Dad, James Coy Watson, Sr., who was a resident of Edendale, was born in Belleville, Ontario, Canada on April 14, 1890. He came to America with his family when he was five years old. He lived with his parents, four brothers and three sisters on a two-acre farm near the end of the streetcar line, on the north edge of town.

Dad as a young man, age 17

Like most kids of his time, Dad did anything to earn a nickel. He watered the neighbors' cows in Echo Park Lake, ran errands and sold newspapers on the streets of downtown Los Angeles. The San Francisco earthquake and fire in 1906 were good for newspaper sales. He attended Logan Street School but dropped out while in seventh grade when he didn't like his report card.

At age 12 he went to work to help support his family. Dressed in a gray letter carrier's uniform, he rode his white pony, Billy, delivering Special Delivery mail for the U.S. Postal Service to the residents in the hills and around the "City of the Angels."

There weren't many good roads then and horseback was the best way to get around. He liked meeting the people but the job didn't pay enough for a boy helping to support his family, so he turned in his suit. With a letter of recommendation from the Post Office Superintendent, he was hired to deliver packages for the Ville de Paris Department Store, the largest in the territory. It was more fun and it paid more money.

Dad on "Billy"

The James Watson Family (early 1900s). Left to right, top row: Bill and Vic. Center row: Rally, Coy (my dad), Grandpa James, Herb. Front row: Ethel and Grandma holding Amy.

Watson family at Sunday dinner (1905). Left to right: Uncle Bill, Vic, Aunt Amy, Grandma holding baby Hazel, Coy (dad), Grandpa and Aunt Ethel.

With mixed feelings he gave up his pony for a one-cylinder, gasoline driven motorcycle. That put him in the "jet set" of his day!

EXTREME DANGER

1908

It was just another one of those sunny, cloudless days in downtown Los Angeles in 1908; nothing unusual was expected to happen but something strange was going on at the old Chinese laundry.

On what had once been quiet streets, the town folk and their horses were getting used to progress and learning to live with the disturbing sounds of noisy combustible engines. Rolling along Broadway, my dad sat astride his motorcycle as it popped puffs of gray smoke swirling out behind him. His black tie fluttering over his shoulder was flapping against the large canvas bag of packages strapped on his back. Carefully he rode through the slowly moving street traffic made up of horse-drawn vehicles, automobiles and bicycles. He was glad to be working, and even though he liked his job, he knew he could do better. Surprised at a busy street crossing, he laughed and waved in answer to a loud, "Ride 'em Cocky!" from a couple of cowboy friends waving their hats.

As he putted down Olive Street at Seventh, he approached the Chinese laundry building. To his surprise, he could see a group of people gathered beside the old, wooden structure. Rolling closer, he saw eight or ten men and women standing dead still along the weather-beaten picket fence with all their eyes focused on something happening in the rear yard. He cut the engine power and coasted to a stop. He got off and cautiously pushed his motor up to the fence beside the watchers.

"What's going on here?" he asked. An old woman at his side put a shaky finger to her puckered lips and gave him a loud "Shush!" Just 20 feet from where he was standing, under a large white umbrella, near a polished wooden box atop a tripod, two men stood talking. A camera lens stuck out one side of what had to be a camera.

A man, wearing a cap with the visor down the back, stood beside the camera. A man in a white shirt, leather leggings and a straw hat walked from the camera toward an odd looking structure: a large room with a floor, only three walls, and no roof or ceiling. It was built of lightweight lumber with long, wooden boards bracing the walls from the outside. Inside the room, it was like a theater scene—drapes, a carpet on the floor, walls decorated with strange designs and furniture to look like the dwelling of some foreign country.

The man in the straw hat seemed to be the boss and he was gesturing with his arms as he spoke, giving orders to two men and a woman dressed in heavy foreign costumes, standing in the center of the open set. Facing the camera and the sun, the three watched and listened carefully, then responded with nods of understanding. After a few minutes, the instructor turned and walked back and sat down in a folding chair next to the camera. He looked up at the cameraman, then over to the actors. He put the small end of a three-foot megaphone to his mouth and to the surprise of the watchers, in a loud, booming voice, he yelled, "Camera! Action!" The cameraman started to turn a crank on the side of the camera. The actors began to move around acting very disturbed, talking to each other and making broad, dramatic gestures with their arms and hands. Yes, the moving picture camera was photographing the scene for a motion picture.

The fascinated, silent viewers had never seen such actions. As the crank turned they heard the boss pleading dramatically with the actors. "Put more feeling in it. You are in extreme danger. You could be killed. Look worried." And they did!

A jeweled saber and a long rifle taken from behind a drape caused the actors more distress. Sparkling articles were lifted from

Sunset Boulevard, Los Angeles, 1908

a large chest on a table and handled cautiously. The scene was taking on a mysterious atmosphere when the commanding voice shouted, "Cut! Cut! That's good!" The crank stopped turning; the actors stopped acting, put down the props and began fanning themselves. "Let's move in, Tommy," the boss said to the cameraman. "We need a close-up of the sultan with the jewels." He carried his chair and megaphone onto the set, followed by the cameraman with the tripod and camera.

At the picket fence, the thoroughly entertained audience had become California's first gathering of moving picture fans watching history in the making—scenes photographed for what was to become the first complete moving picture filmed entirely in the western United States. Dad was impressed and stuck around to learn why the moving picture company had come to Los Angeles to make the picture.

Moviemaking had started years earlier in New York and Chicago. From the beginning, movie producers found making motion pictures to be expensive and time consuming. Due to the low sensitivity of the film to light, they learned early that in order to obtain well-exposed pictures it was necessary to photograph all scenes in bright sunlight. The weather was unpredictable and waiting weeks for blue skies and sunshine was downright discouraging and costly. Then, one historical rainy day in Chicago, moving picture producer Colonel William Selig, head of Selig Film Company, heard there was a place in Southern California where the sun shone every day. What an ideal place to make movies! The rumor proved to be true. Selig had an idea for a picture story to produce, so he sent a company out west to film it. The director rented the drying areas of a laundry, and after the clotheslines were removed and a set constructed, the shooting began. The director and cameraman found all the locations and backgrounds they needed to photograph the picture in and around Los Angeles—in the hills, parks, mountains, canyons and on the beautiful sandy beaches of the peaceful ocean. They discovered the place where more moving pictures would be photographed than any other area in the world.

The first picture was *The Power of the Sultan*, directed by Francis Boggs and photographed by Thomas Persen. The star was Hobart Bosworth; the co-stars were Stella Adams and Tom Santshi. During the 1920s, I worked in two pictures with Hobart Bosworth and one with Tom Santshi.

Selig's studio—and Edendale's first studio—1909

Mr. Bosworth, Dad learned, had been a well-known stage actor back east. At the peak of his career, he contracted tuberculosis. After the removal of one of his lungs in order to save his life, he came west to regain his health in the warm, dry Los Angeles weather. Unable to speak with his formerly strong stage voice, Bosworth believed his acting career to be over. To his surprise, director Boggs rediscovered him. Bosworth's ability to act in silent moves, the new entertainment business, without the need of his stage voice, earned him starring roles in many early California silent pictures. Dad believed Mr. Bosworth was the west's first moving picture star.

When the picture was completed and ran before audiences back east, it was a box office success. Selig was surprised and pleased with the low cost of photographing the picture. Director Boggs gave full credit to the reliably endless days of valuable sunshine.

Convinced that California was the place to make movies, Selig bought a block of land in the center of a little place called Edendale, a half-mile from my dad's home. It was ten miles east of an agricultural community called Hollywood, and five miles northwest of the Los Angeles City Hall. There, in Edendale, in 1909, years before filmmakers C.B. DeMille or D.W. Griffith came to Hollywood to make pictures, Selig built the first permanent motion picture studio in California and started making motion pictures.

A RIDE WITH TWO PRIZES

1909

The movie business did interest Dad, but he wasn't an actor and he knew nothing about movie cameras. What he had learned behind the laundry, however, did make him think about his future. He gave notice and quit the store to learn the plastering trade from his motorcycle buddy, Lawrence "Hooley" Webb.

Starting at the bottom, he mixed the plaster, called "mud." He carried it in the hod and learned to spread it on building walls and ceilings. Dad stood only 5 feet 10 inches, but he was well built, muscular and wiry. "Hooley" Webb and "Cocky" Coy Watson made a good team and spread a lot of mud. They worked hard and their friendship grew stronger.

"Hooley" and Dad head for Oregon

The moviemaking in Edendale didn't hold the pair and in 1909 "Hooley" and Dad decided to go north. On their motorcycles they headed for Deschutes County in Oregon to stake a claim on some good farmland. Motorcycles or automobiles had never before made the trip they planned. The wagon roads were bad and some sections they traveled were without roads. Dad said they sometimes felt they carried their motorcycles as far as they rode them. The lack of gasoline and the absence of bridges over streams made the going tough. At times, a dry creek bed made the best course; they had to move carefully along the deep rutted horse and wagon roads.

Dad and Hooley never made it to stake their claim. They

stopped in Medford, Oregon, where their arrival into town caused quite a stir. "Two boys rode motorcycles from Los Angeles to Medford," the newspaper story said. It went on to give all the interesting details on how they braved the elements. They were famous and became quite popular overnight. A couple of days after their arrival, the local motorcycle dealer staged a race to promote sales.

Dad (1910); Mom (1908)

Dad signed up to race, then borrowed a cook's hat from a local chef and bought a four-ounce can of ether from the drugstore. As the racers neared the starting line, Dad put the hat on his head and the ether in his gas tank. When the gun fired, the field of about eight motors and riders were off to a running-and-push, then into-the-saddle start! The crowd cheered as the motorcycles began popping. A cute, little girl named Golda Wimer was one of the excited spectators.

Dad's practice on pushing his motorcycle for much of his 700-mile trip got him into a good place up front with only one rider ahead of him. As Dad had expected, the ether was burning hot, making the one-piston engine fire like a pecking woodpecker. They came to a turn and Dad looked back over his shoulder in time to see the two goggled riders behind him weaving and swaying. A second look back and the riders ran off the track onto a plowed field, overcome by the ether fumes! At another turn there was nobody behind him but one rider ahead and Dad was about to overtake him. As Dad fired past him, he realized that his burning ether fumes had put some of his competitors to sleep in their saddles. He had not counted on that, but

A dream Mom couldn't imagine—nine children. Top, left to right: Gloria, Louise, Mom, Vivian. Middle: Coy Jr., Harry, Billy. Front: Delmar, Bobs, Garry and Dad.

he was laughing as he crossed the finish line as the winner! The prize was five gallons of gas and a case of oil, which was gratefully received. Later, Dad only smiled when one of the riders asked, "What kind of gas were you burning in the race?"

Mom and Dad had not met at the time of the big race, but she had seen him race and he had noticed her and liked what he saw.

My mother, Golda Gladdis Wimer, was born in a little town called Stayton, near Salem, Oregon. She later moved south to Medford, where she attended school and was a good student. She was a little girl—slight, feisty and full of zip! If there was any real rugged work to be done, Golda Gladdis could and would do it. She made all the quick trips to the grocery store. When volunteers were needed to pick blackberries for a few cents a pail, my mother was first in line. Her oldest sister, Lollie, was a more prim and proper girl, but they loved each other. Baby sister, Ola, was too young and

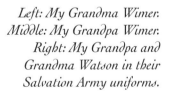

Left: My Grandma Wimer. Middle: My Grandpa Wimer. Right: My Grandpa and Grandma Watson in their Salvation Army uniforms.

brother Newt was younger. So, "Call Golda," or "Let's send Golda, she can do it," was the way she grew up. Doing it all for everybody! Her mother was sickly and in bed much of the time and depended on Golda the most. The good Lord must have planned her early training to prepare her to bear and raise nine children. What a loving, well-prepared, understanding mother she became.

A couple of nights after the big race, Mom and some girlfriends were standing on the street talking to some fellows. Dad came along, saw the happy group and there was Mom. He wanted to meet her but he did the wrong thing. He stepped up behind her and ran his finger up her back, hoping to get her attention and have a pleasant introduction. Instead, she turned her 5' 3" self around and with a mean, Irish eye-to-eye look, she said, "Stop that you mutt!"

She was ready to fight! He apologized but stood his ground. He told her he just wanted to meet her. I never heard if she excused him, but he asked for a date and got it. They went roller-skating. The two good skaters made a nice-looking couple. The rink was in the natatorium, a part of the town's sport center. During the summer, the indoor swimming pool was the popular thing. When winter set in, the roller rink floor was put over the pool. On the cold, snowy days and nights, the smart set mixed and kept warm. On one such night, my future Mom and Dad sat for a rest and talked. Dad learned that Mom's folks were Pennsylvania Dutch. They came west on the Oregon Trail in covered wagons in the 1800s. Mother's grandfather, Jacob Wimer, a typical little, long-whiskered Dutchman, lived to be over 100 years old. After the Wimers settled in Oregon, Mom's Uncle Jones (an Irish Methodist Circuit Preacher) built one of the first churches in Oregon. As he traveled his territory, he took up collections on the street and in saloons—taking donations from farmers, miners and lumbermen. One night in the small town of Jacksonville, near Medford, he received a big donation from a winner of a blackjack game that was played in a barn. That money, plus what he had collected, was enough to build a little, wooden church.

Dad liked her story and the way she told it. She was a proud, little lady. With a smile, he told her his family background. About the same time, her uncle was building his church in Jacksonville, Oregon; his dad (my grandpa, James Watson) was helping General Booth start the Salvation Army in London, England, Grandpa's hometown. He and Amy Kate Ball, from Bath, Wales, were members of a group of young Army soldiers selected and transferred to Canada to start the Army there. Amy helped start the Army's first home for unwed mothers. They were married and after 10 successful years, with 5 children, they were transferred from Canada to Denver, Colorado. Then to Salt Lake City, and finally to Los Angeles, where they did settle down.

Dad and Mom's wedding picture

I think my dad and mom fell in love that night.

On September 23, 1910, in Jacksonville, a small town near Medford, the two were married. Dad was 21 and Mom became 18 the next day. Dressed in their best "Sunday" clothes, they stood in the office of the Justice of the Peace, which was also the office for his feed store and livery stable. Dad's brother, Herb, and Mom's sister, Lollie, stood with

*"George" pulled Mom, me and
Sitka in the wagon*

The Echo Park Avenue horse-car

them. It was a quiet wedding. They both always remembered, with smiles, the scent and sounds of horses as they repeated their vows.

After a few goodbyes, Dad and his little bride, he called her "Goldie," with two suitcases, boarded the train in Medford for Los Angeles and the start of their new life together. The passengers were singing along with them when they arrived four days later. What a day! They were met at the depot by Dad's mother and father with a horse and express wagon and taken to the family home in Edendale.

Later, Mom and Dad rented a small house (Mom called it the "Honeymoon Cottage") on Morton Avenue in the Echo Park District, not far from Edendale, near the entrance to Elysian Park.

Dad had come home and went to work plastering houses. But, for Mom it was a strange place, among new people. She was homesick at times, even though she met and liked some of Dad's friends. Dad helped her overcome her feelings as an outsider and she picked a few friends of her own. Years later, she told me how happy she felt when she learned that she was carrying me. She was so pleased

to think she would have a baby—someone that would belong to just her and Dad. I was made to realize how sad and alone she must have been in those first days with Dad off to work all day.

When Mom wanted to go shopping in downtown Los Angeles, she took a small horse-car, a streetcar about 10 feet long. With a twinkling smile, Mom enjoyed telling how she walked to the car line and for five cents rode the horse-car down to Sunset Boulevard, boarded the Sunset Boulevard car and, with a transfer, rode into Los Angeles.

The horse-car rolled on tracks and was pulled by a horse up the two-mile gentle slope of Echo Park Avenue from Sunset Boulevard to the end of the line. It was operated by a uniformed conductor, who stood on the front platform driving the horse up the avenue, stopping for paying passengers to get on and off. When the car reached the end of the line, the conductor set the brakes and unhitched the horse, who then stepped up onto what had been the front platform, but which had now become the rear platform. A feed bin filled with oats and hay allowed the horse to enjoy eating while the car rolled back down the slope. The conductor had only to apply the brakes for stops as the little trolley coasted down the avenue back to Sunset Boulevard. The well-fed and rested horse was then hitched again to pull the car for another trip up the avenue.

DAD BECOMES A MOVIE COWBOY

1911

My dad entered the picture business in a typical way. In addition to plastering houses, he was earning extra money from stockmen for breaking wild or unruly horses and teaching them to stand, ride, or pull a wagon. One afternoon in 1911 (before I was born), following a breaking session with a tough, strawberry roan, he rolled a cigarette and stood chatting with a couple of cowboys at McGraw's corral on Fargo Street. They were approached by a man wearing "city clothes," who said he was a representative of the Selig Motion Picture Studio. This man could have been California's first motion picture casting director. He was rounding up men and horses to ride in some scenes for a movie to be shot just over the hill from Edendale, near Silver Lake, later known as Mixville. He offered $1.00 a day for each man and $2.00 for a horse! The boys

Dad dressed as New Yorkers thought a Western cowboy should look. Note the cuffs, chaps and six shooter (1911).

A group of California's first motion picture cowboys. Dad is on the lower right.

Buck Jones; Hoot Gibson

laughed and couldn't believe it. It was the best pay for a day's work they had ever known. Two days later, for a day he would never forget, Dad was at the scene with several other cowboys.

He rented out three of his horses and hired himself out to act in one of Hollywood's first "western" movies. That day, working with the makers of early movies, fired his desire to get into the business. It was a new game for everyone and everyone enjoyed it.

Dad rode with his Edendale cowboy pals, some of whom later became "movie stars." Buck Jones, Hoot Gibson, Art Acord and Jack Hoxie—all accomplished rodeo performers and/or expert riders before coming to Hollywood—started in pictures by riding their own horses in this same way for directors like Selig, Griffith and DeMille.

On a typical morning, cowboys chased back and forth over the country's bush-covered rolling hills. After eating a company-supplied paper bag lunch, Dad and the new movie actors took the saddles off their horses and removed their hats, boots and six-shooters. They stripped to loincloths, and donned wigs

The typical silent movie western saloon set

and feathers to become the Indians being pursued. Using stage actors' make-up sticks, the Assistant Director helped them paint each other's faces and bodies with war designs and then handed them bows and arrows. The cameras turned, they rode their horses bareback and chased themselves (the morning's cowboys) over the same hills, yelling and waving the props. Called back the next day, the same cowboys, on the same horses, riding in the same saddles, put on Cavalry uniforms, with sabers at their sides, and carrying an American flag, rode as horse soldiers. They chased the Indians in still another direction over the same hills until the sun went down.

GRANDPA HELPED DAD BUY A HOUSE

1912

Like all young people of their day, Dad and Mom wanted a house of their own to make into a home for

My grandpa, James Watson

a family. Dad also wanted to contract plastering jobs on his own. A horse and wagon to haul his scaffolding and a place to keep them was a necessity.

My grandfather, James Watson, who dabbled in the real estate business, knew my dad and mom were renting a house but wanted a home of their own. He heard of a good property for sale. A little house, on a large lot in a good area, that was reasonably priced. It was on a slightly sloping road, four blocks north of Sunset Boulevard where Berkeley Avenue and Allesandro Avenue crossed.

After work one evening, Dad and his dad drove over for a look at the place. It was an old ranch layout

Above: Berkeley Avenue, looking west from Glendale Blvd. (1912)

Right: Berkeley Avenue, looking west from Glendale Blvd. (1982)

and quite run down, but Dad liked it, even though he knew it would take a lot of fixing. Grandpa wanted him and Mom to have a home, because he knew I was expected to arrive in a few months. Father and son talked things over. Dad didn't have a down payment to start the deal, but he knew he could make monthly payments. To Dad's

Mom and Dad's first home

amazement, Grandpa proposed an offer to the seller.

"My son will buy your property if you will keep my commission as his down payment," Grandpa promised. "He will start making monthly payments in thirty days and will continue to do so until he has bought your property." Dad and the seller agreed. It was a deal! They signed the papers with no money down. Dad and Mom got the house, the man got his money each month and everybody was grateful.

The house was an old, typical early California, ranch-style building with a weathered exterior of

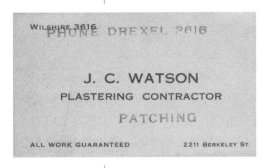

PHONE DREXEL 3616

WILSHIRE 3616

J. C. WATSON
PLASTERING CONTRACTOR

PATCHING

ALL WORK GUARANTEED   2211 BERKELEY ST.

Dad's business card

Dad and his first horse at the new home

A friend of Dad's. Note Dad's corral and wagons. The house on the left and the hill in the background were on Mack Sennett's property (looking northeast).

vertical 1"x12" boards and 3-inch battens. It was set back from the street. The barn, harness shed and corral were also "old timers." Old eucalyptus, apple and loquat trees hinted of the years the structures had stood in the sunshine. There was a vacant lot on each side of the homestead. On the lot above, there was a dying orchard of plum trees and a beautiful, young, bearing fig tree. The lot on the downhill side was planted in alfalfa.

A few months before I was born, Mom and Dad moved in and had an address: 2211 Berkeley Avenue. The house wasn't great, but it was theirs and they appreciated it, even though it needed lots of repair. They immediately began to clean it up and work to make it into a home. Dad bought (and traded) for a wagon and some horses. Successfully, he took on plastering jobs with a pal, Buck Champion, working as his hod carrier.

A HOUSE BECOMES A HOME

1912

Shortly after Dad and Mom cleaned up the house and moved in, Mack Sennett wanted to buy their place so he would then own the entire block. He offered a good price. Dad and Mom considered his offer. It was a tough decision to make, for they were sentimental about the place. They had bought their little one bedroom house in such an unusual deal. Dad had worked hard to improve it. But to sell it? Where else would they live? Such as it was, it was home. They had come to love it, and they refused to

Above: Dad and his friend Mack Sennett

Dad as a Keystone comedy sheriff

Dad as a Keystone comedy outlaw

sell. Mr. Sennett understood, respected Dad, and offered him a job. Dad accepted and became an early member of the happy Keystone family.

Dad never ceased to express his gratitude to his father for the help he gave him, without which he might never have made moving pictures. Years later, Mom confessed what she really felt about the house.

"We never would have bought that house if I'd seen it before they signed the papers. It was the most awful place I'd ever seen in my life! It was dusty and dirty, with filthy old wallpaper hanging off the walls and ceilings. But, a house, a barn, sheds and a corral were what we needed at that time. Dad wanted some horses and a wagon. Renting horses to the studios and working in the pictures himself, he knew was a way to get into the business. From the beginning, he believed movies had a great future." However, in that rustic little "love nest," starting in 1912, over an eighteen-year period, nine Watson "birdies" were "feathered." First a boy, then three girls and then five more boys.

Dad (on left) in an early movie with Madeline Hurlock, Joe Young and Andy Clyde

(1944) Old cowboy friends continue to visit. I'm playing the guitar, Mom is at the piano and Charlie Miller brought his violin. Charlie drove the six-horse stagecoach team in Fox Studio's first sound-on-film western movie, In Old Arizona.

We were all born there. It was the way Mom wanted it; within the walls of that old ranch house in the northwest district of Los Angeles. There were no cement walks or driveways, no fancy green landscaping. Just paths of packed, worn earth in summer and sticky mud in winter. The house was covered with vines of beautiful morning glories and honeysuckle. Other houses on our street, and in the rolling hills of our neighborhood, were more modern and more expensive—but at the end of the day, when the sun had passed over Glendale Boulevard and was setting at the end of Sunset Boulevard, my dog, Sitka, and I headed for that cozy, old home. I couldn't wait to get inside, because I didn't feel that any of those modern houses had the love our home had. Here, we had that feeling known only by loving families.

Dad and Mom showed me early how we lived for each other. "All for one and one for all," was our family pledge. It was love. What else was there? I knew when I got inside that house and closed the door, I was safe. I had shut out all the frightening, scary, unknown things of the world. I do now remember feeling that peace. I never knew anything else. Years later, I came to realize that our

Friends come to visit

home had always been truly happy and full of a real understanding love. It was so real that people came from all around to be near, to be with us, and to be a part of the tender feeling that Dad and Mom had created. Visitors must have felt the kindness and the warmth that was always there.

Our happy and unhappy neighbors and friends were all gladly received. Troubles were heard with caring ears and eased with words and deeds of sincere concern. Much was given from that place, humbly and unselfishly, just for the taking.

The Watson family, still at home in 1932

They came: cowboys, plasterers, muleskinners, circus performers, tramps, hobos, ex-convicts and many silent movie pioneers. Often they were "flat broke." Nearly always they were hungry and sometimes sick. I remember one came with a broken leg. They were welcomed and cared for because Dad and Mom "felt" for them. All comers left feeling a bit of the caring those two people had for each other and their children. Folks sensed the simple, honest love that filled that old Western home, "Where seldom was heard a discouraging word" from anyone!

A MYSTERIOUS CALLER THE DAY I WAS BORN

1912

When asked, Dad remembered what he called one of the happiest days of his life! He liked the way Mom told about the unbelievable, strange thing that happened the morning I was born, November 16, 1912. She had to be in the "right" mood to tell it. Here's her story:

My Grandma Watson

"I was lying in bed almost asleep, when I thought I heard the strange sound of heavy shoes stepping on our old, wooden porch. It was odd. Then a knock at the door was scary. We weren't expecting anyone. The doctor had left an hour before into the cold, November morning. But now, who could be at our front door? Was I dreaming? Or, could I have been half-asleep? No, I heard Coy walking to see who was there. I strained and heard low voices over the soothing sound and smell of the burning wood crackling in the stove that warmed our home.

"I was weak and woozy. Little Coy had been born about 6:00 A.M., two hours earlier, at day break. Grandma Watson had wrapped him in a blue blanket and laid him beside me.

"'This woman wants to see the baby,' Big Coy's voice shook my eyes wide open and I stared. There, walking behind him toward my bed was a very little, strange looking, old woman. The brown knitted stocking cap pulled down to cover her ears matched the long, heavy coat that buttoned up around her neck.

"Who was she? Coy stepped beside me as the old gal slowly pulled off one glove, then the other and put them in her coat pocket. She stopped at the foot of the bed and just stood there. If Coy

I took a look at the world and liked what I saw

Big Coy and Little Coy

hadn't been there, I would have screamed. I was afraid of her. She looked at me, leaned over the bed, screwed up her wrinkled face and strained her blue eyes to get a good look at my baby. What did she really want? Why? Nobody knew I had a baby—only Coy, Grandma Watson, the Doctor and I. How did she know? Who was she? She stood there looking at us. Then she slowly turned to Coy. Did he know her?

"'May I hold the baby?' she asked in a clear, soft voice. My heart jumped. Hold our baby? I looked at Coy and before I knew it, as if hyp-notized, he bent over and lifted Little Coy up from my arm to his and turned to the woman. I was horrified when I saw her hold out her arms to take my baby from Coy.

"Grandma Watson just stood in the door of the kitchen and smiled peacefully. Coy told the old woman how proud he was of his baby boy and me. I couldn't believe what I was seeing! Then it dawned on me, Coy and Grandma Watson both thought I knew this woman—that she was a neighbor or a friend of mine from up the avenue somewhere. I knew Coy didn't know her. There the old thing stood with my baby in her arms.

"I started to speak when she looked at Coy and asked, with her eyes half closed, 'Do you have a silver dollar?' As Coy put his hand into his pocket, she opened the blanket and brought out Little Coy's left arm. Wondering 'why,' Coy pleasingly picked the only silver dollar he had from what I knew was a handful of pennies and nickels. She reached out her bony, wrinkled, old right hand and took the coin from him. What in the world will she do next?

"I watched with amazement and fear. What's going on here? I was frightened. Grandma and Coy moved beside her to watch. I raised my head from my pillow. Then the mysterious, old woman tenderly took that little pink hand and tiny fingers into hers, care-fully opened it and pressed the big silver dollar on it. She lowered her face close to Little Coy's and in a low, strange soft voice said something like, 'There—that is a good sign for the little fellow.' Then, with her hand over his, she squeezed the little hand around the dollar. 'May you always be happy and healthy. I know you will never want.' She looked down at me with such tenderness; I tried to smile back. Then she looked back at the baby and handed the dollar back to Coy. As she patted the baby on the back, I heard the dollar drop back into Coy's pocket of change. Tenderly she handed Little Coy back to Coy. I settled back onto my pillow. What was that all about? Had she performed some sort of ceremony or ritual? Or was it a blessing?

"The old woman took her gloves from her pocket and slowly pulled one on as she glanced at Grandma, who stepped back smiling. Coy put Little Coy down beside me. The old woman stood very still, looked straight into my eyes and with a tender smile nodded to me and turned to leave. I wanted to speak. What could I say? Then I raised up on my elbow. I wanted to see her feet. The poor soul was wearing a pair of men's heavy work shoes. She pulled on her other glove as Coy followed her to the door. 'Thanks for the visit. Come again anytime.' I heard him say, as he closed the front door. I lay back, closed my eyes and heard the sound of those heavy shoes stepping across and off the creaky, wooden porch.

Dad with motorcycle (1912)

"'Who was that nice old lady?' Coy asked, smiling as he came into the room. I didn't even open my eyes, just said, 'Coy I never saw that old woman before in my life!' I pulled my baby to me and put a big kiss on his forehead, took a slow, deep breath and tried to go to sleep. We never saw that mysterious, kind old woman again."

Dad told me, "After your Mother and you went to sleep, I left you in your Grandma Watson's care. Anxious and pleased to spread the good news of your arrival to our friends and our early honeymoon neighbors, I fired up my motorcycle. In the cold morning air, as fast as the thing would safely roll, I putt-putted up Echo Park Avenue and then up quiet Morton Avenue. With a chuckle to myself, I took a deep breath and over the noisy sound of the engine, I started calling out; 'It's a boy! It's a boy!' Riding along, every two or three seconds—'It's a boy!' At the end of the road, I turned around and came back down still yelling. To my surprise, doors were opened and faces were looking out smiling. What a proud day it was for your mother and me."

SITKA, MY FIRST PLAYMATE

1913

One of the most significant "players" in my early life was my dog, Sitka. He was my first friend. We were about the same age. After "Billy" the dog was killed, Mom would say: "Dad brought Sitka home about six months after you arrived. A man heard that Dad had a new baby and asked him if he would like to have a dog for the baby. Dad asked, 'Why do you want to get rid of the dog?' The man replied, "Because I got the dog for my baby, who died last week. The dog misses the baby. I thought it might be good if the dog could be with a new baby—he was very attached to the baby.' Dad asked the man what kind of a dog it was. The man said he was three-quarters Malamute and one-quarter wolf and was about six months old. His mother had been the lead dog of a sled that carried mail into the Klondike during the gold rush in Alaska. Interested, Dad went to the man's house, liked what he saw, and brought Sitka home.

"He was very alert, even as a puppy. You two got along so well from the very beginning. You played together and were constant companions.

"Later, when you started to try to walk, he helped you learn. You would stand up and hang onto his collar and as he walked slowly around the room, you took steps with him. Later, you walked around outside in the yard, still hanging on.

"If we looked out and you two were nowhere to be seen, we figured you had gone for a walk up Allesandro Avenue toward Sennett's Studio or up the hill to Mohawk Street. We never worried. We knew you were safe with Sitka. I'd just call, 'Sitka, come, bring him home,' or Dad would whistle for him. We'd wait and watch. It wouldn't be long till we'd see you two coming down the path across the field, you clinging to his collar!

"Often we could see that you didn't want to come home, so Sitka would be pushing you to force you to step and walk toward home. It was a cute sight, watching that dog bring you home. The neighbors marveled at Sitka's sense. He wouldn't let anyone near you for any reason. Sitka and you grew older and closer day by day."

My first trips to the "show" or movies were made in a baby buggy pushed by my Mom. Here's how she told the story. "I always tried, but never could make Sitka stay home. I'd go to the theater and park your buggy in the lobby. I'd sit down, with you on my lap, settle back to watch the show while you went to sleep. Just

when the picture got interesting, down the aisle, shining his flash-
light over the audience, would come the theater manager looking
for me. I knew it! Sitka had arrived, entered the theater, and was
again lying beside your buggy. 'Mrs. Watson, would you please
come up and put your dog out? We're afraid of him. The men can't

Playmates

pass near him and the
buggy to get into the
restroom.' I'd go to the
lobby and make Sitka
go outside. He'd wait
near the exit door until
somebody opened it
to leave and then he'd
slip back in. After I
made three or four trips
up and down the aisle,
in response to, 'Mrs.
Watson, he's in again!'
the management de-
cided to allow folks to
exit by the entrance
door and leave the
dog and buggy alone.
When the show was
over and we were
ready to leave, the manager would hold the exit door open for us.
Many a time, as we passed out, he would remark, 'That dog sure
loves that baby, doesn't he?'"

Fortunately, such proceedings only occurred when Dad wasn't
home to baby-sit Sitka and me. More often, Mom, on her own with
a friend or neighbor, was able to enjoy a bag of popcorn and a movie
without concern for the men's room problem.

MOVIES CREATED JOBS

1913

Many families in the Edendale area took an early
part in making their town the west's first motion picture colony. The four studios—Selig, Bison, Norberg and Sennett
took over New York Moving Picture Company's Studio. They offered
a variety of opportunities, with new lines of work for talents in many
fields. The first movie crews from the east were very few in numbers.

Increasingly, more and more people were needed to make more and more pictures. Directors and writers were needed to create the stories. Carpenters built sets to look like rooms. Painters decorated and dressed the sets with drapes and furnishings. Tailors and dressmakers made the costumes. The prop men supplied the props for the actors. The cameramen photographed the scenes that showed the combined work accomplished through the efforts of each separate department. Finally, the directors and cutters edited the scenes of film to make them into finished motion pictures.

There was work to be done in Edendale and the people learned to do it. Many newspaper writers became top directors. Frank Capra and Craig Hutchinson were two of them. Making motion pictures in Edendale had become a wonderful way of life. Most of my neighbors had something to do with the picture industry. Dozens of us in school were the sons or daughters or the brothers and sisters of folks in the movies. Davey and Jack Crockett's dad, Ernie, became a cameraman. Bub and Carlos' dad was a carpenter. "Pinky" Bowman's dad worked in the mill. Leora's mother, Sunshine Hart, became a character actor. My next-door playmates were Sonny and Sister Holmgren. Their dad was foreman of the Keystone carpenters.

Mom's dad was a cabinetmaker in Medford, Oregon. With a little persuasion, my dad got him to pack up Mom's younger sister, Ola, and brother, Newt, and come to Los Angeles to live. Grandpa Wimer became the maker of the windows and doors for the sets at Mack Sennett's Studio.

My third grade classmate, Don Black, had a brother, Art Black, who started in pictures at Mack Sennett's Studio and later became Frank Capra's assistant director on *Mr. Smith Goes to Washington* and *It's a Wonderful Life*.

I traded postage stamps on Sunday afternoons with Billy Hornbeck, whose folks helped settle Edendale. Billy started as an errand boy at Sennett's, where he learned to cut film. He became one of the world's greatest film editors and went to England to edit many of Alexander Korda's classic pictures—*The Four Feathers* was just one. In America, he edited dozens of big productions. For one of his best remembered, he teamed with Frank Capra. Their levels of perfection were seen in *It's a Wonderful Life*.

Benny Coleman, our neighbor, and his brother Ed, became photographers. Ed shot the *Dragnet* pictures for Jack Webb. Dad's pal, Ray Hunt, lived across Effie Street from Sennett's. We kids gathered there and his cute wife would let me pump her player piano for "Yes, Sir, That's My Baby!" She helped me sing "I'm

Forever Blowing Bubbles." Dad encouraged Ray and he became one of the best comedy prop-men in Hollywood. Later he propped for the Three Stooges' pictures directed by Jules White and Del Lord.

Jules and his three brothers, Jack, Sam, and Ben lived in Edendale when they were young. The four made movies into the 1960s. In 1904, before movies came to Edendale, Dad remembered that he took a special delivery letter on his pony, Billy, to the Whites. He then treated the White brothers to rides on his pony along Allesandro Avenue. A small story for a smaller world: During World War II, Jules' son, Harold, served with me in the Coast Guard Photo Section, 40 years after our dads laughed together in Edendale!

Chester Conklin

Most of the original actors came west from New York and Chicago, where they had performed in vaudeville or acted in plays on the legitimate stage. Many settled in Edendale, near the studios, if they could find a house for rent. Others took apartments or flats a couple of miles south down Alvarado Street in the Westlake Park area.

Some of the first people to arrive in the new colony were Gloria Swanson and her husband, Wallace Beery, who became our neighbors across the street. There were also Mabel Normand (Sennett's girlfriend), Charlie Murray, Mack Swain, Bobby Vernon, Dot Farley, and Ford Sterling, who became the Chief of the Keystone Cops. Later, Marie Dressler, Slim Summerville, Chester Conklin, Charlie Chaplin, Roscoe (Fatty) Arbuckle and his wife, Minta, joined them. Louise Fazenda lived with her mother on Alvarado at Scott Avenue. Louise was the first funny, slapstick comedienne. Dad liked her and Gloria Swanson enough to name my sisters, Gloria and Louise, after them. Polly Moran, cross-eyed Ben Turpin, and Buster Keaton came along too.

Among the home grown "stars to be" was Bebe Daniels, a classmate of my Aunt Ethel. They rode a donkey to school together. A local boy, Joe Young, Robert's older brother, was a very early actor, a great guy and a good swimmer. I'll always be grateful to Joe for teaching me to swim in the "Tank" on Sennett's lot.

Other early arrivals were Al St. John, Billy Bevan, Alice Day,

Louise Fazenda

Lew Cody, Wallace Reid, Bull Montana, Natalie Kingston, Wheeler Oakman, Heinie Conklin, Hank Mann, Marie Prevost, Harold Lloyd, Madeline Hurlock, Jimmy Finlinson and Harry Langdon. Ralph Graves, Tom Kennedy, "Slow-burn" Ed Kennedy, Ade Linkoff and George Spear.

Charlie French lived on Duane Street. He was a character actor who played a sheriff or a judge in most pictures made by Colonel Selig, D.W. Griffith and William S. Hart Studios.

It was interesting for us kids to watch the people shooting scenes and talk to them on the sets. I came to know them. When I saw them on the big screen at the show, I felt I was a part of "the wonderful game!"

In 1912, the year I was born, Dad and Buck Jones, who also became a star, helped Hoot Gibson butter his new saddle to take to Pendleton, Oregon, to compete in the National Roundup Rodeo. Hoot won the "Champion All-around Cowboy" title. When he returned to Los Angeles, the movie business was getting a good start and Western movies were going over big in the east. Some of the studios were looking for handsome men to star as cowboys. What could make a better Western movie star than a real honest-to-gosh cowboy, who could ride, rope and bulldog a steer? Carl Laemmle had just built Universal Studio in the city with the same name. He heard of Hoot's success and offered him a job. Hoot accepted, but it wasn't easy! Acting was tougher than bulldogging. He learned to act and shoot blanks at rustlers and became a Western movie star as good as Tom Mix and William S. Hart.

Art Acord was another of Edendale's tough, handsome cowboys, who became a Western star at Universal. In their days before stardom, Hoot and Art were great pals and, like all boys in Edendale, they played tricks on each other. Dad told me, "One day, Hoot had packed his trunk to make a move into another place. Art heard about the move and rode his horse up Branden Street, a dirt road, to Hoot's house. He saw the trunk with the initials 'H.G.' on it. It was beside the road in front of the house waiting to be moved by someone with a wagon. Laughing to himself, no doubt, Art roped the trunk, took 'dallies' (turns) on his saddle horn, kicked his horse and jerked the trunk down the hill on the run. The trunk burst open on the third bounce and Hoot's stuff rolled out and laid in the dust all over the road on the side of the hill. Hoot laughed, but I'm sure he got even."

I came to know these cowboys as any kid learns to know his Dad's friends and neighbors. I never missed seeing a picture when Hoot and Art were starred at "the U."

In about 1922, Art was featured in an 18-episode serial titled, *In the Days of Buffalo Bill*. The serial ran at the Garden Theater on Sunset Boulevard at Mohawk Street one night a week and we kids wouldn't miss it. As advertised, the night the first episode ran, the theater manager gave each of us a 2"x3" *In the Days of Buffalo Bill* card. Fifteen squares were printed around the edges of it. Each night, when we bought our 10-cent tickets, the box office girl punched out that night's episode number from our cards. When 15 holes were punched out, we were allowed to go in and see the last 3 episodes free! It was a big savings of 30 cents for each of us.

For 18 weeks, rain or shine without a miss, on Monday nights my sisters Vivian and Gloria and I, with our playmates, Sonny and Sister Holmgren, hurried up Alvarado Street to the theater. Eating a five-cent bag of popcorn helped us endure the anxious wait until we saw how Art and Buffalo Bill got out of last week's dangerous situation. I never tired of watching them beat the feathers and wigs off a band of made-up Indians that I knew were my cowboy friends wearing loincloths and carrying tomahawks.

Along with Tom Mix, Buck Jones became William Fox Studio's second cowboy star. Years later, I worked in a picture with Buck called, *White Eagle*. Many of Dad's cowboy and cow-

Art Acord

girl friends came from the rodeo and circus to work in pictures. Mike Braham owned and trained eight "educated" horses that traveled with the Barnum & Bailey Circus. One night he gave us tickets to the "Big Top" to see his wife, Alice, dressed in her fancy clothes. She put the horses through their paces, and got a big applause when she made the horses all stand up together on their hind legs in the center ring, as she passed her long whip under them!

Our neighbor, Buff Jones, not related to Buck, was a top trick roper and rope spinner, who also performed in circuses and rodeos.

He could rope six horses running abreast with one long rope. For hours, I watched him practice his rope spinning tricks on our vacant lot. Claude Elliott, another of Dad's pals, was a champion bucking horse rider. Years later, in 1953, when he and Dad had retired, Claude helped me buy the first 55 head of cattle for my ranch in Elk Grove. Dad said, "Claude was the best bucking horse rider in the world, and I don't say that because he was one of the guys that rolled cigarettes for me when I was busted up!"

After 1913, nearly everything that happened in Edendale had something to do with the motion picture business. Mornings when we went to school, we carried our brown bag lunches up Allesandro Avenue. When we passed Aaron Street, we spoke to the cowboys who had ridden their horses to congregate at the corner. Usually six or seven waited around, each hoping to get a call to work in a picture. Some were shooting pool in Davie's Pool Hall. Others were having breakfast next door in Kate's Little Cafe. Folks from Sennett's would later come across the street to have lunch at Kate's.

I knew most of the men as pals of Dad's or fellows I'd seen at the studio. They were all real horsemen. Some were known as "daredevils," who would double for actors. They took the places of stars, doing the dangerous scenes, preventing risk to the actor. Small sized cowboys, wearing a wig, often doubled for girls in dangerous rides. The double received three dollars a day and two dollars per fall!

Getting bucked off a horse or a steer, or getting shot and taking a fall off the top of a stagecoach, wasn't an easy way to make a living. I always admired those quiet, confident guys. They were in a class by themselves. Dad said they analyzed each stunt carefully and figured out just how they would make the fall. "Stunt men," as they were later to be called, came to play an important role in the making of exciting moving pictures.

The years passed and by 1960 the real, hard-riding cowboys, who had made the original Western pictures famous, were gone or too old to ride. Casting directors had a problem when riders were needed for a Western picture. To hire men to form a sheriff's posse or to make up a gang of outlaws was tough. The casting director would plead for honesty when he interviewed for the jobs. "We need some good riders. Do you know how to ride a horse? Please tell me the truth." Bandits and outlaws falling off their horses, while holding up the Wells Fargo stagecoach, had convinced producers that a dude wearing a big Western hat, boots and spurs would never make pictures like the silent-day cowboys had made. "Where do they ride tonight?" In old movies on TV screens.

MY FIRST MOVIE ROLE

1913

In 1913, on a warm August morning, Sitka and I were on our front porch enjoying the weather. A man wearing a blue suit came walking up the path. Sitka gave a low growl and the man stopped at a safe distance from us, near the big eucalyptus tree. The intruder nervously called, "Anybody home? Hello there." Sitka kept a suspicious eye on the stranger until, after two or three calls, Mom came out and gave Sitka the, "Okay boy."

"Are you Mrs. Watson?" the stranger asked.

"Yes, I am."

"I'm an assistant director from the Selig Motion Picture Studio. I've been told you have a baby."

"Yes," Mom answered, curiously. "He's nine months old."

The man took off his hat and spoke as he moved cautiously toward the porch, with his eyes on Sitka. "The studio needs a baby. Would you let your baby be photographed to appear in a motion picture?" He explained the picture, *The Price of Silence*, would feature two new actors from New York, Lon Chaney and Dorothy Phillips. (Note: Motion Picture history relates that at least five films titled *The Price of Silence* were produced in the early days of the industry. Memories, as well as studio P.R., can be fuzzy.)

Dorothy Phillips and Lon Chaney

"If you will let your baby work in the picture, we'll pay five dollars for the day's work." Mom thought it sounded interesting. It would be fun to see me on the big screen, she thought, but she was also cautious.

"What would he have to do?" She asked about the action and where the scenes would be taken. She knew the kind of movie-making Dad was doing. Riding, chasing and being chased over the hills, near Silver Lake, in the hot sun, was rough and dangerous work and she didn't want me involved in any of that kind of action.

The man assured her my scenes would be quiet and easy and

Ready for my movie debut in
The Price of Silence

without any risky business whatsoever. Reassured about the offer, she thought about it and finally agreed to let me make my debut in the movies. It would be the first of 65 pictures I'd work in before I was 18 years old.

Mom was told what I was to wear, the day and time we were to be at the studio, and thanks were exchanged. She could hardly wait to tell Dad the news. By this time, Dad had been pioneering in the business for two years. When he came home and learned I was getting into motion pictures too, they both fairly danced for joy. They wanted me to look my best for the picture, so the next day Mom took me on the streetcar to Grandma Watson's house at the end of the car line.

"Could Little Coy borrow his 11-year-old Aunt Ethel's fancy baby dress to wear in a motion picture?" Grandma Watson listened, but was hard to convince. She didn't like the movies or the movie people, nor did many of her Salvation Army co-workers. Mom assured Grandma that she wouldn't let "those crazy movie nuts" do anything that might hurt Little Coy. Fortunately, Mom didn't know at the time of her persuading talk that I was to be the illegitimate child born to the unmarried, leading lady of the drama. Had Grandma learned that, she would have had no part of my debut and I would have had to wear my own, not so classy, baby clothes. Grandma let us take the dress.

On the day of the shooting, Mom, excited as a would-be star herself, scrubbed me pink, dolled me up, packed a bag with diapers and cookies, and set off for a four-block walk to the studio. Sitka jogged at her side as she carried me up Allesandro Street. A couple of Dad's cowboy friends greeted us as we passed the pool hall.

When we reached the studio, Mom sent Sitka home and the gate man let us make our first entrance onto the studio lot. After being introduced to the director, Joseph De Grasse, we met Miss Phillips, the star who was to play my mother. Mom watched her put on her makeup as they talked about babies. Mom said I got a laugh from the crew when I pulled my new mother's nose.

The first scenes were photographed on a tiny open bedroom set in sunlight because there was no electricity in Edendale then.

Making "flickers" in Edendale
without electricity was not easy.
Some of the first cameramen were
forced to photograph all the pictures with crude, hand-cranked
cameras that punched the sprocket
holes on the edges of the film to
move the film through the camera,
at the same time the pictures were
exposed on the film. The tiny
blanked-out dots of film were
caught in a small tray at the bottom of the camera that had to be
emptied after each roll of film
was exposed. Then the camera
was reloaded.

In a medium shot, my movie
mother finished dressing me on the bed, packed her bag, put on her
hat and picked me up. In a long shot, she left the poorly furnished,
drab little room with me in one arm, and a suitcase containing all
her worldly possessions in the other. For the next scenes, we left the
studio. The actors and crew were driven in big open automobiles
to a street in Glendale. On the way, Mom learned the picture's story.
It was about a courageous, young girl, who had been shamed and
was leaving town alone, and hopefully, unnoticed. She had refused
to admit that the baby was the son of the town's wealthy mayor,
who had "done her wrong." She was paying *The
Price of Silence.* It was a typical early flicker plot for
a drama of that time. Mom guessed, when the picture ran on the screens of neighborhood theaters
across the country, the piano player would no
doubt render "Hearts and Flowers" or similar sad
music to help bring tears to the eyes of the sympa-
thetic audience.

*I made my first appearances before
movie cameras on open sets. There
was no electricity for light. The
muslin overhead softened the bright
rays of the sun.*

*Below: Early film producer Mack
Sennett and his cameraman Hans
Koenekamp with an early motion
picture camera (1913)*

The next scenes were to show the heroine
leaving town and walking to the railroad station.
The cameras were set up in the street to pan along
and follow my movie mother with me in her arms.
She would walk slowly, passing the various store-
fronts, as people, horses and wagons moved about.
Speaking through a megaphone, the director explained the action of the scene to all the extras

who would walk or ride on the street. Then all the action was rehearsed. When they were ready to shoot the scene, Mom handed me to Miss Phillips and took a place behind the camera and director to watch the action.

To her surprise, the director got up from his chair and asked Mom if she would like to be in the scene. He said he thought Mom was a cute, little lady. Mom always was attractive, especially at the age of 19.

"He wanted me to walk into a saloon with a couple of cowboys to create some action in the background as the unwed mother with the baby walked past," Mom recalled. Being a good sport, she said, "Sure," and took her first directions. "Now, Mrs. Watson, don't watch your baby and don't look at me. Talk to the cowboys, as if they were old friends. Just act natural!"

On a Mack Sennett Studio three-walled, open ceiling set, two cameramen and an assistant cameraman stand on the right. Extreme left is a prop-man. Coy Watson, Sr., Assistant Director, standing. Director Frank Griffin, seated. Comedian Harry Booker and baby sister Vivian on the floor. The movie was Twilight Sleep.

On the cue, "Cameras! Action!" the two cameras cranked, and the horses and people started to move along the street. The lonesome girl, carrying me, made her way through town, and my mom, laughing, entered the saloon. When the scene was shot, the director yelled, "Okay," thanked everybody and said, "That's all."

Finally, the cameras were set up and focused on the little railroad station. The brave girl slowly approached the ticket window. She sat me on the counter, opened her purse and bought her ticket. She went to an old wooden bench and sat down with her suitcase at her side and me on her lap. In a close-up, she talked to me, tickled my cheeks and nose and made me laugh. Then, a last long shot of the lonely station showed her patiently waiting for the train that would take her and her baby away to a happier place. Fade out.

My always-happy Mom, holding me and Vivian (1914)

Mom said the day went well. The director was pleased with the way I had behaved. He thanked Mom for her bit. She was overjoyed. It always tickled her so and she'd laugh when she told about our working in our first moving picture together.

"Can you imagine?" she'd say. "Here I was letting Little Coy leave town with a gal I didn't know and I was going into a saloon to have a drink with a couple of cowboys I'd never seen before. No, I didn't get paid for my bit, but I got a five dollar gold piece for Little Coy's day's work." That day was one of the highlights of Mom's life.

A DANGEROUS RIDE FOR DAD

1913

About a year after I was born, Dad rode in the picture that darn near killed him. The Selig Studio movie starred Tom Mix, who became Hollywood's best-dressed cowboy, and his horse, Tony.

The script for *Logan of the U.S.A.* started out to be a story about a band of ruthless outlaws who for months had run unchecked, robbing and killing ranching families, burning their homes and barns. The Governor, to bring law and order to the Los Angeles Territory, called Marshall Logan from Wyoming. The two-gun lawman immediately deputized fifty-five cowboys to ride with him and bring in the dangerous bad men, dead or alive! The new deputies, none with a star, but all well armed, were ready and able to help

Tom Mix, early Western movie star

Dad on "Buck" as he appeared in one of the earliest movies made in California

restore justice and peace in the land they were trying to settle.

In a long shot, the huge posse had gathered at the crossroads as designated by Logan. The cowboys and their horses waited quietly in the warm, California morning sunshine for their leader. Real Westerners, this bunch, in their wide-brimmed hats, Levis, high-heeled boots and chaps. In close shots some stood quietly talking. Others squatted thoughtfully as they smoked their hand-rolled cigarettes. The only movements were the horses moving a leg, shaking a head or switching a tail at a disturbing fly. The tense, waiting scene was in the rolling hills near Silver Lake, a mile from Edendale.

At the sounds of an approaching horse, heads turned. The

hard-riding Marshall arrived and as the dust settled, he received stern attention. A quick "Howdy" to his posse and the handsome lawman immediately gave the details of their ride. He warned of the dangerous battle they were about to encounter.

"If anyone wants to change his mind, we'll understand," announced the Marshall. "Now is the time to drop out. Otherwise, stay together and wait for the order before using your six-shooters or Winchesters." No one spoke or left.

"Alright boys, mount up!"

The actors quickly mounted, settled into their saddles and waited for the final signal to ride out. The signal would come from the director, seated in his chair under the umbrella near the camera, two hills away. At the top of the nearer hill, a cowboy mounted on a pinto pony watched and waited for the director's cue to start the scene.

A motion picture company on location photographing a Western movie (circa 1911)

My dad was one of Tom's 55 real cowboys, acting as deputies, riding their own horses, making movie history in another of Hollywood's early Western motion pictures. Edendale was changing fast!

The story was only a movie, but the action would be very real. The posse was to ride up the first hill into view of the movie crew on the side of the next hill, then charge down the other side, straight into the cameras. It would be a thrilling scene. Many of the cowboys were making their first appearance before the cameras and enjoying it. They laughed and joked with good reason. Each was receiving a big one dollar a day for himself and two dollars for his horse. It was a week's pay for a day's work! The assistant director, also mounted and ready to ride in the lead with Tom Mix, noticed the joyful attitude of the posse and called for attention.

"Hey boys," he yelled. "Listen! This is a serious scene we're shooting. We don't want any laughing. We're supposed to be on our way to round up a gang of dangerous outlaws, killers."

The cowboys received their first lesson in acting: "You gotta be serious. In this scene you're supposed to be riding to save your homes and the West, so look mean, as though you mean business. Ride hard and don't laugh!" Then he reminded them to pull their hats on tight. He didn't want anybody going back to pick up a lost hat!

My Dad, unaware of the terrible accident that was to happen, sat confidently astride Buck. Then yip-pee! The posse's wait was over. Atop the hill, the lookout received the signal, waved back and yelled, "Let's go boys!" Every rider and horse kicked into action, moving up the slope, riding easy at the start. As they made the hill, riding four abreast, the posse picked up a faster gait.

"Start camera! Action!"

Over the crest they came now at a full gallop, each cowboy riding hard down the hill straight for the cameras and the director on the hillside across a ravine, a half-mile away. The silent, hand-cranked cameras were grinding to capture the great ride. The only details not being recorded were the exciting sounds of the thundering hoofs on the dry hillside and the slapping and pulling of leather on the saddles and bridles. The happy, new actors descended the slope on a dead run. Their intense expressions showed they could act. Inwardly they laughed at being paid for doing what they and their horses enjoyed most.

Fifty-seven hearts thrilled as fifty-seven horses leaped forward on powerful legs. Their neckerchiefs and big, wide-brimmed hats fluttered and flopped in the wind as they bent forward in their saddles with their chins bobbing in the flying manes of their wide-eyed cow ponies. With each lunge forward, the horses extended their necks and heads, gasping for breath with expanded, pink nostrils. The director and crew grouped around the tripods, eyes and cameras focused on the action racing toward them.

Then it happened! A horse running just behind the four leaders stumbled and fell broadside, throwing and rolling over its rider.

The following three horses were tripped and went down head-over-legs. The next four tumbled over them, then five more! In seconds, 13 horses and men were down in a horrifying pile. Some horses tried to stop short, rearing and twisting and throwing their

Accident scene in Logan of the U.S.A.

riders into the heap. Others, charging up from behind, crashed hard into each other as they tried to pull up. Frightened horses reared, twisted and fell over backwards. Some, throwing their riders, ran off with saddles dragging at their sides. Screams of pain came from the churning heap of arms, legs and heads. Horses squealed and grunted as they rolled and pawed the air, flashing the bottoms of their shiny shoes in the sun.

The director yelled, "Keep grinding! It's awful, but let's get it all on film!"

The rear ranks coming up, with more time to see ahead, slowed down and reined off to the sides to avoid the gruesome pileup. Mix and the leaders received frantic waves from the director, looked over their shoulders, and then rushed back to give aid. The cameraman kept shooting as the director and crew ran to help untangle bodies.

Dirt-covered cowboys, saddles, horses, chaps, hats and bridles were pulled from the mangled mess as quickly and as carefully as possible. One cowboy was unconscious and another was dizzy, wobbling around. Wagons and automobiles were loaded with the seriously injured for the trip to the hospital in Los Angeles. No one was killed, but there were many broken bones.

Dad's horse, Buck, one of the first to flip over the fallen horse, threw Dad, causing two breaks in his right shoulder and a broken arm. The ill-fated horse that caused the accident had stepped into a

Dad

In this blow-up of the above photo, you can see my dad

gopher hole, had broken a front leg and had to be destroyed by its owner at the scene. Other horses received serious bruises and minor injuries. A horse is a tough actor if he can keep his legs.

The day's shooting was over. The cameras had caught the entire scene, the first disaster of its kind. Shooting of the picture, at that point, was stopped and the script was rewritten. The spectacular scene of the falling horses became the decisive part of the exciting climax to the picture. The horses had fallen about 75 yards from the cameras. When the scene was projected on the screens of New York and Chicago, the big audiences were spellbound. They had seen cowboys and Indians chasing each other, but never action like this. Ticket sales shot up. Directors and producers were delighted with audience reaction. It started a trend terrible for horses, but one good for riders, who became known as "stunt men." Directors started tripping horses to create sensational scenes. Hard-to-see ropes or wires were stretched a foot or two above ground to trip and throw horses and riders, as they charged into the cameras. Not only the horses but also several of those first fallen cowboys paid a dear price for the privilege of being the originators of such scenes. Some were months recovering from their injuries; others carried them for life. Later, horses were trained to fall on cue.

It had been a bad accident for Dad. He lay flat on his back, in bed at home for three weeks, with his right arm bound across his chest to keep the arm and shoulder immobile. He couldn't move or roll to either side. As a right-hander, his left was of little use. His cowboy pals came to see him every day and kept him up on corral gossip of scenes being shot and upcoming pictures' work. They also rolled cigarettes for Dad, a favor he appreciated. The boys rolled as they talked. Dad furnished "the makings," a small cloth sack of Bull Durham tobacco and a pack of Wheat Straw cigarette papers. There were no "ready made" or "store bought" cigarettes in those days. In typical cowboy fashion, they opened the sack with both hands, then held the cigarette paper in one hand and carefully, with the other, shook a portion of tobacco from the sack onto the paper. Then, holding the sack's drawstring tag between their teeth, they pulled the sack closed and put it into their shirt pocket. With two hands, they leveled off the tobacco, rolled up the paper, and with a moist tongue, licked the edges to seal the cigarette. The final touch was to fold over, at an angle like a dog-ear, the end to be lit. The other end was pinched closed. They rolled a dozen or more while they visited. Mom was grateful to the cowboys for a chore she hadn't learned to perform. With his one hand, Dad could light up and enjoy a smoke with plenty of time to think things over!

"Just lying there day after day could have been boring," Dad told me. "But you didn't let that happen. You were just learning to walk. You'd crawl over to the bed and stand up, holding onto the side and we'd jabber baby talk to each other. That was cute. But, it was not funny when you showed up for a little visit asking questions and pounding me on the head with a big wooden spoon given to you by your mother to amuse you. You always came to my right side where I couldn't reach you and I was helpless." He laughed, "Often you appeared jabbering a blue streak and wanting to share your crackers or bread and butter with me. My kindest refusals didn't stop you from reaching over and pushing your goodies into my face as you tried to locate my mouth. Your mother had a big laugh when I called her to please come and remove the cracker crumbs from the bed and the buttered bread from my ears."

The fall and the pain didn't change Dad's mind about getting into the movie business. He was more determined than ever to do so. He did recover to ride again, like all good Hollywood cowboys.

I BECAME "THE KEYSTONE KID"

1913

I don't recall working in any pictures before age three, although Dad and Mom remember some. My earliest memory, a vague one, was a scene where I was sitting on the sidewalk in front of a house on a hillside. I was surrounded with a lot of toys: a fire engine, a jack-in-the-box, a teddy bear, some blocks and some little cars. A man in a Santa Claus suit handed me toys

Mack Sennett's Keystone Comedy Studio, looking east across Glendale Boulevard in 1913—the year I became "The Keystone Kid"

from his pack, acted silly and excited, and jumped all around. I was disturbed when he kicked some of the toys and they rolled down the hill. I remember the director laughed and yelled at us. Santa jumped up and down as he laughed at me. I guess they were trying to make me laugh but couldn't. Mom remembered it was a funny scene. "We all laughed," she said.

I can't recall the name of the picture or the director; there were so many pictures. We lived next to the studios, and whenever a director or gagman needed a kid for a scene, on the spur of the moment, the assistant director came to our house or phoned. He would be representing Director Dick Jones, Craig Hutchinson, Eddie Cline, Del Lord or any one of five or six directors.

Unknown actress and Fatty Arbuckle

"Mrs. Watson, we need a baby for a scene," he'd say. "Can we use Little Coy for a couple of hours?"

That's the way it was. I became "The Keystone Kid" before I knew it. Before I was two years old, I had worked in scenes with most of Sennett's stars: Mabel Normand, Marie Dressler, Harry Booker, Gloria Swanson, Charlie Murray, Billy Bevan, Joe Young, Wallace Beery, Chester Conklin, Ford Sterling, and Fatty Arbuckle, to name a few.

I played Arbuckle's baby in a picture called *Fatty's Gift*. Fatty's real wife, Minta, played my mother. It turned out to be a bad experience for me. Mom told me that I was doing great and everything was fine until the director wanted me to cry in a scene.

"You were in a good mood and didn't feel like crying," Mom recalled. "I started onto the set to tell the director that if I waved goodbye to you and started to leave, you would possibly cry. But, before I got to the director, that fool Fatty yelled, 'I'll make him cry,' and he leaned over into the crib, yelled and growled right in your face. I was six feet away and he even scared me! It made me angry. You began to cry all right and you cried hard. They got their scene but you were very upset and wouldn't stop crying. For weeks after that, every time Dad or I took you onto a set, you became frightened and uneasy until

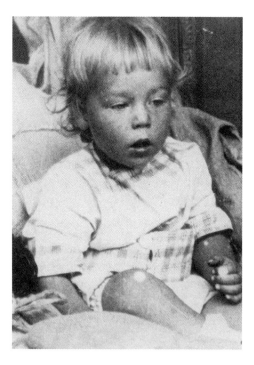

Left: As Fatty Arbuckle's baby — just before Fatty made me cry

Below: Lost in Echo Park wearing Fatty's gift — a watch on a ribbon

you became familiar with the place and the people. You were not a crybaby. You were good natured and happy or the directors wouldn't have had you back on the set as often as they did."

After the episode with Fatty Arbuckle, Mom always asked about the action and with whom I would be working. Even in those silent days, there were some impatient directors, who couldn't and wouldn't waste film or time with kids that cried or fussed. A kid was no different than an animal to some directors. If it didn't behave, take directions and do what it was told, they got another animal. The same went for kids. Directors with more patience, who liked working with children, became known as "kid directors" and they made most of the "kid pictures." I worked for many of them from 1913 to 1924.

THE FIRST FILM EDITORS WERE DIRECTORS

1914

Editing film was the first thing a would-be motion picture director learned. The directors who began as editors were the ones that became the best directors. Frank Capra, George Marshall, Eddie Cline, Del Lord, Lloyd Bacon, Brick Enright and my uncle, Bill Watson, were some of the first who learned to edit film.

A director could get the actors to do the things in all the scenes for his story. But, could he edit the film to keep the story moving *and* tell his story? The actors looking at each other, then a look off to the right for a second! And when he sees her, cut to what he sees. Editing actually was a forerunner to scriptwriting. (The writers later laid out on paper—"He looks in this direction, cut to what he sees, cut to what she sees . . ." etc.) Directors who couldn't edit made room for men and women who became "film editors."

All the other studios absorbed the people from Mack Sennett. Eddie Cline went to Fox, Lloyd Bacon and Ray "Brick" Enright went to Warner's. They all knew what to do with the film, what

My Uncle Bill Watson directing Keystone bathing beauties on Santa Monica Beach

scenes to get, so when they sat down to edit a picture they had what they needed. It was there. They didn't have to shoot retakes or add scenes. Lloyd Bacon, long before Hitchcock, chose to always appear in a scene in each of his pictures. Today, if I watch a Warner Brothers picture, I still watch for Lloyd.

I can usually tell by the fast pace of the picture if it was directed by Lloyd or "Brick" (called "Brick" because of his red hair). Their pictures moved faster because they were sensitive to editing.

Director Hampton Del Ruth and Assistant Director Coy Watson, Sr., on location for the William Fox Studio picture, Skirts

CHEERS FOR MY "PONY BOY"

1915

The trust and love and confidence that I had in Dad and Mom just made me want to have fun with them and do anything they wanted me to do. They taught me poems and songs. For an evening's entertainment, Dad would stand me on a chair and ask me to sing "Pony Boy" for his cowboy friends and neighbors.

My audience—Dad's rodeo and movie cowboy friends. Left to right: Arley Harr, Hank Potts and "Hippy" Burmeister.

I was too young to remember the first time I sang that cowboy song. Bobbing up and down like riding on a pony singing, "Giddyap, Giddyap, giddyap! Whoa! My Pony Boy," I gave it everything I had and enjoyed it. They'd all laugh and clap for me. So did I.

Another little number with actions and tune was "Thus the Farmer Sows His Seeds." With my left arm held as if holding a sack of seeds, I swung my right hand from under my left arm, out to my right side, as if throwing out seeds. Under and out, under and out, I went through the motions as I sang. Then, "Thus he stands and takes his ease." With that I folded my arms and stood up straight. The farmer "Stamps his foot," meant a quick hold onto the back of the chair to keep my balance as I stamped my foot on its seat. "Claps his hands," was easy. Then came, "Turns around and views his land." With my right thumb pressed against my forehead, I turned and looked around the room.

Years passed before I really understood what I was singing about or doing. It didn't matter. I just did as I was told. I'm sure that early training gave me a head start in school and in taking directions for scenes in motion pictures. At age four when on a set, the director, with Mom or Dad's help, would explain the action for a scene, tell me what to do and I did it. It was always fun, just like at home, only for a bigger audience and more applause.

Even in the early days, the big costs in making movies were time and film. The question was asked, "How would kids do in pictures? Would

An early entertainer in his sand pile

they do as they were told?" Scripts seldom included kids' parts. When they did, too much film and shooting time was lost getting the youngster to do a satisfactory scene.

Dad believed the time would come when a child who could do and say what he was told would be in demand by impatient directors. So, long before 1929, when sound was added to film, Mom and Dad were training me. Brothers and sisters arrived and learned to act, recite poems, sing songs and perform skits. We trained our minds to memorize. We had fun together and learned to take directions and to do what we were told. When we were employed in the movie industry, we knew how to behave as well as how to act.

A RIDE IN MY DOG WAGON

1915

I had the happiest and most interesting childhood a kid could ever have wished for. From the beginning, I believed my dad and my mom could do anything. They made my life, gave me their time, patience and love. I was four when Dad made me a dog-team wagon, using Mom's old wooden ironing board and four baby buggy wheels.

The wagon's tongue was a four-foot piece of 2" x 2" hardwood that ran out from the front wheels. My two dogs, Sitka and his new playmate, Lunk, also part malamute, were hitched to Dad's creation in their handmade leather harnesses, like a team of horses fitted to pull a buckboard. Strapped in the bucket seat, I was off for a ride up Allesandro Street, past Mack Sennett's studio and onto Glendale Boulevard. Dad ran along on the left side of the dogs with a short rope tied to Sitka's collar. In my little seat, I enjoyed the ride and laughed as Dad called directions to the dogs, "Mush! Gee! Haw!"

What a ride! The dogs' tails bobbed up and down as they trotted along. I knew they had smiles on their faces, as their tongues flapped from side to side. The spinning rubber-tire wheels made a light, grinding sound as they rolled on the asphalt pavement. We were having as much fun as a team mushing a sled on the snow-packed trail in the Klondike! Sledding up the boulevard, crossing street after street in alphabetical order, Aaron, Branden, then across Clifford Street. "Mush!" Dad cracked out, laughing as we heard folks on the sidewalk yell, "Go get 'em. Mush! Mush!" At Duane Street, "Haw! Keep to the right you pups! Look out for that Model T. Ford."

We passed Ewing Street and Dad was running like a cross-country Olympian. Then Fargo Street. "Gee! Gee!" He yelled to the team. Here we made a left, hairpin turn and headed back down the way we'd come. We didn't go over the hill to Silver Lake and Tom Mix's ranch. We were headed for home now, and the dogs knew it. They whined out their happy, little barks and grunts and increased the pace. No need for a "Mush" from Dad now, only a "Haw" to keep them to the right side of the street. We passed Selig's Studio, the Norbig Studio and then Sennett's again. On Allesandro, Dad slowed them to a jog. Then off the street to the right and up across the lot and into our front yard we went.

Dad, wearing his putties, with me and sister Vivian on his knees

Mom was waiting on the porch with a big smile as we pulled up and stopped. The dogs whined and wiggled with excitement as Dad gave them some rewarding words and a pat on the back. "I know you're all having fun with that thing," Mom said, "But Coy, you must be careful." She unbuckled the belt and lifted me out of the seat. Dad unhitched the dogs and they danced around him with their tails waving. From a bag in his pocket bits of cooked meat were given to each dog. With time and patience, Dad trained the dogs to pull my wagon and do many tricks. With his understanding and love for animals, he trained horses, lions, bears and dogs to perform in scenes for many movies in the years that followed. I always felt that the same caring and understanding he used working with animals since his boyhood had made him the patient, teaching and loving father he was. It was his nature to think and look ahead to anticipate what might happen.

Several movie people with whom he had worked told me how he was prepared for and/or prevented many unexpected mishaps during the shooting of tricky and dangerous scenes. It was his reputation. He cared about people and people cared about him.

A MOVIE COWBOY'S LOVE NEST

1915

One crisp, winter night, a full moon shone down on our little Los Angeles ranch house. A thin, gray column of smoke rose slowly from the clay pipe chimney and swirled its way up into the clear star-filled sky. In the living room of our tidy home, the air was warm and the scent of burning wood was part of the quiet, peace and contentment that prevailed.

I held my open hand flat against the glass of the French door. It was cold! Mom reached for pieces of firewood from the wood box with one hand, as her other held open the lid of the black stove in the corner of the room. As the wood tumbled in, the old heater was puffing and poofing, making sounds like a kid blowing out his birthday candles. She walked toward the kitchen, rubbing her hands on her apron as she left the room. I moved toward the stove and held my open hands up to feel the heat coming from the corner. Sitka, my dog, was lying on the floor in front of the bookcase, his head between his paws, flat on the linoleum. I knew he was warm and glad to be in the house. I turned my chair and sat down with my back to the warm, crackling stove. The glass lamp on the table, half full of coal oil, seemed to softly push its quiet yellow light up to the ceiling and out to the walls of the room.

Dad was sitting in his Morris chair with a lamp by his right shoulder. He was reading a Zane Grey Western story. He raised his eyes from the magazine and watched me as I moved toward the hot stove. Not until I had sat in my little chair did he go back to his reading. Sitka's wolf-like eyes had also followed my move. Without lifting his head, his gray, stalking eyes followed me with concern for my safety. This caring between us was deeply felt. I'd known him all my life. We had always been together. As I moved toward the stove, he was ready to "speak" or move with a warning to Dad or me.

Me, Dad, Vivian, and Sitka

"Oh, oh, here comes my Mom!" I could hear her footsteps. She was through the door, heading straight for me. Kneeling beside me, with her hands over my ears and pulling my face to hers, she kissed my forehead. I didn't know what love was then. Her gentle hands began to unbutton my shirt! I knew what she was going to do. As I leaned forward in the chair, she pulled off my shirt. I felt the heat more now as my right shoe came off, then the left and the socks, and so quickly! She knew what she was doing. She had done this before. Yes, now she was holding my hands in hers. Dad laid the magazine on his chair and walked to the kitchen.

I reached out and touched Mom's cheeks with my warm hands as she loosened and dropped my pants. They were off. She stood and moved to the stove to close the damper. In a few seconds, she was back and my underpants were off and I was bare. I liked that. She put her hands on my ribs, under my arms, pulled me to her and gave me a big kiss on the cheek. Then she lifted me up and stood me on the table beside the big, galvanized wash tub.

"If it's hot enough, bring it in," she called to Dad.

"Here it comes!" he answered.

He came to the other side of the tub with a big teakettle in one hand and a bigger steaming pot of water in the other. Ma's hand was slushing the cool water already in the tub as she held me with her other arm. Dad slowly poured the hot water into the tub. Then Mom sat me down into my warm Saturday night bath! They both seemed to be having fun. Little sister Vivian, 1½ years old, had her bath earlier and was sound asleep in her crib in the corner of the room. Mom scrubbed me as if she enjoyed it. She called me her "Little Movie Actor," her "big boy with the cute smile." She had to be proud. I was her first child, born when she was 18. She washed my hair and face carefully. No soap got into my eyes. Dad stood watching with a smile on his face. She scrubbed me all over; the arms, legs, everything, talking to me all the while.

When she said, "We're ready for the cold shower," Dad headed for the kitchen with the big pot in his hand. The scrubbing was over and Mom was wiping my head and face with the wrung out wash cloth. "Now, stand up."

What else could I do? She lifted me and I stood in the tub. Dad came in with the cold water. "I'll pour," he said.

"O.K., but not too fast."

"I know how to do this, Goldie," and he smiled as he took hold of my right arm. Mom held my left. "Be a big boy," they said together. "Here it is!" and the cold water hit my head. I closed my eyes as it ran down over my shoulders, back and tummy. My breath was gone and I started to shake. Dad kept pouring and Mom rubbed me. When the pot was empty, I opened my water-filled eyes. I was cold and shaking like a leaf, but I started breathing again. Mom kept rubbing and patting me all over and making warming remarks like, "Now warm up," and "That's my big boy. This will keep you healthy." Dad was laughing and reached for a towel. "This will make you strong and tough."

I looked at Sitka, sitting up now, his head tipped, his ears "up," watching with wonder. Was I having fun or not? I was not laughing.

I might have cried, but Dad with a towel in both hands was drying and rubbing me like Mom scrubbed clothes on her washboard.

"Not too hard, Coy" she said.

Dad lifted me out of the tub onto a towel on the table. I was still shivering, but he was rubbing so hard, I had to feel warm.

"How's that now?" He chuckled. "That's the stuff. He's tough! He can take it!" They were laughing. I couldn't.

"Careful, don't hit the lamp," Mom said.

Vivian had slept through my bath and Sitka was lying down again. I was dressed and warm in my outing flannel nightshirt when she held me up at arm's length. "There, now to bed!" She gave me a big hug, kissed me "goodnight" and handed me to Dad. Then she headed for the kitchen to heat more water for Dad's bath.

Next, fixed deeply in my memory, Dad knelt with me beside the old, double bed. I don't remember when I didn't know how to say, "Now I lay me down to sleep." Leaning against Dad, my hands together, "I pray the Lord my soul to keep." His voice was low and soft as he helped me remember each word. "If I should die before I wake, I pray the Lord my soul to take." And always, "God bless Daddy and Mamma and Vivian and Grandpa and Gramma Watson and Grampa Wimer, and all my aunts and uncles." And, "Help me to be a good boy and thanks for Sitka. Amen."

Dad, still on his knees, lifted me gently and easily into the turned-down bed, settling my head on the pillow and with a pat on the tummy pulled the covers over me, up and under my chin. His hand, ever so lightly, rubbed my forehead. "Now you go to sleep like a big boy and tomorrow we'll have some more fun. And be real quiet so you don't wake sister, okay? God bless you, sweetheart. Goodnight."

He stood up, bent over and pressed a big kiss on my forehead. This was the stuff that tied Dad and me together for all time. A little ways from the table, he reached and turned down the lamp wick. A gray veil, slowly and gently, slipped up the walls and came together in an orange circle on the ceiling above the lamp. I couldn't see Dad, but I knew he held the lamp from beside his chair and was walking to the bathroom. The ceiling and walls grew darker and seemed to move closer to my head. The room was more peaceful now. The tiny lamp flame became misty and started to move away, growing smaller and smaller. My soft, heavy eyelids slowly closed. I knew all was well. My world was at peace.

Years later, we three calculated this experience was one of the first early events in my life that I can remember. "You were about three-and-a-half years old," Dad said. "As I sat in the corner opposite

Mom loved kids. Here she is smiling with sister Gloria.

the stove, I well remember watching your mother undress and bathe you. We four were very happy."

My parents' memories of details gave me these stories.

DAD WAS "FIRE, WIRE, AND WATER WATSON"

1915

Before electronics and computers, the special effects sequences in movies depended on the ingenuity and remarkable inventiveness of a handful of brilliant, behind-the-scenes technicians. Some of their props and techniques are still used, like "break-away" bottles and windows that look like glass but are made of candy so no one is hurt, and the mashed potatoes which simulate ice cream and do not melt under the hot studio lighting. Other special effects have become lost or forgotten over the years as the old generation of special trick effects men have retired or passed on, taking their secrets with them.

Prop box money

Some of these effects date from the earliest days of silent pictures, when my Dad was one of the first of these specialists. He left behind, in stories and photographs, details of some of his outstanding feats, notably the pioneering and still impressive special effects in Douglas Fairbanks' movies, *The Thief of Baghdad*, *The Black Pirate* and *Around the World in 80 Minutes*, as well as the crazy stunt sequences in the first Keystone Comedies.

In Dad's early days, he did virtually all the work on a picture production that would keep an entire back lot crew busy years later. He was mechanically inclined, creative and quick of mind, hand, and foot. From the start he proved to have the natural ability to foresee what would be needed for a scene. He built a big prop box and stocked it with everything imaginable. Working as they did at that time, without a script, the director or any member of the company could come up with an idea for a gag on the spur of the moment to get another laugh in a scene. The gag could call for some fake flowers, ladies' bloomers, gunpowder, a baby's bottle, a sling shot, balloons, a rubber hammer, wires, ropes, spectacles, umbrellas or roller

Dad with one of his first trainees from the zoo

A lion acting in an early Keystone comedy

skates. The prop man had to have them ready to go!

Dad earned two nicknames, "Quick Watson" and "Fire, Wire and Water Watson." "He can do it," they would say. He experimented with ways to use very fine but strong piano wires to create unbelievable effects for scenes. From off camera, he pulled the almost

invisible wires to open or close doors, move chairs, flip hats, lift car tops and sway trees in phony windstorms. He slid baseballs, arrows and knives on wires through scenes to make sure they hit on target. He did a little of everything. He was good at working some of the first animals used in pictures. He got them to do what was wanted. Dogs, horses, goats, donkeys, pigs, lions, and bears in training respected and worked for him.

Above: Dad fighting a cinnamon bear in a Keystone Comedy, The Snow Cure, *filmed at "Dr. Coolem's Snow Vapor Baths," 10,000 feet above sea level! Truckee, California, 1914-1915.*

Left: Dad and some cool actors

"It is a new business," Dad said. "Everybody is a pioneer, not just the stars. So much of the mechanics have never been done before. We are doing things for the first time. Every picture offers new challenges." Now, over 80 years later, some of Coy Watson's ideas are still used in making movies.

DAD PUT STARS IN THE SKY

1915

Dad's success in producing new and unbelievable tricks with his wires got lots of laughs from audiences and inspired the directors and gag writers to dream up still more wire stunts. They wanted to put everything up into the air on wires.

Sooner than Mack Sennett or the growing audiences could imagine, they saw pieces of furniture, farm equipment, pigs, goats, parts of houses and automobiles pulled up into the air to follow funny scenes previously shot on the ground. A mad inventor's smoking rocket zoomed through the air, a strongman's 1,000-pound weight floated up into the air, and a winged bicycle flew through the air, all on piano wires!

By this time and after much experimentation, Dad had perfected a special tie or knot that wouldn't slip or break when the wires were put under strain. This reduced the chances of possible accidents. Then, as he had expected, the day came when the fathers of the world-famous American motion picture comedies asked him to put actors and actresses in the air on wires, and he did!

A hilltop behind Mack Sennett's studio was hundreds of feet above the street. It was simply called the "Keystone Hill." At the top, two telephone poles were planted. They stood about 45 feet tall and about 75 feet apart. A heavy wire cable was strung across the top between the two poles. In the center, heavy pulleys were attached to the cable. Ropes joined to piano wires were run through the pulleys.

To lift actors into the air, Dad designed a special belt for them to wear (like jockey shorts made of leather). The wires were tied to metal eyelets fastened to the belt. The actors, airplanes, rockets or whatever were pulled up and suspended in the air a few feet above the crest of the hill. Cameras were set up to photograph the hanging subjects and the houses on the ground hundreds of feet below.

The cameras were angled so the top of the hill was not visible in the picture.

One of Dad's first "wires in the air" pictures was a comedy about a mad inventor who became impatient when surrounded by a group of doubting investors. He decided to prove the capabilities of his brainchild. He sat straddling his eight-foot, pointed-nose rocket, as it waited on its launching pad, angled and ready to be fired into space. His assistant lit the fuse. The short fuse didn't allow the inventor time to dismount. To his surprise, and that of his soon-to-be-convinced investors, the rocket took to the air with the bearded "screwball" aboard.

A pair of wires was tied to the comedian's belt and a separate set to the rocket. From each, the wires ran up to the top end of a 20-foot loading crane, which was extended over the scene, out of the camera's view. When the lighted Roman candle shot its first ball of fire, the rocket and the comedian were lifted and swung out of the scene.

The next morning the crew and the inventor—with his mis-launched, unguided missile—were up on Keystone Hill. The next scenes of history-making subjects shooting through space were to be photographed. For a side shot, the rocket and rider were hung on wires as before, about six feet above the crest of the hill.

Off camera, a wind machine (an automobile engine that turned a three-foot airplane propeller in reverse) was mounted on top of a six-foot stand. It was aimed to blow a heavy wind at the head of the rocket and the clinging rider. In the scene, the strong wind current made the yellow smoke streaming from a smoke pot out the back of the rocket look like the afterburner of a solid fuel jet engine. The frantic professor had trouble clinging to his creation. His clothes, beard, hair and necktie flapped in the wind. As he tried to stay aboard, he went through one comical maneuver after another. He slid and twisted from side to side, nearly falling off, as the take-up on his wires, held by three men, was slackened and tightened, allowing him to move about.

After some careful rehearsing with the actor and the men working the wires, the scene showed the rocket flying a thousand miles an hour, 500 feet above the houses below.

For the final scene the rocket was hung higher, turned with its nose pointed skyward and its tail toward the camera. Now, shooting upward, no houses were seen below. The camera was on a sled ready to slide down a greased, wooden track laid flat straight down on the slope of the hill for 200 feet.

The wind machine was moved to blow from above. The smoke pot was lit. "Ready! Action!" cried the director. As the camera photographed the rocket, the sled and camera slid down the hill on the slick track, at a good speed, leaving the rocket. On the screen the rocket appeared to be leaving the earth on its way into outer space, the final scene before the end of the picture.

The size of the wires used for each trick depended upon the weight they were to carry. The smaller the wire used, the less chance it would be seen on camera. The average actor weighed 150 to 200 pounds. A wire the size of an average sewing needle would carry up to 300 pounds. Two wires were always used. Often, a couple of guide wires were used to turn or twist the actor in action. For heavier loads, wires up to the size of pencil lead were used.

Doreen and me high above "Keystone Hill"

By actually adding weights, pound by pound, to hanging wires, Dad learned the amount of weight each size wire would carry before breaking. After the wires were hung for a scene, they were swabbed with a special colored paint. Photographic tests were made to determine the best color to blend with the sky or with the background of any upcoming scene.

Dad never veered from his rule, "I always used two wires each, twice the size to carry the load I was putting up in the air." For over 20 years he rigged hundreds of scenes. If a wire happened to get kinked during his rigging procedures or while the scene was being rehearsed, he stopped everything and took the time to replace that wire. The kink didn't break, but weakened the wire. He usually heard complaints from the director, who spoke of losing time.

"To pull people up into the air on wires, from 3 to 20 feet above the ground was a risky, serious business."

There were no books on how to do wire work. From the first use of wires, there were stars and comedians, male and female, who flatly refused to go up for "wire scenes." However, there were other actors who agreed to work up on wires without fear if Coy Watson did the rigging. They believed in him. They knew he planned, engineered and carefully tied every wire for every stunt he worked.

As time passed, more stars came to trust his wires, but never all of them. Dad felt that, when he had people up in the air, he alone was responsible. He had helpers with the set-ups, but he tied all the wires himself. It became his specialty. He never undertook the simplest scenes lightly. Each job was different and dangerous. Each took careful planning and execution. His conscientiousness, interest and ability earned him an undisputed reputation. He was unequaled by any other mechanical effects technician in motion picture history.

During his 25 years doing wirework, he pulled some of the biggest stars in the business into the air on his wires. When he was asked about using his dangerous and never-publicized, unknown secret skills in moviemaking, he quietly said: "I am very pleased and grateful to say that while working many impossible, crazy and dangerous scenes, I never injured anybody. I did pray a lot. I tied all the wires myself because I didn't want anyone to feel the pressure or deep responsibility that I felt for the people that put their lives in my hands."

THE PIANO-WIRED GOAT

1915

Some of the first movie special effects started on our kitchen table as Dad experimented in miniature before making a full-size rig out on the lot. Mack Sennett had a motto, "Nothing is impossible," but he needed "Fire, Wire and Water Watson" to live up to the boast. Often Dad would sit in our kitchen until late at night puzzling through a director's idea for a scene to find a solution by the time the cameras started rolling the next day. He had to come up with quick answers on the spot. Many of the best effects came during actual shooting, like the classic butting-goat sequence.

They were shooting a Keystone two-reeler set on a farm, featuring a farmer and a very large and uncooperative billy goat. The movies didn't have skilled animal trainers in those days and the goat refused to do even a simple scene of running into the barn. It was his first time in movies and he'd never been trained to do anything before, just to eat the grass on an Edendale dairy farm.

"That goat has to run into that barn," growled the director. "Send for Watson!"

He arrived and the director asked, "Coy can you get that big goat to run, not walk, into that barn?"

"Sure, I'll tie a wire on him."

Shooting was held up while Dad carefully tied one end of a 75-foot length of piano wire to the goat's horns with padding. He ran the other end of the wire into the barn. A four-inch steel ring was tied to the end in the barn to which two three-quarter inch ropes, six feet long, were fastened so that two husky men with good, firm handholds could pull the wire.

The director shouted, "Camera! Action! Go!"

The men ran full speed out the back of the barn. The ropes tightened, and the iron ring lifted off the floor as the piano wire became taut. The billy had watched all the preparations with disinterest and was placidly chewing its cud with all four feet planted squarely on the ground. When the energy of the two heavyweights, now building up speed on the other side of the barn, was transmitted down the ropes and wire to his horns, the effect caught all of us by surprise. The wire twanged as the slack was taken up. The goat's head went down and he was yanked at high speed across the scene into the barn, as if shot from a cannon!

"Print it! That's great, Coy!" said the director. Then he had a typical on-the-spot inspiration. "Coy could you make the goat butt the farmer when he bends over?"

"Why not," answered Dad as he dug into his self-created prop box and came up with a pulley which he fastened to a stake driven into the ground. Then the two grips took hold of their ropes and the piano wire that ran through the pulley and back to the goat, out of camera range. He was a slow learner and still recovering from his first experience of movie magic, so he allowed the wire to be fastened to his horns a second time.

One of Sennett's actors, Andy Clyde, wearing long whiskers and dressed as an aged farmer, stood legs astride over the pulley. He bent over to lift a cage of chickens onto a wagon. The camera started rolling and the director yelled, "Action!"

The two ring-pullers again charged off toward the hills, the ropes and the wire tightened and once more the old billy found himself in involuntary rapid forward motion, like a rocket. He charged head down and bang, right on target. Another score for Dad!

That old goat was probably the world's first wire-guided missile!

Certainly he was the first to be seen on screen as he streaked across the set, made contact with the farmer's fanny and propelled the actor up, forward and down into the dirt. The crate popped open and the squeaking chickens shot into the air, feathers flying in all directions.

Everybody was laughing and Andy was rubbing his bottom! We used to laugh a lot making silent comedies, but the wired goat was a highlight. It wasn't even intended to be a gag sequence in the movie, but it was hilarious shooting it. The crew laughed and cheered. The goat-pullers remarked they weren't in shape to do many more 100-yard dashes!

THE FLOATING BATHTUB

1915

Dad was soon churning out other piano wire special effects, which got big laughs on the screen and helped Sennett keep a competitive edge over rival studios. It took awhile for them to puzzle out that it was piano wire again which made possible another unbelievable Keystone comedy sequence, where a comedian fell asleep in a hotel's second floor bathtub. He left the water running until it overflowed the tub and filled the bathroom with water.

The scene was shot in the "Tank" (a swimming pool on the studio lot, 20' x 40' x 10' deep). The bathroom set was built in the "Tank" and the "Tank" was filled with three feet of water from a nearby fire hydrant.

The next scene was the hall outside the door. The housemaid entered carrying a tall stack of towels. She stopped at the door and reached for the knob. The action which followed had to be filmed in one continuous scene where the hotel lobby was filled with a crowd of milling people.

The cameras were set up over the hotel set's front door. To rig the scene, Dad fitted four small wheels under the legs of the bathtub and carefully tied three piano wires to each front leg. He then ran the wires through pulleys at given points on the floor down through the set, a hundred feet to the hotel door. There the ends of the wires were tied to the steel ring and ropes to be handled by three husky men. A couple of "dry runs" were rehearsed by the crew and the actors. This gave assurance that the actions of such an expensive, one-chance-only scene were well timed and ready to be photographed. A camera was also set up in the room across the hall from the bathroom to get a close shot. Behind the wall in the bathroom was an enormous, hidden water storage tank.

When the director yelled, "Camera! Action!" the maid opened the bathroom door, threw the towels into the air, fell back and did a "pratfall" to the floor. On that cue, the hundreds of gallons of water were released from the hidden tank in the bathroom. As the water flooded through the door, the three men below took their cue and started running from the set, pulling the wires that pulled the tub through the door at the same time the water surged into the hallway. As if washed before a tidal wave, the tub rolled down the hall toward the stairs. The now awakened, bare and embarrassed bather, unhappy to appear in public, waved his arms in distress.

The director yelled cues through his megaphone to the actors. Appearing to be pushed by the flowing water, the floating bathing craft took its big nosedive down the stairs, splashing the hotel guests into a panic as it bumped the lobby floor. Rocking and rolling, it continued to skid its way across the floor, scrambling and tumbling actors and acrobats into flips and pratfalls. Finally the frantic bouncing bather and his tub were zoomed from the scene, out the front door, for more rides down the street!

"O.K.!" yelled the director. "A great scene, everybody did great!"

It was scenes like this that got high ratings for entertainment before the twenties. In theaters, Dad's work was considered movies' secret magic. The trick work was never revealed to the public. Who could have guessed that over 80 years later, those first silent movies

Traveling by tub!

would be transferred to videotapes? Dad might find it hard to believe, if he were alive today, that scenes he helped create as early as 1913 are still popular with the entertainment public.

Many of the old black and white films have had sound and color added to them. Over background music, narrators recognize and call attention to the creative ingenuity shown in early flickers made by those imaginative pioneers who started the motion picture industry.

Some of the tricks Dad devised for 1913 comedies were to come into use years later. In 1924, Douglas Fairbanks trusted his life to Dad's secret piano wire knots and took off on his flying carpet and performed other mystifying tricks in the *Thief of Bagdad*. Dad made everything fly, often soaring on piano wires strung between two telegraph poles on the hill behind Sennett's studio with the Edendale skyline in the background. The company had such confidence in Dad that they never used to think of the danger, but there was tension on the set the day Sennett shot the famous "floating bathtub" sequence!

THE FOUR-YEAR-OLD MAILMAN

1916

I truly enjoyed working in some of the first silent pictures made before 1929 when sound was added. The first flickers made for kids' theater audiences didn't need much of a script. The first producers of children-and-animal pictures learned early that these movies were entertaining to audiences of all ages.

Performing at home before visiting friends was great training. Speaking in classrooms at school, or to any audience, was never a problem for me. I learned to like people early. I felt others liked me, so I enjoyed them. It has never, ever been any other way, thanks to Dad and Mom.

By the time I was four, Dad said I had learned to take directions during the shooting of a scene without looking at the director or the camera.

"Do as you are told, but don't look at the director," Dad had taught. I knew to stay in a fixed position when I spoke my lines, so that later the text of what I said could be edited in on a subtitle to inform the audience before the scene continued.

I remember making *The Mailman*, a two-reel comedy for the L.K.O. Studio. The director and producer was Henry Lehrman. After a brief explanation of the action wanted, and without a rehearsal, I heard him say, "Camera! Action!"

From camera right entered Bernie, a big St. Bernard dog pulling my express wagon carrying me, a 3-foot ladder and a bag of letters. On my head I wore a postman's cap. A postman's whistle hung on a string around my neck. The wagon stopped at the first mailbox post. The dog looked back at me as I got out of the wagon.

As the camera filmed the scene, the trainer was calling commands to Bernie, "Stop. Stay. Hold it there."

The director spoke to me, "That's fine, Coy. Get out of the wagon. That's good. Take the ladder out of the wagon."

As directed, I leaned the ladder against the post under the box. The dog sat down. Back at the wagon, I looked through the mail pack, picked out a letter, put the others back into the wagon. Then I walked to the ladder, checked to make sure it was steady, climbed up, opened the mailbox, put in the letter and closed it again. Holding onto the ladder with one hand, I reached for the whistle with the other. The owner must be signaled that mail had just been delivered.

The "Mailman" blew his whistle, smiled and descended the ladder.

"Okay, keep going," softly cued the director.

I didn't look at him. I remembered.

I picked up the ladder and put it back into the wagon. The dog stood up. I looked toward the house. Nobody answered the first

The toothless mailman

call, so I blew my whistle again, then got back into the wagon, picked up the reins and gave them a shake. "Let's go, Bernie."

As we started out of camera range, on cue a woman actor, drying her hands on her apron, came rushing out of the house and down the steps to the mailbox.

"Cut! Okay!" called the director. "That was fine, Coy."

The next scene involved a similar set-up: another house, another post and box and the same routine. In fact, for a couple of hours there were more posts and boxes, some taller.

Whenever a scene started, I didn't know what the director might want me to do. During one shot, he saw me having trouble standing the ladder up straight and steady. The camera continued filming.

"Oh, you've got a little problem there," the director said. To keep the action going, he said, "Put your hand up by your ear, you're thinking." So, I pushed up my cap to one side.

"Scratch your head. Look up at the sky. That's good."

"You've got an idea. Move the ladder a little." He waited for me to complete the action, then said, "That's it. Let's have a smile."

As the camera continued grinding the director laughed. "Now straighten your cap. Look at the mailbox. There, that's okay. Now go over to the wagon and get a letter."

Like the other scenes, I continued up the ladder, put the letter in the box, closed it, blew the whistle, climbed down and put the ladder in the wagon, got in and, with Bernie pulling, rode out of the scene.

As the cameraman cranked the camera, the director would talk me through the scene—changing it, as he liked, all without rehearsal. I just did what I was told. This is how I remember making silent films in the early days.

A STREETCAR RIDE

1916

When I was about four years old, as big a thing as working in pictures was riding on the streetcar to visit my Grandpa and Grandma Watson. They lived on a two-acre farm on Allesandro Street, about two miles from our house, at the end of the Edendale Red Car Line. I don't remember the first time Mom put me on the car to travel alone, but I remember other trips very well.

One day after lunch our wall phone rang. Mom sat down to answer it.

"It's Grandma Watson," she said.

They talked awhile as I rolled my toy car on the floor. Mom hung the receiver on the hook and looking at me said, "Would you like to ride the street car to see Grandpa and Grandma Watson?"

"Yes, I would." I was on my feet. The only thing I didn't like about it was leaving Sitka home, but it had to be. Grandpa liked Sitka but as Dad had explained, "Grandpa doesn't want Sitka chasing and killing any more of his chickens." I understood that.

"Take off those clothes. I'll help you wash your face and hands. Put on a clean shirt and overalls."

Before I could ask . . . "Yes, you're going to wear your shoes."

"Oh gee, do I have to?"

"Yes." She helped me put them on. When I saw her carefully fold my nightgown and put it in a paper bag, I knew I was going to stay overnight. She handed me the bag and took her purse from the dresser in her bedroom.

On our front porch, her teenage sister, my Aunt Ola, sat playing with my little sisters, Vivian and Gloria. She often visited us from her house around the corner on Mohawk Street, where she lived with my Grandpa Wimer and Uncle Newt. They had all moved from Medford, Oregon about a year before.

Mom told her we were walking to the car line and asked her to watch the little girls until she returned. I told Sitka and them good-bye. Sitka knew why he couldn't come with me! He remembered the last time he went to Grandpa's house. Mom took my hand as we walked on the dirt path across the vacant lot and down to Berkeley Avenue. With every step she told me again what not to do and how good boys acted when they were visiting away from home without their moms and dads along.

A wagon team and two automobiles stirred up the dust around us as they passed. When we reached the car line, we had to stand close to the track or the streetcar wouldn't stop for us. Mom put the nickel for the "can-duck-door" (the conductor) in my pant's pocket and reminded me to be sure to give it to him.

The car finally came along and stopped. Standing at the rear of the car, by the two high steps, Mom picked me up in her arms and gave me a big hug and a goodbye kiss. As I clutched my overnight bag in my hand, she said, "Hello, Mr. Wooley," and handed me up to the man who always wore a funny kind of cap and the same black suit and vest with shiny brass buttons.

"Well, little Coy is going to take another ride to see Grandpa, is he?"

"Yes. He's been a pretty good boy and his grandpa and grandma want to see him again."

Mr. Wooley lifted me up and over to the hard, wooden seat at the rear of the car and sat me down near where he always stood. He told Mom he'd watch me. I gave him my nickel and waited for him to reach up and pull the string that rang the bell to make the car go. When he did, we started to move. I looked out of the window. Mama was waving goodbye and saying, "Be a good boy. Stay in your seat." And, as she did all my life, "Be careful!"

"I will Mama," I called as I waved to her.

Rolling up the tracks through Edendale, I saw Mr. Walker, the gate man, leaning back in his chair in front of Mack Sennett's studio. I waved to him, but he didn't see me. We passed store buildings and people walking beside the street. Two cowboys on horses waved back to me. A dog ran along beside one of them.

I was enjoying the ride as we rocked along. We stopped at Fargo Street to pick up a lady carrying two big fishnet shopping bags. I could see they were filled with groceries, fruit and vegetables. She was a big lady wearing a little, brown hat.

The driver rang the streetcar bell; we were rolling. The car was moving again when she put her bags on the seat across the aisle from me and sat down with her big purse in her lap. She took a good look at me and bobbing her head, asked, "Is this brave, little boy taking a trip all by himself?"

The Edendale car from Los Angeles

I just looked at her, then out the window. We were rolling through the "cut," a place where the tracks cut through a hill and for three blocks we rocked along between the high walls on each side.

"What's in the bag?" the lady asked, leaning over toward me, her head tipped back as she peered through the bottom of her eyeglasses.

"My nightgown. I'm going to stay with my grandpa and grandma." I noticed Mr. Wooley was watching as he stood swaying behind us.

"Oh, isn't that nice! I'll bet you'll enjoy that."

I told her I always had fun at their house. That seemed to please her.

"How would you like an apple?" she asked and started digging through her bags. "I've just bought some very nice ones and you can have one if you like." She held a big, red one across the aisle to me. I reached out with both hands to take it.

"Thank you. I won't eat it now." I put it in my bag with my nightgown.

The car driver in front rang his bell. I leaned out the window and saw Grandpa waiting for me. As soon as we rolled to a stop, I quickly slid off my seat. I told the lady and Mr. Wooley goodbye. I stood in the door as Grandpa held out his arms, I jumped to him. He squeezed me in a big hug and whispered in my ear, "I'm glad to see you. How's my big grandson?"

"I'm fine."

"Did you have a good ride?" he asked.

"Yes," I replied as I pointed to the lady stepping down the steps. "She gave me a big apple."

"Did you thank her?"

"Yes, he did," she answered and walked away saying, "He's a brave, little boy."

"Was he a good passenger today, Mr. Wooley?"

"Yes, and he remembered to give me his nickel this time. He's a good fellow." He waved to me and called, "Goodbye, young fellow." I waved to him.

Hand-in-hand Grandpa and I took our time walking. I heard the streetcar bell ring as we stepped down the long flight of wooden steps in the hot sunshine to the street below.

PLAYING MARBLES WITH GRANDPA

1916

Grandpa's house sat way back from the road, just across the newly paved black street. One day during my last visit, I had watched the men put the black, smoking, stinky stuff all over the dirt roadbed and then flatten it down with a big steamroller. As we crossed it, Grandpa said he liked the new street.

He carried my bag and held my hand as we walked up the path toward the house. He called my attention to his garden of nice vegetables growing in long straight rows on one side of the path. On the other side of the path stood a line of pretty peach and plum trees that he liked very much. I was disappointed to see all the fruit had been picked. I remembered how much fun it was when I had climbed up in the tree I liked best. I sat on a limb that just fit me and picked all the ripe, yellow peaches I could eat. I knew when the bees buzzed around my

Grandpa Watson's farm in Edendale

head they wouldn't sting me. I just sat there that warm summer day and ate peaches while the sticky, sweet juice ran down my arms to my elbows.

"Look who's there!" Grandpa pointed. Standing on the front porch, Grandma was waving to us wearing a happy smile and her blue checked apron. I waved to her. Grandpa let go of my hand, gave my shoulder a little push and said, "Go to her."

I ran up the path waving. It was cool when I ran into the shade of the big bottle tree. The white jasmine blossoms growing up the side of the house put a good smell in the air.

Grandma bent over, clapped her hands and held them out to me. I bounced up the steps and into her arms. She squeezed me tightly. She smelled good like my Mom; nice and clean like a bar of white soap. I felt her hand patting my back. I hugged her hard too.

Grandma Watson

"I'm glad you've come to see us." Then she put her hand on my face and leaned back. We looked into each other's eyes.

"Did you have a good ride on the car?"

"Yes, and a lady gave me a big apple. Grandpa has it in my bag."

"She must have thought you were a good boy."

"She said she thought I was a brave boy. You don't have to be brave to ride on a streetcar, do you Grandma?"

"I think you are brave and I know you like to ride on the streetcar. I've made you and Grandpa a plum pudding for supper."

"Oh good, thank you."

Grandpa was on the steps as he put his hand on my head. "The 'can-duck-door' said he was a good boy today."

"I stayed in my seat all the way. Yes, I did. Can I take off my shoes now?"

"Oh, yes," said Grandma as she opened the screen door for us. "Come in."

I went into the room where I always slept (even before I knew how to walk) to hang my nightgown in the closet. Rolled up in my nightgown, I found my little, red cast-iron fire engine. Mom thought of everything! I rolled it across the polished, wooden floor a couple of times and then put it on the dresser that had the broken looking-glass. Shaking his bag of "emmies," "dough-babies," and "aggies," Grandpa called, "Who wants to play marbles?"

With a hand on the arm of a chair for a little help, he kneeled down in the living room on the only carpet in the house. I dropped down beside him as he rolled the different colored "migs" out onto the soft rug. We chose our "taws" and "lagged" to a line to see who got first shot. We clustered the marbles in the center of what was like a big ring in the design of the rug. Grandpa won and took first shot, knocking two migs out of the ring. I couldn't shoot very hard, so when it came my shot, I didn't knock any out. Grandpa let me "fudge" and get up closer. Then I knocked out four! We were having fun when my aunts, Ethel and Hazel, came in and gave me a big kiss and a striped bag of candy lemon drops. We all had one.

Grandpa Watson

Grandpa and I played until Grandma called from the kitchen, "Come boys. Wash your hands. Supper is ready!" Aunt Ethel clapped her hands and Grandpa laughed as I helped him stand up and rub his knees.

At the table, just like Dad did at our house, Grandpa asked us to bow our heads and pray before we touched our food.

"Our Father, we thank You for this food and pray You will bless it and nourish it to our bodies. God keep us well and strong and help us to be loving, kind and true. Amen."

All the plates that Grandma had heated in the oven were on the table in front of him. Starting with Grandma, he handed each of us a plate with a slice off the roast. We helped ourselves to the potatoes and gravy. I didn't take any vegetables. That started it again!

They all told me I should learn to eat them, as they were good for me. I'd heard all that before. I did eat some that Grandpa made Ethel put on my plate. It was all good and I cleaned my plate. Then we finished our dinner with Grandma's plum pudding.

DEVELOPING PICTURES IN THE PANTRY

1916

After dinner, Grandpa said he was going to develop some photographic plates he had exposed in his camera the day before. Did I want to help him in the darkroom?

Before the end of the 19th century, after studying some books on photography that he had sent for and received from the U.S.

Army Signal Corps, Grandpa became one of California's first photographers. He learned to develop his 5" x 7" glass plates and make his own prints. I loved my grandpa and was always pleased and thought it was great when he asked me to help him. He worked in Grandma's little five-foot square pantry which he used as a darkroom. At the end of a narrow bench, he placed a big tin box the size of a five-gallon can, with a red glass on one side. He lined up three white trays next to the glass and from the three bottles he filled the trays with developer, water and hypo-fixer. Opening the door on one side of the tin box, he set in a lighted coal oil lamp, for there was no electricity in the house.

"Well, Helper, are we ready to 'go dark?'" He looked down at me. I was in my place sitting on a little wooden box that had a picture on it of a cowboy fry-ing pancakes. My back was against a wall of glass jars filled with Grandma's canned peaches, plums, tomatoes, beans and corn.

"I'm ready, Grandpa." He closed the door. We were in the dark.

"Now we go to work," he said and explained what he was doing. "I'm taking a plate out of a holder."

As my eyes became used to the dark, I could see Grandpa's head and shoulders bobbing by the red light as he rocked his tray of developer. It wasn't too bad at first, but after a while I could smell the stinky chemicals.

"Do you see any light?" he'd ask.

"Yes, I can see little cracks of light around the door."

"We won't worry about 'em." He assured me that they wouldn't fog his plates. He talked to me about many things and asked me questions as he worked. I think he wanted to keep me awake. I didn't get sleepy, but I got tired, and the box got hard.

Grandma knocked on the door, "Are you two still alive in there? Don't stay too long, Jim. You don't have much air." She was right. The air was stuffy, but cool.

After a while, the red light became brighter to my eyes. I could see Grandpa holding a plate up to the light to get a good look at it.

On the beach at Santa Monica. Front (left to right): My dad, Vic, Ethel, Grandma. Middle: Rally and Bill. Back: Grandpa and Herb. With his camera set up on a tripod, Grandpa had a bystander click the shutter.

"Ah yes, that's a good one," he'd say, or "Oh my, that is quite over-exposed," whatever that meant. I got tired, but I never let him know I wanted to open the door and go out.

Sometimes we'd sing songs like "Way Down Upon the Swanee River" or "Jimmy Crack Corn."

"Oh Coy!" He said with delight. "Here is a good negative I got of the river. Come have a look!" I stood up and squeezed between him and the plate he held close to the red glass. Developer was dripping from his prize into the tray next to my nose.

"I don't see anything, Grandpa."

"See all those little black spots across the center? They are reflections from the sun on the ripples of the flowing water. This is only a negative, you know. You must envision all that's black and white on here will be white and black on the printed picture."

"I just see some black and white smudges!"

A 1903 Grandpa Watson photo of the world famous Buffalo Bill Wild West Show moving down Broadway in Los Angeles

"You will learn to read negatives in time," he assured me. "Sit down again." He dipped the plate into the water, then into the fixer. I felt around for my box and sat down by the string beans. Happily Grandpa took another plate from a holder and put it into the tray of developer.

As he waited, he told me how he helped his dad care for horses in England when he was a little boy and how one of his uncles took care of the King's horses. It was a very serious thing when a horse got sick and his uncle had to know what to do to make it well.

"Your daddy is a good horse doctor, too. He likes to take care of animals."

"I know that, Grandpa."

Grandma knocked hard again. "Jim, it's been thirty minutes. You must come out before you and that boy suffocate."

"I'm about finished, Amy. Please don't open the door!"

Only thirty minutes? It seemed like hours before Grandpa finally opened the door. The light from the lamp on the kitchen table seemed bright and made my eyes squint, but the fresh air smelled good. I stood rubbing my eyes.

"There now, we'll wash the plates in Grandma's sink and after they dry in a couple of days, we'll make some prints from 'em."

His pictures were usually of pretty landscapes, rivers, mountains and some of the family on picnics at the beach or in the mountains. He also enjoyed taking pictures of parades and sailing ships in Los Angeles Harbor. He had taught my dad and Uncle Rally photography and laughed when he told me they called him "Snapshot Willy" because he enjoyed making pictures so much.

We enjoyed being together as I helped him wash and dry his trays in the kitchen. We bottled and corked his solutions and stood them back on the floor in the pantry.

"Some day all my plates will be yours," he said as he looked at me, gripped my shoulder and patted my head. He was right. However, at that time I didn't know how important still photography would become in my life!

WHEN MY STICK HORSE RAN AWAY

1916

We little boys took our early broomstick horse-riding very seriously. I'll never forget one particular ride. After a couple of days of cold winter rains, the weather let the warm sun come out and mothers let us go outside to play. A few puffy, white clouds floated swiftly across a clear blue sky carried by a crisp, high December wind.

Bundled up in our winter coats and stocking caps, Sonny, Sydney and I were astride our stick ponies. With Sitka at my side we were riding around the big vacant lot, our imaginary cowboy-and-Indian country. The neighborhood had been washed fresh and clean, but the ground was still damp and slippery with puddles of muddy rain water here and there.

After the water holes and the tears dried up. Vivian, Dad and a happy cowboy.

As we broke into our second gallop up a hidden canyon looking for Indians, I saw a camera car coming down Allesandro Street from the studio. A company was shooting a running scene for a Keystone comedy. We pulled up and watched. Standing up in the rear section of the loaded, open touring car was the crew, shooting, with Ernie Schoedsack turning the crank to photograph a car behind him as they moved along. The director, Hampton Del Ruth, was calling directions through his megaphone. Prop man Ray Hunt was holding a reflector to reflect sunlight onto Gloria Swanson and Bobby Vernon, following closely in a Model T Ford touring car with its top down. Teddy, Keystone's big Great Dane dog, sat up in the back seat. His owner, Joe Simpson, stood on the front seat of the camera car waving his arms and telling Teddy, "Smile!"

We three cowhands trotted quietly with them along the curb as we watched. Gloria had an arm around Bobby and with the other hand was patting his cheek. They were smiling and talking. The director yelled, "That's good, now a big laugh!" They rolled their eyes at each other as the cars rolled past us and made a left turn at the corner along Berkeley Avenue and out of sight.

We sat in our saddles and made up a story. We pretended we chased and caught a train robber and put him in jail. He beat up the sheriff and got away. We chased him again and things got very exciting. My stick horse, Buck, Sitka and I had to splash our way through several muddy lakes and rivers before we cornered our man in a box canyon. When he was locked up again our game was over.

Then I realized I had a real problem. My shoes and pants were soaked with muddy water. We took a slow jog up to the house. Sonny pointed. There stood Mom on the front porch. It didn't look good for us. We pulled our ponies to a stop. Mom wasn't smiling and took a long look at her little cowboy. She folded her arms as she gazed at my feet. I hurried to explain how during our big chase my pony had run away with me, right through water puddles, to catch the bank robber!

I'd hardly finished my story, and before I could dismount, Mom was off the porch, took hold of my shoulder, pulled my pony from between my legs and carefully stood him next to the porch. My saddle buddies, wide-eyed, sensed trouble and rode for cover. Sitka knew what was going to happen and backed off. Mom spoke softly in my ear to remind me.

"This is the second time in two weeks that your pony has run away through muddy water holes."

Seated on the porch, holding me firmly with one hand, she bent me over her knee and with the other bare hand she quickly landed six good, hard, stinging swats right where she always put them! On my bottom! They hurt! I knew cowboys didn't cry but this one did. Released, I stood with tears running down the cheeks of my face and with both hands I rubbed the cheeks of my sitter. Bending down, with her face near mine, Mom held a very red finger close to my nose. I'll always remember what she said.

"There cowboy, I don't think your pony will run away through any more water puddles again, will he?"

I got my breath back, dried my face and managed to sniffle an assuring, "No."

"Good. Now take off those muddy, wet shoes and socks before you catch your death of cold."

The faces of my worried saddle pals peeked around from behind the big eucalyptus tree. Sitka came up beside me as we watched Mom open the door.

"Your pony will stand easy while you come in the house and put on some dry clothes."

My pals waved. I signaled back for them to wait, I'd be out.

That night Sitka lay warm on the floor in the corner near my bed while Dad and I knelt and said our prayers. "Amen." I jumped into bed. Dad tucked me in and gave me a kiss on the forehead.

"There now, goodnight, sleep good, God bless you! Mom will see you soon."

I waited, closed my eyes and was almost asleep when I felt Mom's hand on my head. She sat on the side of my bed with her arm across my chest.

"Are you nice and warm?" she asked with a smile.

I nodded. She hadn't talked much at dinner.

"Are you ready to go to sleep?"

"Yes," I said, "I'm tired."

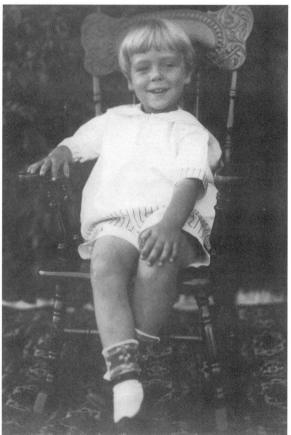

I cleaned up pretty well!

"Did you say your prayers with Daddy?"

I answered, "Yes."

She lowered her face close to mine. Looking kind of sad, she spoke softly, "I spanked you today because your pony didn't get your feet wet. You ran through the water and got your feet wet. Didn't you?"

"Uh-huh."

She moved closer, our noses almost touching, and with her finger tapping my cheek, she said, "You know I love you and have to teach you to keep your feet dry because I don't want you to get sick and feel bad and have to stay in bed all day. You wouldn't like that would you?"

We were looking into each other's eyes. I shook my head and pulled my arms from be-neath the covers and put them around her neck.

"I love you, Mama."

She put her lips to mine for a big, long kiss. I held her tight and then let her go.

"What a big hug from my big boy!"

I patted her cheeks, then put my hands under the covers. She pulled them up under my chin.

"There now, cowboy, go to sleep and you can ride Buck again tomorrow. Goodnight Sweetheart."

"Goodnight Mama."

"Sleep tight and God bless you!"

"God bless you."

She blew out the lamp. The room went dark. I closed my eyes and thought about the day. Mom was right, my stick horse never ran away again!

COWBOYS LOVE THEIR HORSES

1916

I liked to have Dad tell me stories and to have Mom read me stories from books. One cold night after supper, a few days following my last ride through lakes and rivers, Mom was in the kitchen washing the dishes. I was wrestling with Sitka on the floor. Baby sister, Gloria, was asleep in her crib and Vivian, wearing her nightgown with little pink flowers on it, was playing on her bed with her doll.

The house was warm. Dad was sitting in his Morris chair. I jumped to my feet and hurried to stand at his knees. He puffed on his newly rolled smoke a couple of times, then held the burning match down to my puckered lips and I blew out the flame. We watched the curling matchstick smoke and go out.

"Thank you," he said and dropped it in his ashtray.

"Daddy, tell me a story, please?"

Our eyes met. He smiled. "All right. What'll it be this time?" he asked and I answered quickly as he lifted me onto his lap. "A cowboy story." Sitka rolled over on his side and looked at me. I waved a finger and he moved his tail.

"More about cowboys, huh?" Dad tipped his head to one side, settled me onto his lap and lightly patted my leg. Well, let's see, cowboys are funny guys. They are a lot different from men who live in cities. They even dress a whole lot different. A cowboy is not much without his pal, the horse, is he?"

A Sunday get-together in our alfalfa field. Left to right: Claude Elliott, Dad and friends.

"No." I snuggled close and laid my head on his chest. His arms folded around me and I patted his hand.

"A good cowpuncher takes better care of his horse than he cares for himself, because he knows he's only as good as his horse. When he's not riding his horse, he always loosens the saddle cinch. When it's hungry time, he sees that his horse gets fed before he takes time to eat. He only allows his horse to eat what's good for it." He glanced down at me and cleared his throat. "And, of course, you know a good cowboy never lets his horse run away with him!"

To that I squirmed a little and rolled my eyes to his.

"In fact, a thoughtful cowboy will never run his horse too hard or too long without letting it stop to have a rest. We must remember a horse is trained to do what its rider wants it to do. Good horses have been known to keep running and have sometimes run themselves to death because the riders didn't care enough to stop."

"From the early cattle herding days, cowboys who really liked horses had their own way of seeing that horses were cared for. If a cowboy ever saw another cowboy running a horse too hard or mistreating it, especially if it wasn't his horse, one of the boys would quietly remind the abusing cowboy to take it easier on the horse and be kind to it. After that cowboy had been told, if he continued to abuse the horse, the other cowboys rode up around him, got off their horses and pulled him off his horse. They took him roughly into hand to teach him and give him a good "Chapping" (pronounced "shap-ping"). This meant, wherever they were, even under a hot sun out in the middle of a lone prairie, one of the cowboys would kneel on the ground, down on all fours, while the other cowboys, as many as it took, wrestled and got hold of the "meanie's" arms and legs. They took everything from his pockets and held them for him in his hat. Then they would bend him over the kneeling cowboy.

"Standing ready, near the dusty huddle, was a suntanned, husky cowboy holding in his brawny hands one leg of a pair of cowboy's chaps. On a 'Let's teach him, Mack,' the huge cowboy proceeds to take big swings and swats with the chaps at the upturned bottom. Now, a pair of chaps are the heavy, leather leg protectors that cowboys wear over their pants to keep their legs from getting scratched or cut when they ride herd on cattle through high, thick, sticky brush. So, the heavy spanking must have really hurt that cowboy! Each time the chap hit his seater, the boys all counted out loud together, 'four, five, six.'"

"Mom didn't count my swats," I chimed in.

"Other cowboys rode up to watch and laugh and waited to hear their thoughtless saddle pal speak up and say he'd had enough and that he would not mistreat his friend the horse any more. Sometimes, if the punished cowboy wouldn't speak up soon enough, to make the swats hurt a little more, one of the cowboys would pour water from a canteen onto the seat of the upturned Levis. The caring herd drivers were always glad when the cowpuncher finally grunted and spoke out. Covered with sweat and dust, he painfully promised to be kinder and not mistreat horses ever again. When they let him up, he stood rubbing his seat and was handed his hat."

Very concerned, I asked, "Did the cowboy cry when they spanked him?"

"If he did, he didn't shed any tears. But that bunch never saw him mistreat a horse again."

"That was good," I thought and watched Mom put some wood into the stove.

Dad continued, "The horse and the dog have been man's two best friends for a long, long time. Helping in so many ways, they have been known even to die while trying so hard to do what they thought their masters wanted them to do. That's why people must be careful not to expect too much of them or work them too hard. We must feel for them. Be kind and take good care of them and love them."

Dad wearing his gray hat, seated in his corral (to right). Keystone Hill is visible in the upper right.

I sat up, looking at Dad. "I love Sitka. I take good care of him, don't I?"

"Yes, you do, and I hope you'll always be kind to all animals."

"Even cats?" I questioned.

"Yes, even cats." I didn't say any more because I didn't think cats were as good as dogs.

"Well, that's the end of that story. Did you like it?"

"Yes, cowboys sure must like horses a lot."

Dad put his hand on my head and shook it.

I said, "I like cowboys."

"Yes, most of them are good fellows like my friends that you know. Now, go get your pajamas and I'll help you get into them." He stood up and took his cigarette from the ashtray and put it between his lips and reached for a match and lit it.

"Was the cowboy mad at his friends after they spanked him?"

"He might have been a little upset with his pals, but he was more likely to be ashamed of himself. He knew he deserved to be chapped."

Dad helped me with my pajamas. Later, lying snug in bed, I decided cowboys were rough guys. I fell asleep thinking about that one, the one with the red bottom, and how bad it must have hurt when he sat back on his horse!

Dad on right. I'm wearing his hat as I play cowboy on a cowboy.

MERRY CHRISTMAS

1917

A couple of unexpected gifts made a cold, Christmas morning warm for this five-year-old. Oh, boy! Was I surprised and happy to find next to the Christmas tree a dandy ride-in toy automobile that I could peddle and drive myself. There was also a sixteen-inch cast iron toy model of a red hook-and-ladder fire truck. I hadn't asked Santa Claus for either one. Who knew I would like them so much? Dad was pleased to tell me the car was a gift from his friend, Charlie Murray, one of Keystone's star comedians. The little fire wagon was from his friend, Louise Fazenda, slapstick comedy's first star comedienne. Sisters Vivian and Gloria also stood wide-eyed at the tree when they saw their dolls and little baby buggies from Dad's friends. Mom and the girls played with the dolls.

Dad and I got a big surprise when we wound up the fire truck and let it run across the floor. When the bumper hit the wall, the three ladders lying on top were automatically released to unfold

Charlie Murray

and stand up, three high, against the wall! I became a fireman making sounds like sirens and bells clanging as my equipment arrived at the scene of a fire. I vividly imagined a fireman climbing the ladder to a window of a burning building and bringing an old lady down the ladder to save her life.

Such excitement was running high when Charlie arrived at our house to watch us have a very merry Christmas. Miss Fazenda phoned to say, "Merry Christmas." I wished her the same and thanked her for the fire truck. The folks that made the early Keystone Comedies in Edendale were much like all pioneers; they felt and worked together as one big, close family. I knew everybody liked my dad and mom.

I peddled my car all over the neighborhood until Dad made a harness for Sitka to pull it. He added a full-sized automobile horn to my "Peerless" sports car. I squeezed the big rubber bulb to make it honk, honk! I rode past the neighbor's houses at top speed pretending I was Barney Oldfield, the great auto racer.

Vivian and Gloria enjoyed their dolls and toys and often asked if they could have a ride in my car. I let them take a short spin or two on the rough, dirt-packed paths around our yard. I didn't play with their dolls. That was a wonderful Christmas for all of us, thanks to Dad and his Keystone Studio friends.

Vivian, me and Sitka ready for a ride in the automobile from Charlie Murray

PICTURE PROJECTORS AND RADIOS

1917

At age five, I was fascinated by projected pictures and played with my Magic Lantern slide projector for hours. I lay on my stomach in a dark closet and projected the image onto the closet's white wall. The tiny, colored, glass slides were of kids and dogs playing with wagons and sleds in the snow. The light in my slide projector was made by a little coal oil lamp. It's a wonder I didn't burn down the house or suffocate myself. I did so love my Magic Lantern!

Later, at age 10, I earned my first hand-cranked moving picture projector by getting 10 subscriptions to the *Gentlewoman Magazine*.

Early radio fans—sisters Louise and Gloria

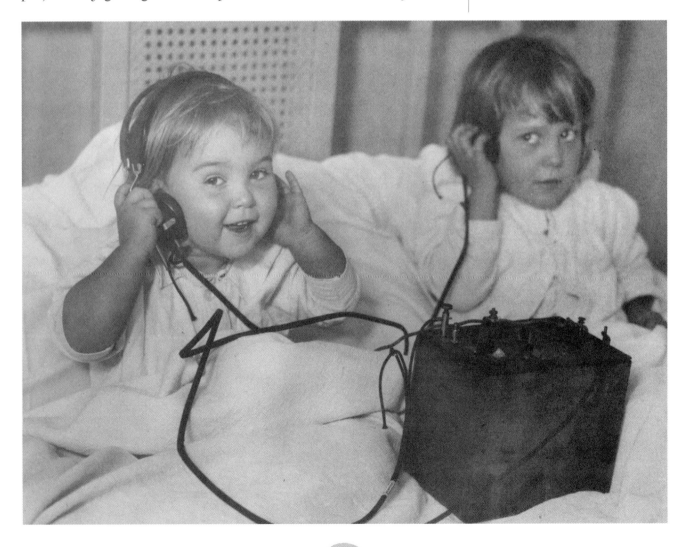

The ad had run on the back of the *Los Angeles Times* Sunday comic section.

Years later, for our first radio, I made a crystal set. Again, the inspiration came from a drawing I saw in the newspaper. I used a black, hard rubber phonograph record for the front panel and tacks with brass heads for the contact points. I wrapped 10 feet of copper wire around an empty oatmeal box and connected it to a 50-cent crystal and listened to my first Los Angeles radio programs.

Uncle Newt (my Mom's brother) was an early licensed ham radio operator and he loaned me a pair of earphones. I soon learned one radio and two earphones were not enough for Mom and Dad, my sisters and me to listen to radio programs. Even though we took turns listening and passed the earphones around during commercials, it was always a problem who got them next!

We all wanted to listen to "Chando the Magician," "Mert and Marge" and "The Two Black Crows." Something had to be done to reduce the number of fuses if the Watsons were to enjoy radio. So, I hustled the neighborhood and got a second crystal radio set with two more earphones when I turned in ten new one-month subscriptions to the *Los Angeles Examiner* newspaper.

SITKA AND I MARCH FOR SCHOOL BONDS

1918

During World War I, somebody decided the school needed more classrooms. I didn't understand it, but we were told some bonds, whatever they were, were going to be floated somewhere in our area and our school would receive some money to enlarge the school. Our teachers told us to spread the word and tell everybody. It sounded like it was going to be a lot of fun.

It wasn't until the principal told us of plans for a big "Vote for School Bonds" parade through Edendale that I got the idea they were not going to "float" these bonds on Silver Lake or Echo Park Lake! To march in the parade, we were all told to dress up in colorful costumes as if it were Halloween. We could decorate our wagons or bicycles, or make "Vote for Bonds" signs.

"Make anything that will look interesting to the people standing on the curbs as we march by," our teacher announced.

I had seen pictures in the paper of army dogs wearing wide, white body bands around their middle with big red crosses. Dad told me these dogs helped the army doctors find the wounded soldiers on the battlefield in France. Mom helped me pin a piece of white cloth around Sitka's middle. Then, on both sides, we printed a big red cross, using a good portion of her lipstick.

For my field doctor's uniform, I wore a brown shirt over my only long pants, my blue bib-overalls. Dad dug up an old hat and a very old knapsack for me. He said it made me look like a soldier. Mom didn't exactly agree. With an empty first-aid kit under my arm, on that warm day in June, when the parade formed on Clifford Street in front of our school, Sitka and I lined up as the only barefooted, army medical search team in the world.

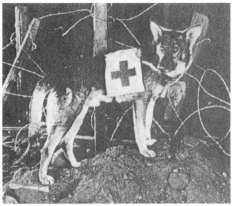

Rin-Tin-Tin as a World War I army medical dog

Sitka and I, and Muriel McCormick dressed like Little Bo-Peep, marched behind a big, outstretched American flag carried by five girls on each side. At the head of the parade was a tall kid wearing an "Uncle Sam" suit. Beside him were two boys in white pants and shirts each carrying a flag—the American flag and the California flag.

As we passed folks standing at the corner in front of Bear's Drugstore, they clapped and cheered for us. Two little kindergarten boys, dressed like brownies, walked behind us carrying and dragging an eight-foot banner that read, "Vote for School Bonds June 4th." We made it to Fargo Street and did a hairpin turn and headed south down the boulevard. All of the straggling three hundred children were out of step and so were the drums. Mrs. Getz and the teachers were flitting up and down beside the line, helping kids that were losing their pants or parts of their costumes. Cardboard "Vote for Bonds" signs were falling off poles, colored crepe paper peeled from wagons and bicycles dragged in the street. Watchers from the curbs stepped out to help.

I looked at Sitka as we walked along. We were enjoying it. We were together. He looked up at me with a smile as we passed Robly's Meat Market. Though a big crowd cheered for the flags, I knew Sitka was thinking of our dear friend Mr. Robly and the big bones and scraps of meat he saved for us.

When we moved by the famous Selig Studio, now the Clara Kimball Young Studio at Clifford Street, a group of actors, in their fancy dinner suits and dresses, had come out to watch the parade. They clapped and laughed and waved to us. They looked kind of ridiculous.

Sitting on the steps of Norbig's Studio was an old bearded

cowboy, who looked pretty "swacked" to me. He was waving his arms and singing, "Three Cheers for the Red, White and Blue." We all laughed and yelled, "Vote for School Bonds."

A man with his face lathered up with shaving soap, wearing the long, white cloth around his neck, stood holding the barbershop door open. He and the barber were laughing and shouting words of encouragement to us.

Vivian, Sitka and me ready to march

Oh! Oh! Here's trouble! A barking dog came running at us down Branden Street. "Oh, gosh!" I put my hand on Sitka and spoke to him. I felt the hair on his neck stand up. He made a little growling sound and looked at the dog. The dog stopped barking and backed off onto the sidewalk. I patted my pal as we walked on. We surely didn't want to cause injury. We were a team searching to aid the wounded. We were unable to attend to the only injury that occurred, when one of the teachers, dressed like Old Mother Hubbard, fell and skinned her knees.

When we came to Dave's Pool Hall at Aaron Street, some of Dad's cowboy friends were standing and sitting on the curb. They recognized us and were glad to see us. "There's Coy Watson's boy!" one remarked.

"Hey, look at Sitka." "Hello, boy," one waved and took a chaw of tobacco.

I was glad to see them, and I waved back. Sitka looked at them with his ears up and his tail wagging. He was enjoying it all. When we passed Katie's Cafe, she was standing on the curb waving. "Hello, Coy and Sitka!" Sitka was so pleased I thought he might stand up on his hind legs and take a bow, or leave the parade! He was remembering her back door handouts!

Then we marched past the west side of Mack Sennett's studio. A couple of companies shooting there had left their sets and were lined along the curb. There were the Keystone Cops and others in their funny clothes, making wisecracks and slapstick faces at us. I

knew them all. I saw Chester Conklin and Billy Bevan as both had
played my father in pictures. As usual, they all looked happy, laughing and being funny.

As we neared the Effie Street corner, I saw Mom standing in
the crowd holding baby Louise in her arms with Vivian and Gloria
at her side. They were watching for us. When they saw us they
broke into a big laugh of excitement and clapped their hands. They
called to Sitka and he ran to them. He wanted to stop and say "Hello,"
so we did. For a few seconds Mom and the girls told us how good
we looked. Sitka wiggled around as they all patted him. Other folks
watching laughed aloud as we ran along to get back into our place
in the line.

At Effie Street, the line of march made a U-turn across the
boulevard and headed north again. Over a hundred of Mack Sennett's
people lined up along the sidewalk the entire block in front of the
studio's main gate. As we paraded by to the drum's offbeat, there
was Mr. Walker the gate-man, wearing his gray cap and his handle-
bar mustache. Even Mr. Sennett stood waving to us with Mabel
Normand at his side. I saw Louise Fazenda waving from her dressing
room window on the second floor. I had worked with all these folks
and I liked them. It was good to see them all waving and calling to
us. I looked for Dad, but I didn't see him.

On the Aaron Street corner, down the hill from the studio carpenter shop, in their dirty white overalls, stood a group of carpenters
and painters. They, too, looked happy to see us and waved. Sonny's
big Swedish dad, foreman of the carpenters, gave me a big "Hello,
Coy!" It looked like everybody in the studio had taken time to come
out to see our parade.

Now we were on the "home stretch" walking the last two blocks.
It was a warm day and the street was hot to our bare feet. Some of
the little kids were crying. The drummers had quit. A few people
on the curb continued to cheer as we passed by, but our lineup
looked tired and sorry. There were no more calls to "Vote for School
Bonds." We moved along, but we were looking for the finish line.
The campaigning enthusiasm had faded away. Even the teachers
were "pooped" and glad the first and last school bond parade was
over. Some of the bigger students carried little kindergartners to
the moms who waited at the bottom of the hill. Sitka was glad to
get rid of the Red Cross wrapper and we were glad to go home.

I never got to see them, but I guess those bond things floated
somewhere, because our school got a dandy new addition built on
the upper ground. School was always fun, but not the studies.

MOVIES MADE IN OUR STREETS

1918

From 1912 to 1926, Edendale's streets must have been the background for more comedies than any other streets anywhere!

I remember one funny scene with a couple of bearded tumblers dressed as painters in baggy overalls and big shoes. While crossing the street in a funny little truck, they were hit by the police wagon and spun around. As their ladders were thrown in the air (pulled out of

The Keystone Cops create a traffic hazard

the scene by piano wires) they did some forward and backward flip-flops. Paper buckets of whitewash flew through the air, landing all over a surprised gathering of nicely dressed music lovers, who stood on the corner enjoying the sounds of a uniformed, four-piece German band.

At that moment, three cops tumbled from the back of the wagon and rolled out onto the street. They struggled to get to their feet, did a little Keystone hop and ran after the wagon. They caught up with their trusty machine just before it banged into a horse-drawn wagon loaded with sweet navel oranges, showering fruit all over the neighborhood! The wagon's driver was flipped (again by piano wires) onto his horse's back, which—wide-eyed, reins dragging—headed

for the barn, leaving the wagon and oranges behind. With a full complement, the patrol wagon sped on to cause more havoc.

Some of the neighborhood women who stood watching the action pulled the hems of their dresses up to their waists, formed sacks, and helped each other fill them with the oranges, trusting their slips would assure their modesty! The film crew laughed as the women waddled off with their loads of fruit. Some of us kids laid our shirts out on the grass and piled on all the oranges we could lift and carry home.

Comedian Jimmy Adams (left), sits with his "dummy" and "double" surrounded by the shooting crew on location

On another day, an interesting scene drew a big crowd. It involved a storefront and a second story window over Moore's Meat Market. A dummy, dressed to look like Chester Conklin, was thrown from the window. It landed on a bed set on the sidewalk as two exhausted furniture movers stopped to mop their brows. In a closer shot, Chester, the live Chester, bounced off the bed and ran out of the scene. Such were the tricks used in pictures. Putting the two film shots together later made the dummy Chester and the live Chester seem to be one and the same.

One Saturday morning I was pulling my express wagon around the neighborhood collecting old newspapers, when I saw a crowd gathered along the curb in front of Sennett's Studio. They were watching director Eddie Cline's company setting up a camera under a big umbrella. When I got closer, I saw all eyes and the camera were pointed up Aaron Street at what looked like a group of actors on the sidewalk. I pulled closer behind the camera where I could watch.

Mr. Kline stood ready, nodded to his cameraman, raised his arm high, waved a broad cue and said, "Camera!" Down the hill, running slapstick style, came a guy in a striped prisoner's outfit. Close behind came eight Keystone Cops in hot pursuit, chasing what had to be an escaped convict.

They all headed for the grinding camera. I recognized the escapee as my friend, Charlie Murray, one of the Keystone's star comedians. He stopped in the middle of Glendale Boulevard and jumped up and down, waving his arms, as he stood between the steel rails of the Pacific Electric Railroad line, which ran through Edendale from Los Angeles to Glendale, 10 miles north. The crowd watched the cops approaching, lifting their feet high and waving their billy clubs.

I heard a "clang, clang" and then I knew Charlie had seen the Big Red 11:15 A.M. streetcar bound for Glendale coming up the tracks, and decided to use it in the chase. From that point on, the action in that running scene would be all "ad lib," unrehearsed. Director Kline told cameraman Ernie Crockett, "Keep grinding. This is gonna be good!"

The convict held a black ball and chain in one arm and with the other frantically waved his black-and-white striped sleeve. He flagged down the car that rolled to a very close stop against his outstretched hand. The action was no surprise to the motorman, who had tumbled into the gag. He had been involved in scenes such as this before and he laughed as the crowd yelled, "Here come the cops!" The escapee quickly tossed his blackened volleyball and rubber chain to the motorman and jumped aboard.

The excited cops arrived on the scene all confused, as usual. The director yelled, "Split up and board the car at both ends." The conductor at the rear of the car learned late of the action, but laughed and stood aside as he let the hijackers run through the car to clash head-on in the middle. The bewildered and frightened passengers were on their feet in a tizzy as they clutched their purses and wallets. The crowd on the street was going crazy with laughter. What next?

Through his megaphone, as loudly as possible, the director yelled, "Charlie, come out the window!" In a second, we saw the ball come out the center window and then, as if pulled by the ball and stretched rubber chain, Charlie flew out feet first and landed flat on the street. Immediately, two fast-thinking cops in the car, George Spear and Ade Linkoff, got another laugh as they dove out the windows, losing their hats and clubs in mid-air and nearly landing on the sprawled man in stripes! The director was delighted and laughed as the cameraman continued to turn the crank. Rolling on the street beside the car, the three comics scrambled around, waving their arms and legs in the air. The curb audience howled with laughter.

A comedy convict leads the cops on a merry chase

"That's great boys! Keep it up!" yelled director Cline. "Now Charlie, get up and run off to the back of the car."

The convict leaped to his feet. Facing the camera, he took time to replace his striped hat on his head, pick up his black ball, do a couple of Keystone hops, wave a silly "goodbye" to his sprawled pursuers and run south. Staggering to their feet, wobbling and bumping into each other, the two cops picked up their hats and clubs and traded hats several times until each was satisfied he had his own. The other cops rounded the front of the streetcar and informed the other two their man had escaped again. As the director yelled to them, they acted out the lines.

"Where is he? Which way did he go? Look around. You spot him. He's over there, that way. Point! Now what do you do? Look at each other. You'd better go get him," Kline yelled.

All together they did a little Keystone hop. (A jump straight up into the air, pulling their feet and knees up high and then back on their feet a bit off balance.) They staggered and bumped into each other, then ran out of the scene after the escapee.

Following their frightening "hold-up," the Red Car men and their passengers laughed and hung their heads out the car windows to watch their beloved, silly, Keystone Cops continue the chase, running and hopping down the tracks, after the weary, ball-carrying escaped convict. The curbstone viewers clapped as the streetcar rolled on through Edendale and the riders waved goodbye. Everybody always got a "kick" out of the moviemaking that was unrehearsed, that simply happened as circumstances developed.

Afterward, while Ernie folded the tripod and camera, I talked with Ade and George. George bruised his elbow during the dive through the window. However, we all laughed, including Mr. Cline and Charlie, at how the scene evolved with the help of the willing streetcar conductors and the frightened passengers.

THEY WRECKED OUR HOME FOR A LAUGH

1918

Dad came home from Sennett's one evening, gave Mom a kiss in the kitchen and told her, "When you've cleaned up after supper I'll help you take all the dishes out of the cupboards and put them in the dining room."

"Why, what in the world are you going to do now?" Mom asked.

"I've made a deal with the 'Old Man' to let him knock down the shed along this side of the house for a scene in a picture."

At first she couldn't believe her ears, yet she had learned to believe anything could happen and did happen in Edendale.

"Oh, Coy, that's awful! You'll let them wreck our home for a comedy scene?"

"But wait 'till you hear the rest. I'll tell you later."

"It better be good," was her reply.

When we went to bed that night the dining room was cluttered with piles of dishes and cooking gear. I was glad the next day was Saturday, no school! Dad had made the wrecking of our house sound strange and mysterious.

The next morning, before we'd finished breakfast, looking out of the kitchen window to the lot next to our house, I saw the studio truck and a company unit setting up cameras, umbrellas and reflectors. Two studio carpenters were tearing down the old back fence between the back of our place and Holmgren's backyard.

I joined a few neighborhood kids as people began to gather on the lot. Two cameras pointed at our old house from two different angles. Director Del Lord and Dad, his assistant, stood talking.

A noisy, big Stutz Bearcat racing car pulled up off of Allesandro onto the lot and stopped. Norman Foy, who had been a real race driver, hopped out and joined Del and Dad. We all moved in close for a good look at the race car. Norman listened carefully to Del's instructions as the three of them looked and gestured toward our house.

The curious crowd grew larger by the moment as folks arrived from all over the area. Mom and the girls came out to watch the action. The director spoke to Mom. "Hello, Goldie. Are your dishes safe?"

"I hope so. What are you going to do to our house?"

"Not the house. Just the shed, Goldie. But we might shake the kitchen."

"I'm ready for that!"

Norm drove the racer into Holmgren's backyard and headed it toward the hole made in the fence in line with the end of our shed. The roof extended out about ten feet and the shed ran the entire forty-foot length of the house. It was held up by five four-by-four posts.

The director told Mom and us kids the story for the scene. The cameras had already filmed the start of the comedy. Drivers in their racing cars had started a cross-country road race. Of course, for comic effect, some of the cars got off the racecourse roads and ran through various scenes. This was to be one of them.

Joe Burdow, dressed as a woman with wig and apron, talked with Norm and then stood ready at the end of the house, out of sight. Norm was in the car and we heard the loud sound of the revved, high-powered engine. A crowd of about 50 people were watching now and waiting for the action to begin. I felt Sitka lean against my leg as we watched.

"Ready?" asked Del. "Alright. Camera!" He waved his arm toward the Bearcat.

We heard the roar of the engine. The racer shot across the fence line and headed for the first post as if fired from a 50-foot cannon! With a crack the car's front right wheel struck the post and flipped it up. The roof started to drop. In a split second the next post was flipped out from under the porch roof. The third post was out and up! The car was staying just ahead of the dropping shed roof. Nobody spoke as we all watched in awe and heard the cracking of the falling timbers.

Norman was moving fast. Honeysuckle was shaken loose and draped itself over the car. The fourth post was gone! The roof was

Vivian and Sitka with our shed to be wrecked in the background

falling fast, but the car was moving faster. The last post was hit and thrown into the air! Down folded the last section of our roof! Norm had to make a sharp left turn to keep from hitting our big eucalyptus tree! While cameras were still turning, Joe, in his woman's outfit, came into sight waving a dishtowel. As if coming from under the roof, he ran across the scene excitedly, jumping up and down, and shaking his arms at the runaway four-wheeled wrecker.

Mom groaned, "Oh, my." The crowd cheered and laughed. The director smiled and said, "Cut." Very Good!" and walked toward the Stutz. Dad was already with Norman, pulling the vines from around his neck so he could get free of them.

"Is he alright, Coy?" asked the director.

"He's okay."

Part of the wrecking crew (front, left to right): Dad, Assistant Director; Glen De Val, Prop man; Norman Foy, Driver; on right rear, Harry Foy, Dad's helper. Three unknown. Seven years later, for a period of four years, Harry was Dad's Assistant Casting Director for William Fox Studio comedies.

"Good job, Norm," Del said. "A perfect shot. Thanks."

"This was easy," said Norman, "compared with Monday's shot when I had to knock down the six freshly-painted, breakaway telephone poles."

Dad told me later, how when Norm had finished that drive, the fresh paint had flaked and spattered from each post as the car hit it, throwing the paint into Norm's face. His eyes became caked, closed with green paint! It wasn't funny to him although it would be to those who saw it on the screen.

Mom told Vivian to watch Gloria and rushed into the house. She came out smiling. To her surprise she had found only a crack in the kitchen window! The neighbor women gathered around Mom to discuss the event.

As the crew packed up, loading the gear onto the truck, I took a close look at our fallen shed. I couldn't see our back door. The vines were on the ground. It had been an exciting scene, but for a six-year-old kid to have his home, such as it was, wrecked, and to hear people laugh and cheer over such action, made me feel sad. Now who cleans this up? What happens now?

Later, Mom was pleased to learn that Mr. Sennett had agreed with Dad to build a new kitchen and a bedroom over the area that had been covered by the old shed. A new picket fence was also added to the deal. A new addition on our house was very welcome! Our old kitchen became part of a closet and Mom and Dad had a new bedroom. Thanks again to Dad's friend and boss, Mack Sennett.

EARLY MOVIEMAKING IN EDENDALE

1918

Life in Edendale was truly exciting. Mack Sennett needed to produce a two-reel comedy every week which was twelve-to-fifteen minutes long. These were the original slapstick, belly-laugh-a-minute flickers. They made the world laugh as the dignified were made to look ridiculous. The best-dressed folks got hit in the face with the biggest pies. Fat ladies sat down on break-away chairs or fell on the funniest, littlest guy on the set.

We kids watched them shoot the first fast-moving chases with horses and wagons, automobiles, fire engines, bicycles and baby buggies running wild all over Edendale and into Echo Park Lake. The Keystone Cops rode in their little police patrol wagon skidding on the soaped streets. Dressed in ill-fitting New York policemen's uniforms, they hit fruit stands, popcorn wagons, telephone poles and chicken coops. They took pratfalls and lifted their knees high as they ran and took corners on one foot, waving their billy clubs over their heads. They were always called to restore law and order to some impossible, funny scene hurriedly created by the quick wit of Hollywood's first comedy gagmen.

The cops drove their wagon through a breakaway wall into a bakery. (Note the cardboard pies, prop donuts and biscuits.)

The director had the story line in mind, but the gags came from everywhere as the shooting progressed. When the crew learned the

Chief of the cops about to send his platoon to create more trouble. Chief, Ford Sterling. Left to right, standing: Edgar Kennedy, Joe Demming, 2 unknown, George Jeskey, Al St. John, Hank Mann, Rube Miller and Roscoe Arbuckle.

Stuck on the train track

themes of the story, each one was encouraged to come up with a funny thought or idea that might suggest an additional gag to help the picture get yet another laugh. Each idea gave birth to another one. Those early comedy idea men set the formula for the way movies, radio and television comedy would be written for years to come.

Edendale became one great big background set for comedy. Folks there watched how it was done right in their own backyards. Early filmmakers didn't build street sets. To save money, they just used the actual stores, shop buildings and neighborhood homes.

With the necessity of making a film a week, Sennett had as many as seven directors with crews, each grinding out a two-reeler somewhere in the neighborhood. A crew consisted of a director, assistant director, cameraman and the prop man who set up the reflectors; and of course, the picture's featured comedians.

There was always an interested gathering of neighbors, young and old, standing on the sidelines watching another new and different comical scene acted out. Laughter from the bystanders encouraged the actors. The directors liked to joke with the onlookers. Often as

we stood by watching, the director would ask us to be in a scene. Some good "hams" were discovered when a group of onlookers was selected to chase a pig into the corner drugstore or to run out of a meat market, chasing after a dog with a prop leg of lamb in his mouth. Director Dick Jones had fun with four women volunteers who were to make eyes at a couple of cops for a scene in front of the barbershop. However, they couldn't keep from laughing. To play the part without laughing was the mark of a good comedian.

A technique originated by the early moviemakers to put more action onto the screen was to use camera cars to photograph running chases. It was interesting to watch a crew at work driving up and down the streets shooting scenes on the move. A camera was set up in the back of a World War I Dodge touring car with its top down. The director and the cameraman stood in the back of the car with the prop man in the front. The driver moved them about 20 miles per hour, along the street beside a moving car, a bicycle, a motorcycle or a baby buggy, to photograph the action in the moving vehicle. As the camera was cranked, the director called cues through his megaphone. The prop man held a reflector—a three-foot square board, covered with tinfoil to reflect sunlight onto shaded faces under wide-brimmed hats.

We kids got a kick out of running along behind the camera car trying to keep up with the shooting. We watched the action as the director yelled his cues to the actors. A chase scene of eight or ten of the always disorganized Keystone Cops riding in their silly, little, overloaded police patrol wagon always got big laughs. The cops wore crepe hair mustaches and eyebrows with heavy make-up and carried billy clubs. Whenever the wagon turned a corner, the cops leaned with it to one side and the bystanders held their breaths expecting the wagon to turn over. Sometimes the streets were sprayed with soapsuds, causing the wagon to skid and spin.

A "soaped" street to skid a car (at the Glendale Blvd./Allesandro Ave. "triangle")

Sometimes the entire neighborhood would turn out standing around watching. The director would talk to women on the porch of a house and ask them to wave when "the fat man on the motorcycle" went past. Others he'd ask to come running out of a house and wave. He'd give all the people watching a little action to do as the comedians drove by. He might ask a man seated on his porch in a rocking chair to stand up and scratch his head. It didn't matter what it was, a runaway motorcycle or a runaway horse dragging a wagon without wheels. Most of the folks got a big kick

36 years later and still having fun

out of acting in scenes and laughing at each other. A week later they'd be down at the theater on Sunset Boulevard to see the finished picture, hoping to see themselves on the screen.

There was never any special costuming. They just wore what they had on. In those days, even the actors and actresses put on their own make-up. I don't remember any make-up men at Sennett's. I don't remember anybody making up Gloria Swanson, Mabel Normand, and Louise Fazenda or checking their hair between scenes. The players took care of their own make-up, hair and wardrobes.

One day, Hampton Del Ruth's company was shooting scenes near our barn on the Sennett lot next door to our house. Gloria Swanson was the star and while waiting between scenes, Gloria's dress became wrinkled. Dad told her to see Mom. She knocked at our back door and asked, "Goldie, can I press my skirt?"

"Sure, Gloria, come in." Mom set up the ironing board and Gloria pressed her own skirt with a two-pound iron heated on the stove top. Gloria knew my mom, and of course my dad, who was a prop-man on many of Gloria's pictures in her earliest days. All the movie people in Edendale knew and helped each other. It was that close-knit relationship that helped start the movie business. Like family, they worked together.

And still later—Dad (front, second from left) gets a laugh from his old Keystone pals

RAISED ON THE MOVIE LOT

1919

As the motion picture business grew, Mack Sennett owned over one hundred acres of land in Edendale. Just south of the studio's main gate and offices, on the west side of Allesandro Street, lay three acres that ran for over two-and-one-half blocks, from Berkeley Avenue north to Effie Street. He owned it all except for one three-quarter acre lot that faced Berkeley Avenue, which was owned by my Dad and Mom. Except for our property and three small rented houses on Allesandro Street, the studio's three acres were covered with movie sets for making moving pictures.

Years before Disneyland and Universal Studios, Sitka and I spent the first years of our lives having fun on movie sets. I got an early education and free entertainment almost every day watching movies in the making. I came to believe it was more important that I learn to make motion pictures than it was to attend school to learn to read and write. On each set and from every scene, I learned a little more about movie magic. They were truly my first learning years. I watched men from all over the country and from all walks of life think and work together. Without a script, on the spot, they came up with original, funny new gags for active scenes.

I spent hours watching with interest the happy spirit with which these fast-thinking men worked. They set the pace and direction for my over 80 years of interest in making moving, still

Below, 1916: Keystone stars, directors and comedians stand on Glendale Blvd., across from the studio's main gate. Behind them is the back of a two-story street set with rough lumber, splinters and rusty nails. Mack Sennett Employees (left to right): Jay Belasco, Louise Fazenda (actress), Mathis Arnold, Arvid Gilstrom, Fred Fishback (director), Dick Jones (director), Bobby Dunn (actor), Slim Summerville (actor), Polly Norman (actress), Charlie Murray (actor), Joe Murray, Gladys Brockwell, Ed Kennedy (actor), Harry Booker (actor), Fred Palwick, Louis Hippe, Chester Conklin (actor), Joe Swickard, Harry Kerr, Bill Campbell (director), Hans Konekamp (cameraman), Pop Keaton, Charles Foy (actor), Mack Swain (actor), Eddie Foy Jr. (actor), Eddie Foy (actor), two Foy girls, William Watson (director), Ed Cline (director), Harry Williams (director), Bryan Foy (director).

and television pictures.

There were several different kinds of sets on the lot. Some were mere fronts of buildings and some had moving parts which added to their realism. One set was a city street, one-block long. It had one and two-story buildings on both sides. The facades, or store fronts as they were called, were just fronts of what they represented. They had no depths, no backs. The fronts of the buildings were all erected and held up from behind by long braces of rough-cut wooden boards.

Signs on the stores, like Bakery, Barber, Butcher, Tailor, Shoes, Hats, Clothing, Drugs and Doctor labeled their fronts. They would all be used in a picture at one time or another. Where Main Street ended was another street across the end with building fronts. Photographing pictures on a street set enabled directors to shoot scenes without the problems they would have on a real city street or its sidewalks. A director could create his own traffic and have it do what he wanted.

It was always fun watching a company shoot scenes on the street. Sitka and I were entertained by wild and wonderful action like a prop man throwing dummies out of a window, funny cars running into stores, or a car knocking over a fake fire hydrant. The studio had its own water supply and could easily control it. It was also fun when no one was working on the street set.

We Edendale kids played some risky runs of "Follow the Leader" when we climbed up and around on the wooden braces. We got splinters in our hands and bare feet from the rough lumber, scratches and holes in our arms and legs from nails sticking out of

boards. We felt there would never be better fun than climbing on those sets. Kids came from other neighborhoods for fun on these sets, and adults came from everywhere in automobiles, to walk around and through the lot. Everyone was interested in looking at movie creations they had seen in pictures.

Then one day we heard some bad news. Mr. Walker, the gate man and security guard at the studio's main gate, came over and told us, "No more climbing on the sets!" He had been given orders by Mr. Sennett to keep a closer watch; nobody on the lot looking at the sets; no more visitors. That didn't stop us guys!

Mr. Walker always wore gray pants, a gray shirt and gray cap. His big gray, handle-bar mustache matched them, so we named him "The Old Gray Fox." So the fun would be more interesting now.

We continued to climb the backs of the sets, but with an organized alarm system for even more fun. If one of us saw the old guy hurrying toward us, we'd yell, "Jiggers, here comes The Old Gray Fox." Laughing, we would drop to the ground and take off in all directions. For years he chased us off the sets.

Years later, Mr. Walker told me he was concerned about us boys. He was afraid we might fall from a brace and be injured. We were lucky. Nobody ever fell!

THE PANORAMA — EDENDALE'S MERRY-GO-ROUND

1919

Of all Mack Sennett's sets used in making motion pictures, we kids thought the "Panorama" was the most exciting and unusual. We called it the "Pano" or the "Rama." It was the only thing of its kind in the movie business. It stood on the big lot at the corner of Glendale Boulevard and Effie Street across from the main gate of Sennett's studio. From the street it looked like a round, two-story building without windows. It was shaped like a high, stiff, straw hat and it turned around freely like a big merry-go-round in a fun park.

The crown of the "hat," on which background scenes were painted, was 30 feet high and 90 feet across the open top. Resembling the flat brim of a hat, the circular stage measured 20 feet from outer edge to the bottom of the background. The stage was steel, covered with a thick wooden floor. Its under-structure was made of steel rods and angle iron. The high circular background was of heavy wire

South side of Edendale's own merry-go-round — The Panorama!

netting covered with canvas. The scenery photographed behind the action on the turning background was always painted to match the background in the earlier scenes shot where the chase started. The Panorama was built to photograph fast-moving scenes on land or in the air without having to leave the studio lot.

On the north side of the Panorama and on the same level with the stage, a broad wooden floor supported the cameras. This deck was where the director and cameras worked. It lay fitted around and up to within one inch of the revolving stage.

Before the "Rama" was invented, running scenes were shot on city streets.

It was a real challenge to coordinate the movements of both camera and subject. A camera had to be solidly set up in a camera car. The director, the cameraman and driver had to move down a city street at 25 miles an hour alongside the moving vehicle in which the comedians acted. It was a costly business and was attended by many headaches. The driver of the vehicle with the actors not only had to watch out for the street traffic, but he had to also match the speed of the camera car. Too close and the cameraman struggled with keeping the subjects in his camera's frame. Too far and the directions might not be heard by the actors. It all took careful timing, lots of rehearsal, film and time. When regular street traffic interfered, a scene might have to be shot eight or ten times before the director was satisfied.

Finally, a city ordinance was passed which required movie companies to obtain a permit before shooting pictures on city streets. Also, a couple of city motorcycle cops had to be hired to direct traffic.

North side view of the "Rama" in action (Glendale Blvd. in the background)

The Panorama was invented to end such difficulties. Running chases could be shot at the studio where the cameras were on a solid deck beside the action on the Panorama's turning stage. All scenes were photographed on the north side of the "Pano" in the shade of the high background. To put more light on the action, six-foot-square boards covered with tinfoil were set up around the set to reflect the bright California sunshine on the action. All day long the reflectors were turned to provide good, even lighting.

I remember standing behind Director Hampton Del Ruth and the camera to watch our beloved Keystone Cops in action on the Panorama. Such a day's moviemaking was a wonder our Edendale neighbors couldn't resist. The little patrol wagon was rolled onto the Panorama's stage headed right, which meant the "Rama" would be turning clockwise. A large, gasoline truck engine that stood on the deck to the left powered the big, revolving set. The engine drove a long, six-inch-wide belt that ran under the stage to turn the entire structure.

The engine was running and the operator stood waiting for his cue to start the "Rama" turning. Ten feet to the left of the engine, just off the stage, mounted on top of a six-foot stand, was a wind machine with a five-foot airplane propeller powered by an automobile engine. Its operator stood by waiting for his cue. Director Del Ruth got the eight cops and their billy clubs into the patrol wagon. The cop driver started the engine.

Onlookers were getting excited. The Keystone Cops' little patrol wagon always drew an audience. The director waved his signals to start the "Pano," the wind machine, and the wagon. It was tricky to get all three started together, but they did. A little acceleration for the patrol wagon and its wheels turned slowly as the Panorama turned under them. The driver had to keep the cops in the camera's frame. Then the director called for more speed. The circular stage turned faster and so did the patrol wagon's wheels. The director asked for more wind across the scene. The Panorama and the wagon were now doing 25 miles per hour! The previously prepared background was a scene of buildings, as they would appear on a city street. The patrol wagon driver was keeping his speed so that it was directly in front of the camera. The turning background made the cops and their wagon look as if they were rolling on a regular city street.

Over the sound of the three engines, the windy propeller and the rumble of the wagon wheels rolling on the turning stage, the

Another way to shoot running street scenes on Glendale Blvd. Top of Panorama in background. Harry Langdon in car.

director yelled through his megaphone, "Action! Camera!" And to the actors, "Look alive. You cops are looking for the bank robbers in their get-away car. Look for 'em! Look all around! There, you see it! It's the robbers' car. Shake your fists and clubs at it. Oh, oh! Look out, the robbers are shooting at you. Start ducking. Tell your driver to speed up. Look mean and brave. That's enough. Cut! Stop everything!" yelled the director. The "Pano" slowed down.

"Good driving there, George, but it went too smoothly, the wagon has to bump." Del Ruth called the carpenters to nail four 2" x 6" x 10' planks across the stage. The scene was started and shot all over again. The planks did the trick. Spaced on the Panorama every quarter turn, the bumps nearly flipped the cops out of the wagon—action intended for more laughs.

My friend Sonny, Sitka and I were standing behind the camera and thought the scene was great. Satisfied with the Cop's second take, the director called for the crew to replace the wagon with the robbers' old, topless Dodge touring car. The robbers got into it with pistols and shot guns heavily loaded with blanks. The "Rama," the wind machine and the robbers' car were started again and similar actions followed. The robbers were photographed hitting the same bumps as they fired at the cops with their heavy, smoking ammunition. That finished the day's shooting.

I knew that to complete the chase sequence, long-shots at slow speed were later taken downtown from the top of a two-story building to show the two cars racing along Los Angeles' city streets. Finally, with all the film shot for the running chase in hand, Director Del Ruth or a film editor would splice the best takes together into one film. Inter-splicing the Panorama shots back and forth from cops to robbers, along with the street footage, made a good, fast-moving chase sequence to cut into a slapstick comedy.

Often when the Panorama was turning, people passing on the boulevard in automobiles, horse-drawn wagons, and even the Big

Keystone Cops in the patrol wagon on the Panorama

Red streetcar loaded with passengers headed for L.A would stop to watch the action on the one-and-only Panorama! Other studios often rented the Panorama to shoot running chase scenes for their pictures. I think I saw everything that could walk, roll, or fly work on the revolving Panorama. Anything imagined was possible!

During the oiling and greasing of the engine, while the Panorama was turning, the carpenters let Sonny and me ride and run around on it — one of the happy events in our lives.

Many times, when things were quiet on the lot, I'd get four or five of the neighbor boys together and on the south side we'd crawl under the "Rama" stage to the open center and push it around. It was no easy task. There was a lot of grunting, groaning and laughing before we finally got it turning fast enough to hop on. Then we'd sit on the iron braces and ride around. When it slowed down, we'd drop off and start pushing again.

We knew it was kind of dangerous and we could be hurt if we fell off and got hit by one of the turning braces. But, we were more worried that "The Old Gray Fox" might see the thing turning and come running over to catch us. We had fun under it until one day I told my dad about it.

"It's not good for you boys to be playing under there," Dad said seriously. "I'd like for you to promise me you won't play under the 'Pano' any more."

I promised and never "rode the braces" again.

A ROCKET IN FLIGHT

1919

A pair of Sennett's funniest comedians (and two of my friends), Louise Fazenda and "Slim" Summerville, were helped onto a 15-foot skyrocket.

The rocket was hanging eight feet above the stage of the Panorama by four piano wires tied by my Dad. They were hooked to cross beams overhead. Clouds were painted on the background and the four wires were painted the same color to make them invisible to the camera's lens.

The day's shooting was to photograph a scene that would follow a previously shot scene for the picture. In the beginning of the sequence the happy-go-lucky couple had attended a rocket launching ceremony. Thinking it would be fun, they straddled a skyrocket that was tilted skyward on its launching pad. Before the pair could dismount, the powerful space vehicle was mistakenly fired. The group of surprised, goofy scientists saw their "baby" with our stars shoot skyward.

Director Craig Hutchinson, now about to shoot the next scene for his picture on the "Pano," called for quiet. It was a beautiful, clear day. The only clouds to be seen were painted on the Panorama's scenery. The camera, set up on top of an eight-foot parallel, was tilted down a bit to the left, which would make the rocket's nose point slightly skyward on the screen. The wind machine was set high to the left on the deck in front of the rocket. It was pointed directly at Louise and "Slim" on the rocket. The prop man, standing on a ladder, fitted a smoke pot into a hole at the rear of the rocket. A group of 50 neighbors stood watching and waiting for the action to begin. When all was ready, the director signaled for the Panorama to start turning the background clouds behind the rocket and its riders. Then he waved to the prop man to light the smoke pot.

I saw the director laugh when he told the stars to just look scared, not *be* scared! They nodded and laughed too.

"Just hang on to each other and give me some funny, worried actions."

When the clouds were rolling by at full speed, the windmaker got the cue for full speed wind. The director called "Camera! Action!"

A one-hundred-mile-an-hour gale blew in the faces of the straining actors. Every inch of their clothing was either pressed hard against their bodies or blowing as if it would be torn away. Every hair on their heads looked stiff, pointing straight out with the wind. The smoke from the rocket was forced into one straight 20-foot stream out of the rear of the rocket. To the camera, the runaway rocket was traveling at two thousand miles per hour, heading for outer space.

Louise Fazenda and Slim Summerville

The excited couple was getting laughs from their live audience. With broad actions the stars were trying to stay aboard the rocket and console each other. Their fearful big-eyed expressions and actions were funny. The director and crew laughed when the riders looked down toward earth, back to where they'd been, and then up to where they were headed.

After a minute of that, the director yelled, "Cut! Stop everything! That's enough! Good stuff!"

The "Rama" slowed, the wind machine stopped, and the prop man dropped the smoke pot into a bucket of water. The crowd gave the company a big cheer as Louise and "Slim" were taken down from the rocket. Another unbelievable scene made easy by the people who originated most of Hollywood's early tricks.

After electricity came to Edendale, night scenes using carbon lights could be shot on the director's favorite merry-go-round. It was wet, but fun shooting a running rain scene at night where a honeymoon couple, wearing tux and tails, rode on a motorcycle and side-car under a heavy downpour from a fire hose!

It was a hot night when an Alaskan dog sled, running on small rollers, was pulled on the turning Panorama stage by six huskies. It was actually 80 degrees when they went through a blowing snowstorm of tiny bits of confetti. Little comedienne, Polly Moran, was in the sled, wrestling a stuffed polar bear. Star comedian, Charlie Murray, in a fur Eskimo outfit, was running (and sweating) behind trying to snap a long felt whip at the dogs.

What fun it was!

RAILROAD STEAM ENGINE CAB

1919

Another set on the lot was an exact replica of the interior of a steam engine's cab as might be seen on any railroad of the time. It was built off the ground as high as a real engine would be, so that it could be rocked by a couple of strong men. The control panel where the engineer and the fireman worked was life-size, too, but made of wood and cardboard painted black. It showed all the gauges and the firebox, even one-inch buttons of wood that looked like the rivet heads that held the boiler together. When not in use, the entire cab was kept from the weather by a big waterproofed tarpaulin.

I remember one clear, summer night when I was about eight years old, the steam engine cab was uncovered. Universal Studio was renting the cab to shoot some scenes for a railroad picture entitled, *The Overland Red.* I believe the director was Lynn Reynolds. The picture starred one of my favorite Western stars, Harry Carey, who was cast as the engineer. I climbed to a perch on the back of a nearby set behind the cab to watch them shoot the scene from the camera's angle. The camera was set up on a scaffold behind, but not touching, the cab floor. It was to shoot past Carey's head and out the window on the right side.

In the scene, the cab was to be rolling through a burning forest showing trees afire as the cab passed them. A heavy wire was strung parallel, four feet from the side of the cab, high and at a steep angle, running down from the front of the cab toward the rear of the train. Eight, ten-foot wooden two-by-four boards attached at one end, hung down from the wire. Each board was wrapped with burlap and thoroughly soaked with kerosene. A wind machine on a high stand stood toward the front of the cab. A prop man stood beside the machine with a four-foot piece of tin bent into a curved tray to

A 1916 railroad engine that Sennett rented from the railroad for a Keystone Comedy

contain burning sawdust. To the rear, outside the cab, two men with a fire hose stood ready. Harry Carey, wearing his engineer's cap, was in the engineer's seat leaning to look out the window of the cab.

When all seemed to be ready, the director yelled, "Alright, let's get it going!"

The cab began to rock, the wind machine started to blow. Two grips with lighted torches quickly lit the soaked burlap wrapped around the planks. "They're burning," they yelled.

The director called, "Camera!" and it was running. "Start the trees and the sparks!"

The prop man began to shake the burning bits of sawdust off the tray in front of the wind machine, which sent them flying along the side of the cab. The two grips started pushing the burning trees down the sloping wire, past the cab.

The director, standing beside the grinding camera, watched the scene. The engineer's cap was fluttering in the wind. The rocking cab appeared to travel through a burning forest. Carey kept his hand moving to keep the sparks from his face, as he tried to look down the tracks that lay before the wheels of his speeding train. It looked real.

The director yelled, "O.K." Turning to the cameraman he saw me in semi-darkness and waved. I waved back. "Print it!" he said. The men with the spray from their fire hose did their job.

Harry Carey remarked, "That's as close as I want to be to a forest fire!"

"Good work, boys!" the director called to the crew. "It looked good. If we did it again do you think you could push the 'trees' a little faster?"

A grip answered, "Yes, now that we've got the hang of it. Give us 15 minutes and we'll do it again."

"Thanks, boys. Let us know when you're ready," said the director.

With a hook on a long pole, the smoldering movie magic trees were pulled back up the wire. The prop man fired up more sawdust on his tray. Everyone was ready for the second take.

What could have been more fun for an eight-year-old barefoot boy?

THE PULLMAN CAR

1919

One afternoon on my way home from school, I walked through Sennett's studio lot. A crew of house movers was setting a full-size railroad Pullman car down on the upper side of the lot about 75 feet from where my friend Sonny and I had dug a cave the month before. Mack Sennett bought the car from the Union Pacific Railway to use as a movie set. It was without wheels and tracks and was being set up on big wooden timbers so that it could be rocked from side to side during the shooting of a scene.

The upper berths were real and had a nice, varnished finish. The seats were upholstered with red velvet and the aisle was covered with carpet to match.

Pinky Bowman's dad was one of the studio carpenters working on the Pullman set. The car looked strange because one entire side was missing. Men at the railroad yards had been requested to remove one side, including the windows and the upper and lower berths, so that studio cameras could film—from the outside—the action that was going on inside the car.

To create a mini-size panorama, two vertical, wooden cylinders eight feet high and eighteen inches in diameter stood thirty feet apart next to the car. A long piece of light canvas, eight feet wide, was fitted tightly to turn around the two cylinders continually. Painted on the entire length of the canvas was a landscape. When a big crank on the top of each cylinder was turned by two men, the canvas scenery moved around the cylinders. When the interior of the car was photographed, the cameras also saw the moving canvas outside through the car windows; it looked as if the train were moving along a beautiful countryside.

The day word got around our neighborhood that a shoot was to be made of the new Pullman car, my sister, Vivian, Sitka and I, together with a dozen or so excited housewives and their children, showed up to watch the traveling Pullman train make its first journey.

It was a nice, warm, spring Saturday morning when the director, his crew and 20 actors arrived on the lot with much commotion. One camera was set up beside the car and another to shoot down into the car. When the passengers and the conductors were in their places, the director put them through rehearsals. Satisfied that every-body knew what was to be done, he said, "Alright, let's shoot it! Start the train and the 'Rama.'"

My friend Sonny and me

Men began to rock the train. The men on top of the cylinders turned their cranks to move the painted scenery. When the train "got up to speed," the onlook-ers were thrilled to see the beautiful passing landscape through the car windows. When everything was prop-erly in motion, the director called, "Action! Camera!"

The passengers started their movements in the seats and in the aisle. Comedians passed up and down bumping into each other as they juggled luggage and packages over their heads. The fat conductor pushed his way through the milling passengers, performing a lot of funny actions. Arriving at the center of the car, he stopped and, making broad motions, reached up and pulled open an upper berth. Bobby Vernon, the star, and two white goats fell out of it and onto the heads of the conductor and passengers. Women screamed as they lost their hats. Afraid of the goats, they climbed up onto the seats. Suitcases popped open and a variety of sizes of clothing fell out, some over heads or faces. Every action to remove the garments was made by the passengers. When the scene looked completely out of control, the director allowed it to run an extra minute and a half before yelling, "Cut! Good. O.K. Print it."

The cameras stopped grinding. The Pullman car stopped rocking. The scenery stopped passing. All of us watchers were laughing. It was a funny scene! The actors too were laughing and trying to catch their breath. Lionel Comport rushed onto the car to collect his excited goats. Bobby Vernon was shaken up, but got a laugh when he shouted, "This going to bed with a couple of goats could be dangerous."

We all laughed and applauded the actors and the director. I clapped for the prop men who had made the scene move, as each man stood mopping his sweating brow. Just then the studio's noon whistle blew and we all went home.

This was truly another one of those happy days on the lot at Sennett's studio. I fondly remember that my growing-up years were always happy. There was always something happening.

KIDS PLAYED MAKING MOVIES

1919

Some of us had watched movies being made before we could walk. We all had our favorite movie stars and we liked to imitate them: cowboys, comedians, whomever. When we were about six or seven years old, during some of our play times, when imaginations ran wild for something to do, it was fun to get a group of neighborhood boys and girls together and pretend we were making motion pictures.

I turned my Magic Lantern slide projector, about the size of a shoebox, into a movie camera. I removed the little kerosene lamp from inside and took the chimney off the top. It had to have a crank, so I attached a heavy bent wire at the side. With the projector's lens sticking out the front of the metal box, my creation did resemble a movie camera of those days. Who would have guessed our camera was not loaded with a magazine of fresh 35-millimeter film? Three wooden laths nailed at one end to a block of wood and spread out at the bottom made my camera's tripod. Magically that equipment turned us into motion picture people. We made lots of pictures!

All of us boys and girls helped decide on the story of the picture we would shoot. The story conference usually took place in our backyard or next door under Holmgren's big palm tree on Allesandro. Like all producers, the gang came up with an action-packed script only after kicking around a hundred ideas. It was interesting that the script always called for a cast with the same number of faces seen in the conference. Agreeing on a story to be filmed was easy compared to deciding on the cast of characters.

Who would take which part? Each producer knew what part he or she wanted to play—the reason some pictures were never made! Usually two girls thought they'd be a good leading lady and there was always more than one boy who wanted to be the leading man. Everybody couldn't star, so who would play the co-stars and the extras? It took a lot of convincing sometimes to get anybody to agree to be the bad guy or the mean girl! Nobody wanted to get beat up, shot, or roll down the rocky slope and lay dead at the bottom of the hill for a close-up in the dirt and weeds. I usually had to promise the boy who would play the bad guy that he could have the lead in the next picture. Assuring him that he would get to hug Sis Holmgren or my sister, Vivian, and they would ride away together on his horse at the end of the picture also helped.

When we made Western thrillers to round up and jail the cattle rustlers, the boys rode stick horses and slapped their sides to give their mounts a four-hoofed sound. The leading man always chased and caught the bad boss and had a big fight with him. These fights often got out of hand when somebody landed a punch and Mom had to come out and stop a bleeding nose. The star never failed to get the girl.

The boys liked doing cowboy pictures and wearing their dads' Western hats and gun belts. We made the big hats fit our small heads by stuffing strips of folded newspaper around the inside of the sweatbands. There were no toy revolvers in those days. We made our own Western justice by whittling our six-shooters out of pieces of soft pine wood taken from the ends of apple boxes. They looked dangerous when we colored them with black shoe dye!

Make-up and wardrobe for the girls was never a problem. They liked working in our pictures because it was the only time their mothers would let them wear their make-up and lipstick. They looked pretty good sometimes when they were all dolled up in the moms' hats, dresses, shoes and handbags.

Sonny liked being the cameraman and looked like one when he wore my cap backwards. I usually directed the pictures, but if Sonny wanted to direct, I wore the cap and did the cranking. We cranked on "Camera!" and stopped on "Cut!" I knew if we were to be considered a good company we had to save film. We only shot retakes if something went wrong in a scene. If somebody laughed, lost a hat, fell down, or a heavy gun belt pulled down a pair of pants then I'd yell, "Cut!" We'd hold the slate in front of the camera to mark the scene "N.G." which meant "No Good"; it wouldn't be printed.

For one of our best dramatic Western pictures, we shot a sad sequence in Dad's old barn, now the garage for his Model T Ford. Bubbles played Hank and sat in a corner on a box behind some strips of wood to look like jail bars, with a jail sign above his head. My sister, Gloria, played Jenny, the female lead who came for a last visit with her most unfortunate sweetheart. She sat down, they held hands and talked through the bars saying lines that could be subtitles on the screen.

"I know you didn't steal Johnson's horse," Jenny said, "But the sheriff thinks you did and he's gonna hang you." The cast stood around watching the action.

"I can't prove I didn't do it," the jailed man replied.

"I'm so worried about you," said Jenny.

Directing, I said, "Lean toward the bars, Hank. Tell her not to worry. You're feeling bad. It's a sad scene."

The prisoner leaned forward and tumbled off the box, against the bars, and pushed the set over onto Jenny, who screamed! I yelled, "Cut it, mark it N.G.!"

Bubbles got up, mad, with slivers in his hand, and wanted to quit. We all helped calm the sweethearts, reorganized the set and started a second take. Soon it was going better than the first take. Jenny was crying real tears. The kids started to snicker, "She's really crying!" Sonny made them shut up and kept on cranking as I directed, "More tears, Jenny. You're gonna miss your sweetheart. Cry more. Your heart is breaking. You'll have to go to the park picnic all alone this year. You'll be so lonesome. Cry! Bubbles, look into her eyes! Cry Jenny! Lean toward the bars. Now both of you say your last good-byes."

Gloria's nose was running, so we cut. "It was a great scene folks!"

We didn't hang Hank!

We all had fun acting. When I took a part in a picture, Sonny got to direct and Benny or one of the girls got to carry the camera around, set it up, wear the cap and turn the crank. Sitka was always around watching and often played in a picture with me as my side-kick. He liked to run along beside me as I trotted on my stick-horse.

The girls would only consent to do comedies if we boys promised not to act too slapstick or get carried away and start to throw

Happy members of our own motion picture company attend my sixth birthday party. From left mid row: Sonny, me, Sydney and June. In front: Mom with Gloria, age one. Behind her, with bow, is 'Sis' Holmgren. Lower right: Vivian and "Bubbles."

things at them. Doing comedy meant getting dressed up in old, baggy clothes, Dad's crushed felt or frayed straw hats. We had fun making our own Keystone Comedies.

From the roof of the barn we threw buckets of water, bundles of hay and paper boxes down upon each other. That was a big scene and we got lots of laughs from the girls, our folks and usually a group of passers-by. We took pratfalls on the wet ground and threw gooey mud pies that sometimes landed on our audience for extra laughs. However, when it was all over, there were no laughs when our moms had to wash us off with a garden hose and slap our faces for tearing our clothes. But the game was too much fun to abandon and in a couple of weeks we would be at it again.

A BIRTHDAY CAKE FOR LOUISE FAZENDA

1919

Dad and Mom thought Louise Fazenda was special and they liked her very much. One day between scenes, on a set with Louise, Director Dick Jones, Dad and the crew kidded her about her age. Was she old enough to work in pictures? They didn't know her age, but knew she lived with her mother. Louise happily took their ribbing, the good-natured gal that she was, and joked right back with her witty tongue. The challenge got hot and before she knew it, she blurted out her birthday and age. The crew was happy to learn it and without rehearsal, but with good voice, rendered a "Happy Birthday, Dear Louise." The favorite comedienne sat red-faced, but laughing.

"If you boys are trying to make this a birthday party, where is my banana cream birthday cake?"

The next day was not her birthday, but a cake appeared on the set.

Dad told Mom the story, including Louise's birthdate. A few months later, on the given day, Mom made a big, three-layer cake. She covered it with real whipped cream and put thin slices of banana all around and on top. To assure protection, she carefully placed her afternoon's work down into the center of a deep cardboard box.

When Dad came home from the studio, he was pleased to see Mom remembered the date and had made Louise her favorite cake.

"Why don't you and the kids take the cake over before Louise and her mother have their supper?" Mom suggested, as she stood at the sink peeling potatoes. "The kids have all washed their hands and faces, go ahead!"

"O.K., kids! We're going to Louise's house. Get in the Ford!" Vivian picked up Louise, my youngest sister. Mom carried the cake and we headed for our Model T touring car. After Dad and Vivian got into the front seat with little Louise on her lap, Gloria and I dived into the back seat. With serious words and instructions, Mom handed me the boxed birthday offering. "For the love of Mike, Coy, be careful of this cake. Sit up straight. Hold the box tight and keep the cake level!"

Dad backed us out of the driveway onto Berkeley Avenue. We rolled down the hill for our three-block ride to Louise's house. With my nose resting on the edge of the box, I kept my eyes on the cake. Dad immediately suggested we practice singing "Happy Birthday Louise." For once we started together and were sounding good until we turned the corner onto Glendale Boulevard. The Ford leaned, I leaned, the box leaned, and just as we sang the "Dear Louise" part, I watched the two top layers of the cake slowly slide from the centered cake plate until banana and cream squashed against the side of the box! My eyes bugged out. I waited. The car straightened up. I leveled up. The box leveled, but the cake did not. We finished the song as we pulled up in front of Louise's duplex at the corner of Alvarado and Montana Streets.

I was afraid to look at Mom's masterpiece! Vivian and Dad got out of the car. I handed Dad the box and got out, too. Dad looked at the cake and laughed, "A slapstick cake for Louise!"

"I'm sorry Dad, you took the corner too fast."

Gloria stepped out onto the running board, got a look at Mom's gooey, tilted creation, screamed and started to cry. "Oh Coy, look what you did to Mama's cake. She's gonna be mad at you!"

We stood grouped on the sidewalk as Dad tilted the box and carefully shook the layers back into place. With a piece of the cardboard torn from the box, we watched him scrape the cream and bananas from the side of the box and stick them back onto the cake. It didn't look too good, but Dad said, "There, you'd hardly know anything has happened to it. It looks as good as before."

"No, it does not, Daddy." Gloria blubbered out, wiping her tears. Dad took a patient look at her. "Now Gloria, don't say anything about this. Let's just play like it didn't happen. Okay?"

He lifted the cake out of the box and handed it to me to carry. "All right, let's go in." I felt bad and a little shaky even though Dad didn't bawl me out. I led the way up the steps to the left apartment where we all waited at the door for Dad to knock. He wiped Gloria's cheeks and nose with his handkerchief and straightened Vivian's hair as she held little Louise.

We heard footsteps coming to the door. Louise's Mom opened the door and with a big smile on her face and with her best

In 1915, Louise was California's first real, slapstick comedienne. She took pies in the face, spilled into mud puddles and showed the frills of her undergarments. She later married Hollywood producer Hal Wallis.

French accent, said "Greetings Vossons. Coom en. Louiees es in thee keetchun."

We all said, "Hello." Dad took off his cap and we walked in. The table in the neat, little dining room was set for two. Louise appeared.

Dad said, "Now!" We struck up the "Happy Birthday, Dear Louise" in fair time. The two French ladies stood smiling, as if pleased, and when we finished, they gave us a little "hand." I stepped over and handed the cake to Louise. "Mom sends her best wishes, too."

"Oh! My favorite cake. It looks lovely!" She looked at Dad with question marks in both eyes. Dad winked at her with a "what-do-you-think?" look.

"How did your Mama know it was my birthday?" We all looked at Dad who just smiled. "You remembered that day on the set, didn't you?" She gave Dad a peck on the cheek. "Tell Goldie 'thanks so much.'"

She handed the cake to her mother, said, "Hello" to Vivian and took little Louise, her namesake, into her arms for a big hug and a kiss.

"Von't you all seet down?" the mother asked, pointing to the davenport.

"No. Thank you, Mrs. Fazenda," Dad said. "We just came to say Happy Birthday to Louise. We're glad we got here before you sat down to supper. We should get home to ours."

"All right. Den pleeze first zing zee happy burzday zong agime."

As big Louise bounced little Louise, we again sang, but not as well as the first time. Louise thanked us for coming and for the songs. She gave Dad a pat on the shoulder and special "goodbye" as he walked through the doorway.

Back in the Ford, on the way home, Dad reminded us not to mention the cake disaster to Mom. "It couldn't be helped. If we tell her, it will only make her feel bad. So, we will only tell Mama how much Louise liked the cake."

We piled out of the car. Mom had supper on the table and we all sat down.

"Goldie, Louise thought your cake was great."

Vivian added, "Louise said it was lovely, Mom."

Mom looked pleased and smiled. "I'm glad she liked it."

But, Gloria came out with, "And we all just played like nothing happened to it."

We looked at Gloria. Mom looked at Dad. Dad said, "Let's say the blessing before our supper gets cold." We bowed our heads.

TRYING TO EARN AN HONEST DIME

1920

When I was about eight years old, collecting old newspapers from the folks around the neighborhood and selling them to "The Ragman" was one of the ways I earned my spending money. These were bearded men with heavy foreign accents, who rented and drove skinny horses that pulled old wagons.

When I was eight years old

They paid fifteen cents for one hundred pounds of old newspapers, and drove up and down the streets calling, "Rags, bottles, sacks, papers." I never saw them buy any of the first three, but they were always glad to buy my papers.

One day, a gruff-looking ragman, when weighing my well-tied piles of papers, tried to cheat me. He held his scale at an angle instead of holding it straight upright so the spring could pull straight down and give an honest reading.

When I realized what he had done, I tied a rope with a loop at the end to a branch of a tree near my paper shed. The next time the ragman came around, I told him to hook his scale to the loop if he wanted to do business with me. He spoke little English, but he got the message. I don't think he really liked it, but he did laugh when he saw my new setup and he did as I told him.

I learned early that some people don't play fair, even with kids.

About this same time, Mr. Beverage, the grammar school janitor, a nice, old, pink-faced, skinny Englishman with a stiff neck, put out the word he needed a boy to help him on Saturdays. I applied for the job and learned that a beverage was also a drink. He offered fifty cents if I'd clean blackboards, sweep floors and rake leaves for three hours.

"I'll take the job if I can bring Sitka," I told him.

"Okay, but no other kids," and we agreed.

It wasn't easy work, but I liked it. I guess he liked my work, because later during school hours, whenever he needed any help, he always asked for me. We became good friends. When I was called out of class, it made me look important to the kids. Some of them knew I worked in pictures and asked why I worked for his pay on Saturdays. Mr. Beverage had a cute, young daughter named Marian. She became a piano teacher, and years later I paid her to give Louise and Billy piano lessons.

MACK SENNETT PLAYS "MOVIES" WITH US

1920

After promising to do our chores later, one warm Saturday morning the girls agreed to shoot a comedy with us. We got our clothes and props together and the company walked to Effie Street, which ran one dead-end block between two parts of Sennett's Studio. The studio carpenters had built a row of storefront sets along the sidewalk: a shoe shop, a café, a bakery, a milliner's shop and a barbershop. There was no glass in the store windows, but each shop had a regular entrance and door. The Police Station front was in the center of the line with a big jail sign above the entrance. We had watched many companies shoot some funny pictures in front of these sets.

Sonny set up our "camera" and we started to rehearse the sequence. Several kids and grown-ups gathered in the street to watch us. The girls, Sis and Dolores, were dressed in their moms' long dresses, big hats and high-heeled shoes. Sis carried an umbrella and Dolores had a big purse.

Due to a shortage of talent that day, Sonny was both cameraman and director. I was made up with a big mustache to be a Keystone Cop wearing Mom's old navy blue suit coat with a belt around my waist and big white cardboard star on my chest. Dad's old conductor cap with "Police" printed above the visor was the topper! A two-foot length of inch-and-a-half rubber garden hose was my billy club. I stood in the station doorway.

Said Sonny, "Let's run through it," We rehearsed the scene with the camera set up at the curb.

Sonny called out, "Action!"

The girls swaggered to the station door. Sis dropped her umbrella.

I came out to pick it up. Instead of handing it to her, I started to flirt with them. I teased them, holding the umbrella out and pulling it away, waving it around and rolling my eyes at them, acting silly, striking poses and trying to hold their hands. They didn't appreciate my actions of fun and became angry. Dolores wound up and landed a blow on my head with her purse. I dropped the umbrella and took a pratfall to the sidewalk. I got up. She knocked me down. I rolled around. Both girls proceeded to beat the goofy cop until he couldn't stand. Woozy, on my knees, the girls pulled me to my feet, pushed me staggering to the door and shoved me into jail and out of sight. Dignified, the girls straightened their hats and dresses, stood tall and, proudly dusting their sleeves, strutted out of the scene.

Sonny, trying to keep from laughing, said, "It looked O.K. Let's shoot it!"

We got into our places, ready to start, when we heard the studio's twelve o'clock whistle blow, as it did every day except Sunday, to signal the start of the half-hour lunch break. We looked across the

Mr. Sennett, King of Comedy

street to the studio's Main Gate. It was open and Mr. Sennett's Rolls Royce came through to the street. After a car and a two-horse team pulling an empty sand wagon passed up out of sight, the black Rolls rolled over to our corner and stopped. I saw Mr. Sennett and Mabel Normand in the back seat. I waved to Cecil Smith, the chauffeur, and he waved back. So did Mr. Sennett as he got out of the car and walked toward us. Gosh! Maybe he didn't want us to shoot on his street!

There was a half smile on his face as he approached our camera. He looked it over, nodded his head and laughed. He gave the crank a couple of turns and looked at me with a knowing smile.

"Well, Little Coy, I see you kids are making pictures."

"Yes, Mr. Sennett, a comedy!" I introduced Sonny and the girls.

"What's the story line?" he asked.

"The Old Man," as he was known, listened and nodded as we told him. Mabel watched from the car. When Mr. Sennett learned Sonny was shooting and directing, to our surprise he offered to direct the scene for us. We accepted. He was

Mack, the comedian

pleased. The bystanders rendered giggles.

"If you have rehearsed and know the action, get in your places. Let's shoot it!" spoke "The King of Comedy." "You girls walk prim and proper now. Don't look down when you drop the umbrella. Make your swings at the cop broad and don't hit him too hard, but keep it up once you start."

I stepped out of sight inside the jail. Sonny stood by the camera.

"Is everybody ready?" I heard our director ask. "O.K. Let's make it move! Camera! Action!"

I could hear the crowd of 20 people laughing as I waited for the girls to strut into view of the door. Sis dropped the umbrella. I swaggered out and did my bit with them. They did theirs with me. I tumbled around on the sidewalk and heard laughs from our audience.

From the director, "Looks good. Keep it up."

The girls finally got me up on my feet and gave me a big push into the jail. The girls brushed themselves off and strolled off-camera. The "Old Man" with the whitish hair and the pinkish face chuckled and said, "Cut!" He patted Sonny on the back. With a big smile he ordered, "Print it!"

Shaking his head, he pulled his handkerchief from his pocket and wiped his eyes and face. He glanced toward Mabel in the car. "That was good, kids. A funny scene. I'm going to tell Mr. Walker, the gate man, that you kids may use these sets anytime you want."

We thanked him and the bystanders gave him a hand. We walked with him to his car. "You got the right idea kids, keep it up!"

At the car, we all looked up and saw the popular horse-drawn bakery wagon coming down the street. Mr. Sennett saw it too!

"Cecil, stop the wagon." He flipped him a silver dollar. "Buy the kids some doughnuts."

The bakery man put the dollar in the pocket of his white apron as we all waved thanks and good-bye to our three friends when they drove off. We gathered around the rear of the wagon to watch 20 puffy, kosher, sugared doughnuts counted into a big paper bag! In just a few minutes everybody had a doughnut. Some of us sat on the curb munching our treat until the last grain of sugar was licked from every finger. The 12:30 "back-to-work" whistle blew and we all gathered our props and went home to do our chores.

I sometimes heard it said that Mack Sennett was a stern, hard-to-please man. We kids didn't think so. Many times during the 40 years that followed, I talked with Mr. Sennett and always found him to be the same man I'd known as a boy—a real gentleman, good-hearted and a great guy!

I suppose we Edendale kids, like kids all over the world, had fun playing at imitating the people who produced the product made in "our" town. I never saw a scene we shot appear on a silver screen, but I'll always be able to run them on my memory screen.

HOW KIDS LEARNED TO ACT

1920

I played Sammy, William Haines' pal in The Smart Set *(MGM)*

In the early twenties there were no acting schools. Kids that acted in silent movies learned from what they saw on the theater screen. They acted. They didn't say lines. We couldn't even read all the subtitles.

What are subtitles? Silent pictures have no sound, so when the audience needs to know what an actor says, it is printed on the screen. These inserts are the subtitles. So long as the audience can figure out what the actors would be saying, there is no need to use subtitles. At other times, they are needed to give the place of the action, the date, or something important before the start of the first scene. The hero didn't talk much either. If he was handsome, all he had to do was act. The same was true for kids in movies. To pick a fight? A fake punch in the nose worked. Audiences wanted action. They could figure out the rest.

Harry played "Albert" with Fred Astaire in A Damsel in Distress *(RKO)*

Watching stars, we saw how to walk and stand. Looks and actions were the thing. Acting natural helped, and not looking at the camera but listening to the director was essential. If there were two cameras shooting a scene, it meant it was a big picture.

"Eddie Cline's company is shooting two cameras today! Get me a kid who can act; a kid with a little experience who will listen and do what he is told. No smarty! One that's well-behaved."

Directors knew what they wanted. There were no casting directors in the

Billy played "Micah Dow" with Katharine Hepburn in The Little Minister *(RKO)*

early days. My dad later became one of comedy's first casting directors at William Fox Studio.

Acting dramatic scenes with live music on the set helped to set the mood. A portable organ and a violin helped me cry real tears! When sound came in, kids worried about their lines and often forgot to act. Sound changed the picture business in many ways.

Delmar played "Goat Peter" with Shirley Temple in Heidi *(Fox)*

In the twenties on Saturdays, when kids went to the theater, there was no sound. Often there was no organ or piano music either. We just watched the star's every movement, impressed with all he or she did.

Our idols, stars like Buck Jones and Tom Mix, never smoked in the pictures because they wanted to set good examples for us younger actors, for kids like us everywhere in the world. We saw and learned how the good guys stood, dressed, shook hands, and how they talked and acted toward women. The bad guys were all taboo, dressed dirty or in black, with mustaches and beards, easy to recognize. They acted mean.

Kids were very much impressed and influenced by what they

Garry played Joan Bennett's little brother in Wild Girl

saw on the silver screen. Movies had a big influence on our country; they showed us the good and the bad. The good guy's image was important. We also saw how bad girls dressed and walked. If a girl smoked a cigarette in a picture, she had to be a "baddie." I think the later sounds and violent actions in pictures were too much for some children—possibly the reason for so many hyped-up kids!

Some youngsters acting in pictures weren't able to cry in scenes. I had a reputation of being able to cry on cue. While the camera turned, a good director would tell me the story.

"Buck your pal and good friend is going to jail for something you both know he didn't do. He's been so good to you! He loves you; you love him. You're not going to see him anymore. Your pal will be gone. You'll miss him."

As the music played with feeling, I listened to the director and cried tears. The story the picture was telling was enough to make me cry; it had to be sad or a kid wouldn't cry.

When the director said "Cut! That's fine son. You're a good actor. Thank you," you knew he meant it. He'd thank the musicians too.

Bobs played "Peewee" with Spencer Tracy and Mickey Rooney in Boys' Town

Above: Harry, Delmar, Billy and Garry played Guy Kibbee's sons in Mr. Smith Goes To Washington, *starring James Stewart and Jean Arthur (a Frank Capra Production)*

Bobs played "Pud" with Lionel Barrymore in On Borrowed Time *(MGM)*

Dad, with his years of experience in making motion pictures, gave us kids early training on how to take directions. After sound came in, when we boys were chosen by the studio casting director or the picture's director to take a part in a picture, we were given a script to learn the actions and our lines for each scene. Dad worked to teach us every movement and word. He must have done a good job—we were all pleased to work with some of the biggest stars of the time.

EARLY THEATER PREVIEWS

1920

Some of the very first studio sneak previews were shown in our neighborhood at our T.D. and L. Motion Picture Theater on Sunset Boulevard, a mile from Keystone Studios and our house. Many nights, when I was seven or eight years old,

I went with Dad to see some of the first edited versions of pictures on which his company was working. Mack Sennett, the producer and director, the gag writers and the film cutter (now known as a film editor) gathered in the theater lobby with two 800-foot cans of film. Usually the newsreel was running to start the show.

The cutter handed the delighted theater manager the two cans and asked, "Would you please run this picture between your scheduled comedy and the feature?"

We all found seats. The producer's object was to sit and watch his picture with the paid audience and get its reaction. The audience was always glad to see an extra

Mack Sennett's sneak previews were shown in a theater like this one on Sunset Boulevard

picture. Following the advertised comedy, without any notice, the unfinished comedy ran on the screen. Its makers listened and learned what their viewers thought of their picture.

Where did they laugh? What scenes got the biggest laughs? Where did they not laugh? How many seconds passed between laughs? What wasn't funny? Mack wanted "A Belly Laugh Every Second!" Every member of the Keystone group knew that was the motto. When "The End" appeared on the screen, the amount of applause from the audience was taken as a fair rating for the picture. Was it "just funny," "good," or was it "a very funny picture?" The answers were heard by the makers.

When the feature started, we "company people" left our seats and gathered on the sidewalk in front of the theater to discuss what the audience had told us. I stood listening to the serious voices as the men analyzed the crowd's reactions.

The girl in the glass box office waved to me as she put the "Closed" sign over the hole at the ticket window. The night's one show was running, so she turned out the light and slid out of sight. The projectionist, after starting the run of the first of the seven-reel feature, left his stuffy, fire-proofed projection booth and rushed out for some fresh air with the two cans of film. The film cutter took them with a "thanks" and handed him a couple of bills.

The audience's reactions to every second and every scene of the fifteen-minute picture were fresh in the memories of the group. Changes were offered and considered. Anything to make their picture move faster and get more laughs. I heard the traffic on Sunset Boulevard as it headed for Hollywood.

"The opening scene runs too long. Cut to the couple sooner." Each man had a suggestion. Cigarette smoke rose from the center of the huddle into the clear, starry sky.

"Mabel's scene should go until she climbs out the other side of the car," remarked Director Dick Jones.

"Charlie's first close-up ran long but it got a good laugh."

"Leave it as it is," said Mr. Sennett.

"You were right, Clarence. The water gag should come ahead of the pie-throwing in the bakery. It'll get a bigger laugh." They all agreed.

"We need a close-up of her foot on his towel and soap," Mr. Sennett suggested. "And a second shot from the rear of the fat lady on the bicycle could get another laugh before we see the pig in the baby buggy."

For half an hour, each thoughtful, happy creator offered to help make their two-reeler funnier. "Do we have to see so much hotel front before Andy gets stuck in the revolving door?" Dad suggested.

I listened with interest. These men were writing the book on "How To Make Motion Picture Comedies!" The "cause" has to be well established before the full "effect" of the gag will get the biggest laugh. A guiding rule was to come back to the story line as much as possible. Keep it moving. Keep them laughing.

Two weeks later, the finished picture ran at that theater! It did move faster and it got more laughs. And, while it was running, the crew was shooting another side-splitter.

By the early thirties, every week four or five theaters in Los

Angeles and Hollywood were running previews of feature pictures and comedies. Later, the agreement between studio and theater became routine. The day a night preview was to be shown, it was advertised in lights on the theater's marquee: "Big Studio Sneak Preview Tonight!" The title was never given but the sign helped

draw a crowd. Each person entering the theater was handed a rating card. Studio "brass" still sat in the audience. After the preview was shown, the lights were turned on for a few minutes so the theatergoers could check their cards and give their opinions of the picture.

Did you like it? What didn't you like most? Would you recommend it to a friend? What could be done to make you like it more?

The studio producers and directors studied the cards with respectful, careful consideration. The public's early criticism of a picture gave producers a chance to make changes and improve the picture before its final editing and release. The better the picture, the bigger the profits at the box office.

Ford Sterling, Chief of the Keystone Cops, receives a phone call saying his Cops are in trouble again. Fatty Arbuckle is on far right (about 1912).

Moving pictures were like all products, made to make money! The preview idea started in Edendale, like so many other innovations that helped the movie industry improve and make better pictures.

NO BETTER THAN OTHER KIDS

1920

After I was about seven, at least once a week until I was nine years old, I attended Jensen's theater—the same theater where Sitka had guarded me as a baby. I sat in the dark watching pictures and listening to the music from a piano, then later from an organ. I learned to read titles on the big screen and to follow stories told in good motion pictures. I watched and learned about right and wrong, honesty, loyalty, bravery, and who always won in the end.

I had a special feeling for Jensen's. It had a high-arched entrance with posters on the walls and a floor of small, white tiles. The polished brass line-up rails welcomed me to the box office. The entire building was an exciting, impressive place in my life.

When I became nine, almost every Saturday morning at eight o'clock, Sitka and I, and about six other boys, picked up our handbills from beside the theater ticket booth. Then we'd hit the streets and sidewalks to deliver them. Each of us was expected to pass one thousand of the theater's four-by-eight inch, folded, printed programs throughout the district. To houses, apartments and stores we trotted, distributing the list of the exciting pictures to be shown each day of the coming week. It took about four hours to cover our routes and put the show bills in the thousand mailboxes or door handles. We had to go onto the porches because most of the boxes, made of black tin, were located beside the front doors.

It was fun flipping the lids of the boxes and dropping in the bills. Every second counted so Sitka and I kept moving. Even though Mom disapproved, I worked barefooted, just as I did in most of my pictures. With Sitka trotting at my side, we always got a barking reception from a dog inside or outside a house. A fight would have been possible on any of the porches, but we didn't stop. Sitka didn't need to stop because he knew he could whip any dog on the route. I knew how tough my wolf dog was and I tried to prevent fights. When dogs came up to us and saw how mean he could be, they ran off quickly. Their size didn't mean a thing to Sitka. If a mean dog came too close to us, he gave it a warning I didn't like to see.

The hair on his back stood up and he showed his teeth. His ears laid back, he lowered his tail and made a quiet, low growl. If the dog didn't back off, in a flash Sitka grabbed at its throat. I saw him

Dad cut hair and resoled shoes

do that once, but not on the show bill route. I liked dogs too much to see them bite and tear at each other. I knew people liked to watch men fight in a ring, but I never understood how they could enjoy watching dogs fight. I learned a lot from Sitka. He was brave and afraid of nothing and that's the way I tried to be. My pal and I kept going until we'd stuffed all the boxes on our streets. Then we headed for home and lunch.

The manager caught a couple of the boys throwing some of their handbills down the storm drains. They got fired. The temptation to get rid of the bills was strong after two or three hours of running up and down steps and hills on street after street. If I had any programs left over, I gave them back to the theater manager, but I was tempted to pass up a steep street a couple of times.

Thursday night was pay night. I felt like a part of the operation when I stepped up to the box office window and gave the ticket girl my name. I received my fifty cents and strolled, without paying, into the theater to see the first show. To attend any show free at any time was part of my pay for pushing the bills. Often, pictures I was appearing in were listed in the programs I distributed.

The pay I received for acting in the pictures was for the family. The pay I received for advertising the pictures was all mine. Sometimes there were one-sheet posters of me on display in the side panels of the theater entrance.

The manager and the other guys kidded me—a kid star passing handbills that plugged his own picture! They couldn't understand it. That was because they didn't know my dad.

"Just because you work in pictures," Dad said, "doesn't mean you are any different or better than other boys. You have to work to learn the value of money."

Years later, he told me, "I wanted you to be a real boy, unspoiled, honest, natural, healthy, and one who knew the value of an honestly earned dollar or a half-dollar." To me, a fifty-cent piece will always be a big coin!

LEARNING TO PLAY BY EAR

1920

At the theater on Saturdays and Sundays, four acts of vaudeville were billed to play between pictures. One Saturday afternoon, a man with a harmonica band of six boys played and got a big hand. I thought they were great. After a couple of numbers, the man invited any boy or girl with a harmonica to come up from the audience onto the stage and play. Nobody went up. He said how much fun they all had playing and that kids should learn to play the harmonica. He mentioned he would again invite players to come up the next day, on Sunday.

I was impressed as I listened to them play and made up my mind I was going to learn to play the harmonica. When they finished, I couldn't wait to get out of the show. I ran across Sunset Boulevard to the drugstore and, with a hard-earned quarter, bought my first mouth organ. I held it to my mouth as they had and played at it all the way home. I told Dad and Mom of my new ambition. They thought it was fine. I puffed, drew and blew up and down the reeds and practiced in the house until Mom suggested I play outside! That night, I played it quietly in bed until Dad called, "That's enough for tonight."

The next morning, I practiced outside before and after breakfast. My music began to sound like "Home, Sweet Home" and Mom recognized it. After lunch, with encouraging words from the folks, I played my way back to the theater.

My Grandpa Wimer taught me to play the Jew's Harp. I played to put my father, Mack Swain, to sleep in The Shamrock and the Rose *at Columbia Studios. My music was not heard—it was a silent movie! Mack Swain was one of the original Keystone Comedians who came west from New York with Mack Sennett. Swain later was the heavy in Charlie Chaplin's* The Gold Rush. *Leon Holmes whistles on the left.*

I was the first kid in the front row waiting for the man to ask for a boy to play a harmonica. I waited through the news, the comedy and the feature—it seemed like eight hours. Finally, the harmonica act came on. After they had played for a bit, the man asked for a player from the audience, and quicker than he thought possible, I was on stage performing "Home, Sweet Home." I got a little hand and bowed like the band had.

The man put his arm around my shoulder and asked, "How long have you been playing?" When he, his boys, and the audience heard how I had become a mouth organ soloist, they all laughed and gave me a big hand. They wanted me to play again, so I did "Home, Sweet Home" once more. More clapping. The man watched me closely, then pointed out to me that I had learned to play the harmonica backwards, with the bass on the wrong side. The band and everybody laughed again and gave me another big hand.

I still play my little Marine Band harmonica with the bass on the right side instead of the left, the way I taught myself! It made me a good teacher. Later, in junior high, I played for my all-boys homeroom class. It worked out fine when our teacher let me start a class to teach four interested boys to play their harmonicas. When they faced me and held the mouth organ properly, with the bass on their left, it was easier for them to follow my moves and play the harmonica correctly.

THE AMAZING LITTLE MOVIE SCREEN

1920

In 1920, any eight-year-old movie fan could learn a lot just watching moving pictures on the big, silver screen. For a dime, every Saturday afternoon, my pal, Sonny, other playmates and I were at the show. We watched and learned what the writers and directors dreamed up for us.

We liked all kinds of moving pictures, but we saw the best action in Western serials. They were movies with one, good, basic fast-running story. Then the filmed story was broken into ten- or fifteen-minute episodes or chapters. One chapter was shown each Saturday and it always ended just when the story and the action was most exciting. Usually the star of the serial was left in some dangerous, life-threatening situation, like hanging on a cliff or about to be blown up in a mine tunnel. The director or writer made each episode end that way just to get us to come back to the show the next Saturday to see what happened.

Universal Studio made the most Western serials that starred famous cowboys. Ruth Roland, a favorite of mine and a real "cowgirl," starred in many long-running serials. Some of Dad's cowboy pals doubled for stars, doing the dangerous stunts in scenes. They told me Ruth did all her own riding and seldom had a double do any of her dangerous or tricky scenes.

I'll never forget a chapter in one of Ruth's serials. She was playing the part of a sheriff, wearing two six-guns and chaps. In one particular scene, she and two deputies were riding on the trail after two bank robbers. They suddenly realized they had ridden into a dead-end, mysterious box canyon. They stopped and, very concerned, looked up and around at the steep mountain cliffs that closely surrounded them. Could they be trapped? They were looking carefully at the thick brush and rocks, but they didn't see what we kids saw on the screen from our seats—a close-up of a big camera lens carefully hidden behind a rock on the side of the mountain and focused on the three riders below.

Ruth Roland—first on the little "Black Box"

The scene changed and became a long, panoramic picture across the landscape to a scene far away. We saw two horses standing beside an old cabin almost hidden among the trees, then a scene inside the dark, shabbily furnished shack. There was an old stove, a cot and two tough-looking cowboys sitting dead still at a small table against the wall. On the table was a kerosene lamp and a black box about a foot square. With their heads together the men were staring at the box. Why?

To my surprise, the answer was in a close-up of the side of the box. I saw an amazing little moving picture screen the size of a playing card. On the screen was the same scene the big lens was seeing from the side of the mountain a mile away. As clear as could be, there was Ruth and her deputies moving around, trapped in the box canyon. The miniature scene was amazing. It was weird.

The theater piano was playing some scary music and we kids all sat spellbound watching the tiny picture. I couldn't believe what I was seeing. What was that thing? It was a little box with a fascinating, tiny, mysterious movie screen. When the scene disappeared, the two robbers jumped up from the table. They covered the box and screen with a saddle blanket, rushed out of the cabin, got on their horses and rode off into the woods.

I sat staring at the big movie screen hoping to get one more look at the little screen on the side of the black box. It didn't come up

(Left to right) Me, my son Jimmy and Dad. Our first Christmas with a small screen TV set.

again in that episode or in the last four episodes on the following four Saturdays. I wondered, how did the picture get from the big lens in the canyon a mile away to the little screen in the cabin?

With much interest, Dad, Sonny and I talked about the fascinating little screen. "Remember," Dad said, "It was only a movie. Everything doesn't have to be possible. It did tickle your imagination and made you think, didn't it?" He added, "The scene was certainly original and had to have been the 'brain child' of someone with a great imagination and an idea for the future."

"What you saw," he explained to Sonny and me, "was some moving picture magic. Two pictures were printed on one film. First the scene of the riders was printed in the center of the film through a hole in a mat the shape and size of a little screen. Then the scene of the box on the table was printed on the same film. So, what you boys really saw on the big screen was both scenes on the one film. It was a special effect, a double exposure."

I never forgot about Ruth Roland's amazing little screen. Twenty-three years later, in 1943, sitting in a Hollywood office, I was surprised again. I watched moving pictures on another little five-by-seven inch screen on the side of a twelve-by-twenty inch box. The pictures, I was told, were being telecast electronically from a transmitter atop the mountain above the big "Hollywood sign."

As I watched, I couldn't help thinking how unbelievable it was that an idea seen in an early silent movie had become one of the world's greatest and most enjoyable inventions. It was called television!

CATCHING CATS FOR COMEDIES

1920

One Thursday after school we were playing marbles in the lot. Glen De Val, a prop man for Director Del Lord at Sennett's, walked down from the studio with some good news.

"We'll need at least a dozen cats next Saturday to use in a picture. We'll pay 25 cents for each cat you bring to the west gate at 9:00 A.M." He asked us to spread the word and tell all the kids at school because he would need lots of cats. My friend, Sonny, wasn't interested, but Bill Eastman and I were. I told Glen I'd have some cats for him.

Many times prop men phoned or came to ask me to help them get a bunch of cats, dogs, or kids together for a picture. They paid 50 cents for a dog and a dollar for a kid! With Sitka I had a ready 50 cents and I usually found another dog running around, too. I liked dogs, but not cats!

After Sitka was gone, I always had a dog of some kind. If I didn't find them, they found me and I took them home. I trained them to do what I told them. That was before many people had trained animals to work in pictures. At this time, Dad was training bears and lions for Sennett and he encouraged me to train my dogs.

I knew where there were cats, but how would I catch them? I thought about it. All the next day at school I put out Glen's offer. "Bring a cat to the studio and get 25 cents and see your cat in a picture."

At 3:00 P.M., after school, I was off to Mr. Robley's meat market. He had cut up his Friday fish for his showcase display. He gave me six big fish heads and some tails in a paper bag. I headed for home. In our harness shed I found three old gunnysacks that potatoes came in. Then I told Mom I was off for the corner. I didn't say for what and she didn't ask, as I frequently did chores for the store-keepers there. I made Sitka stay home on the porch. With the three sacks and the bag of fish, I went straight to the alley and the rear of the drug store next to Joe's Shoe Shop. Many times while burning papers and boxes for Mr. Proctor, the druggist, I had seen cats mousing around the rubbish bins. I picked a spot near the incinerator, took out a fish head and tail and laid them on the ground near the bin. I ducked around the corner of the building, parked the two sacks and the bag of fish, and stood quietly with a gunnysack in my hand. As sweet as I could, with a high pitched voice like Mom's, I called,

"Here kitty, here kitty, kitty, kitty." There was a smell of fish on my hands and in the air.

I heard Mrs. Proctor open the back door of the drug store. She stuck her head out. "Hello Coy, what are you up to?" She asked with a smile and a big question mark in the middle of her forehead.

"I'm trying to catch a cat for my friend Glen," I answered honestly.

"Good," she said. "He's welcome to all you can take away from here." She closed and bolted the door.

Encouraged, I let out a good, loud, "Here kitty, kitty, kitty," again and waited some more. Then I saw the morning glory leaves at the top rail of the old picket fence move, as a tomcat pushed his head through and walked along behind the incinerator. He stopped, looked at me, then at the fish.

"Hello Tom," I said. He jumped past me and started toward the bait with his head down and his tail swinging from side to side. I walked toward him as he neared the fish head. I picked it up and held it out to him. He came close, took a good whiff and touched his nose to the head. With the other hand, I laid the sack down on the ground and spread the top open, then carefully dropped the smelly fish head into the center of the opening. Tom moved on to the sack for another sniff. With both hands, I jerked the sack up around him. I had him! He jumped and kicked around squirming, growling and meowing. I tied the top of the sack with a string and put my catch around the corner away from my trapping ground. Then, with another smelly fish head and tail laid down on another open sack, I gave out with more kitty, kitty, kitty calls.

Tom made so much noise I carried him away from the scene, down the alley, and asked him to be quiet and not tell the other cats. I knew he wasn't hurt. When I returned for a look at my baited sack there was the head of a small cat peering from behind a box next to the incinerator. It was eyeing the fish head! I approached the bait slowly. The cat backed up. I knelt down, picked up the fish head and held it out.

"Here kitty. Nice kitty. Have some fish." It looked interested. I guess I sounded right, so it came over for a closer look and a smell. My technique was working. I held the head and waved it slowly over the tail. Just then, Joe, the shoe repairman, came out his back door and threw some leather scraps into his bin. The cat backed off. Joe looked up, saw me, and in his best Italian-English yelled, "Hey, vot you are doing vit dat cat?"

"I'm feeding it, Joe."

"Don't feed et, Coy. Ve don't vant dem around here."

"O.K., then I'll catch it for my friend." He smiled and waved his arm.

"Gude, take dem all avay for him." He disappeared and closed the door.

The skinny cat had crouched and was twitching its tail as it looked at the fish in my hand. I held the fish way out, leaning toward the cat. "Come on kitty, it's a nice, stinky fish. Come have a sniff." At that moment, I lost my balance and rolled onto the sack and the fish tail but managed to hold the head out. The cat took a good sniff, got up, and as I regained my knees it came right over to the tail on the open sack. I held the head in one hand and patted the scrawny thing with the other. Little did it know how close it was to becoming a movie actor! It took a little bite of the fish tail. I jumped up and pulled the sack around it.

Now I had two cats! I was laughing. I placed Scrawny next to Tom and made sack and bait number three ready. I waited another half-hour, but there were no more takers.

So, I picked up the trapping gear and my two catches and headed for home.

As I walked along, I didn't dare tell anybody what I had in the sacks and hoped nobody would ask. I gently placed the squirming sacks in a corner of Dad's little barn, the one he had turned into a garage. He traded four horses for a 1914 Model T Ford.

Pleased with my fifty-cent captives, I left them talking to each other, sack to sack. Telling Sitka to stay home again, I took the third potato sack and my bag of fish to a place up behind Mrs. Bushler's house. I sat down behind her garage. With my eyes on Mrs. Brown's backdoor, I waited for 15 minutes, but saw no cats. No action! I did my "Kitty, kitty, kitty," routine. There were lots of cats in our neighborhood and I wanted a couple more. I waited another 10 minutes and made more "Kitty, kitty, kitty" sounds, but no cats appeared! I knew Mrs. Brown had cats. I crawled closer to her house on my knees and watched.

"Here kitty, kitty, kitty. Come get some fish." I saw Mrs. Brown moving about in the house and knew she hadn't heard me, so I called a little louder, "Kitty, kitty, kitty, come here," and patiently waited. Sure enough, here came a big, fuzzy, silly-looking gray cat, wide-eyed with its tail held high. It came up to me.

"Hello kitty. Want some fish?" I knew it smelled my bait and me.

Posing with "Bubbles" and Vivian in front of Dad's Model T Ford. The barn in the background was the overnight cat hotel.

I talked nice to it as I laid out the sack and fish head on the grass. As the fuzzy cat sniffed the bait I grabbed him, pulled up the sack, and another star was born! Number three got a place beside the other two talents in the cat barn.

Much encouraged, I went off in a new direction with another sack. The Jewish folks across the street ate lots of fish. I'd sold them some carp I'd caught in Echo Park Lake. Perhaps they put out scraps for their cats and I might see some kitties around their door. With my baited trap laid, I crouched in their backyard for nearly an hour, but no would-be actors showed! It was getting near suppertime, so I headed for the barn. I checked the trio and knew they could breathe in the loosely woven burlap sacks. It was only for one night. I went into our house; Mom was frying round steak.

Our cat, Blackie, was stretched out on the floor next to Dad's old Morris chair. I wouldn't think of it! Mom said she could smell fish, so I washed my hands good before I came to the table. After supper I told Dad (on the quiet) about his friend Glen's visit and my endeavors. With a smile, he suggested Mrs. Bibb had cats! With my bait beside her house it only took me a half-hour to give her big, white pussycat a chance to become a star in a Keystone Comedy! Now the meowing in the barn became a quartet.

About a quarter to nine the next morning, after breakfast, I told Mom where I was going. I knew it would be no place for Sitka so he had to stay home again. I easily loaded the four bags into my wagon and started for the studio. As I passed Mrs. Bibb's house she came out onto the porch with a rug in her hands. Gosh! I thought she knew something. She just shook the rug and said, "Good Morning Coy" so nicely, I felt guilty and nervous. I answered, "Good morning, Mrs. Bibb," and pulled on up the pathway. I liked Mrs. Bibb and her boy, Forrest. I thought about them. By the time I neared the Panorama, I'd decided to let their big, white cat go.

I stopped next to one of the sets and looked up and down the street. Nobody was watching so I reached for the sack. Oh, oh, which one held Whitey? It was one of the two big ones. I chose one, opened the top for a peek, but no, it was old Tom. It had to be the other big one, so I lifted it out and put it on the ground and opened the top, rolled it over, and shook it a bit. Whitey came out like a shot! Without a sound, its ears laid back and its tail straight out, the big ball of fur headed straight for home as fast as it could run. I had to laugh as the other three bags sang out their jealous meows.

As I neared the west gate, I saw David Goldburg sitting on the curb with a guilty look on his face, holding a pillowcase which I knew held his catch. Eddie Cline, the director, and a couple of actors waved to me as they came across the street and went through the gate. Bill, a neighbor kid, showed up behind me carrying a cat in a box. In the next ten minutes, six more guys arrived with cats in sacks or boxes. Stanley Holgate had two cats in a big flour sack. When I saw Leora Hart, a classmate, carrying a cat in a cute little basket, I ran out to meet her. Her mother, Sunshine Hart, was a character actress who had played my mother in a picture just the week before. I liked Leora and told her if she left her cat with this bunch it might get hurt. She agreed and took her cat home.

Two more eighth grade guys showed up with meowing cats in big onion sacks. I saw Glen and a carpenter, each wearing heavy, leather gloves, walking toward the gate from the set. They were glad to see me and evidence of so many cats. They asked us all to come onto the lot and bring our cats. A big, four-foot-square box was put up outside the window of a kitchen set. Through a small hole in its top, Glen and the carpenter, just as fast as they could, put our cats into the box, one-by-one until they were all inside. Loud fights began immediately! The box fairly rocked with action!

One of the kids yelled he wanted his cat back.

"After the scene," Glen told him.

We all ran around onto the set to watch the action. The director and cameraman were ready to grind. Andy Clyde was seated at a table cleaning some fish with a knife. Pieces of fish were on the table and floor. The set was completely surrounded by chicken wire. Everybody stood watching. Glen yelled from the window, "They're ready." The director called, "Camera! Action! Let 'em out!" Glen pulled up the sliding door of the box. Our bunch of cats, some still fighting, jumped out of the box, through the window, and into the kitchen. The smell of the fish made some cats feel at home and they jumped upon the table. Others started to eat fish on the floor under Andy. The camera ground away at the fishy scene. As with actors, some of the cats acted better than others. Two of the cats were still in the box fighting until Glen poked them out.

The director laughed, "Andy, just keep on cleaning the fish. It's a good scene, we'll never get it any better." Three minutes later he yelled, "Cut!"

Two men with bags picked up the pieces of fish. The director thanked us and told us to take our cats. Only two guys picked up their cats; all the others were allowed to run for home.

We all got our quarters, and Glen gave me an extra fifty cents for passing the word at school.

ANIMALS IN PICTURES

1920

Lionel Comport, with his wife and four or five kids, had a dairy out beyond Mixville on Glendale Boulevard. They kept a variety of farm animals. The dairy was just over the hill from the Sennett and Selig studios. The prop men would go over and ask Lionel if he had a goat, a couple of roosters or a cow they could rent.

"Sure, here they are. Where do you want 'em?" Lionel would ask.

"Can you bring them down to the studio?"

"Sure, when?"

Charlie Gay, with his arm on the lion, had a lion farm in El Monte, California and did a good business renting his animals to the studios. On the right is Clyde Cook, a star comedian. Uncle Bill is behind the lion.

He would then put the required actors in a wagon and take them to the studio. When Lionel saw what was happening he went into the business and acquired more animals. He owned the famous sway-back horse that was seen in many movies. He supplied bears and chimps. He was the owner of the deer seen in *The Yearling*.

Another Edendale friend of Dad's from the earliest days, "Fat" Jones, wound up owning and renting most of the horses and western equipment like wagons, stagecoaches and buckboards used in pictures. His equipment is used today and probably will be used as

Mr. Hayes, dressed as a woman, works with a lion as Charlie cues off-camera

long as Westerns are made. Dad sold "Fat" one of the first horses he rented to the studios. It was a wonderful, smart, fearless horse that would do anything. It made jumps across rivers, walked upon tables in saloons and jumped through "candy" glass windows.

Horses became popular when Western movies were shown in the big cities for big money at the box offices. Films shot earlier in the East used horses to run around carrying riders shooting at each

The cook hopes the cat isn't hungry

other, but California's pictures showed horses doing all kinds of unusual stunts. Horses like Tom Mix's "Tony" and Bill Hart's Pinto "Ben" and "Fritz" became famous in scenes that saved the picture!

When farmers saw pictures on the screens of animals and farms or ranches, they contacted the studios and offered their animals and locations for scenes. Sometimes they offered a herd of cattle or some big bulls that Lionel didn't have. When the studios later saw how much money it was costing them to rent animals, some began to acquire their own.

Universal Studios was one of the first to get their own stock. They acquired elephants, camels, cattle and horses of all kinds. A fellow by the name of House was in charge of the western movies' animals like horses and cattle. Curly Stecker was in charge of the circus animals like zebras and giraffes. Sorry to say that Curly was crushed to death by a mean elephant named Charley. He pushed Curly up against a wall and squeezed him to death. Charley was destroyed.

There were people with pets watching movies that thought their own animals would be good in the movies. They offered a dog, a cat, a goat that did funny things, a burro that pushed people with his nose and also would lie down on cue.

While Dad was casting director for William Fox comedies, he received calls from such people. Sometimes he would have them come in with the animal, if possible, to see what it looked like and what it could do. He'd tell them, "Next time we have need for an animal like yours you can bring it here and we'll see what he can do on the set." Dad always called two or three of the animals required making sure at least one would do what the director wanted. Some animals were less frightened, smarter and took orders better than others.

I worked in three pictures with a ring-tailed monkey named Josephine and a boxer dog named Pal. Their owner and trainer was Tony Companero, the owner of several animals he kept in Culver City. In his great Italian accent he would tell me "Coy, you be ah careful wit ah Josephine today, she no feel-a berry good."

Tony got into films because Josephine had been Tony's organ grinder monkey on the street. In our Campbell Comedies the monkey and dog were great. The monkey rode on the dog's back as Tony shouted directions at them from off-camera.

Remember, in those days of silent pictures, owners could direct their animals by voice: "Lie down now, Pal. Josephine, tip your hat." Tony would also wave his arm as he called to Josephine saying, "Josephine, jump over on Coy's shoulder, jump over!" Then he'd open his mouth wide and tell her to "Say Aah!" She'd open her mouth and say "Aah" back at him to look like she was talking.

There was always work for obedient dogs. "Sunshine" Hart played my mother in a couple of pictures at Sennett's Studio. Here she is in This Way Out *with Lige Conley and Mack Swain.*

Sometimes a subtitle would pop onto the screen to tell what the monkey was saying.

I remember how Tony had such patience with the animals. Training animals to work in pictures didn't happen overnight. It wasn't learned from books. Animals were needed and some owners saw an opportunity for pets to get into the movie business early.

EXTRA, EXTRA READ ALL ABOUT IT

1920

Before radio, I had fun making money selling Friday evening special edition newspapers called "Extras." They were reprints of the day's regular last edition, but with the added results of any big news that had happened that night — usually a prizefight or wrestling match.

One night about 9 o'clock, an hour after the Sharkey fight was to finish, Sitka and I waited to buy my papers at the Sunset bridge where Sunset Boulevard crossed over Glendale Boulevard. Prizefights, which were fought at night, made for the best sales. With our money ready to pay two cents per paper, I waited for the paper drop with eight or ten other boys ten to fifteen years of age. Finally, the route manager, driving his delivery truck, came speeding down the Boulevard from downtown Los Angeles with the papers, giving the story and results of the big fight. Sliding to a stop, he jumped to the back onto the piles of papers.

"I got a dollar," one kid said, "Give me fifty." Another had sixty cents and got thirty. I had eighty cents and asked for forty papers. As we got them, we took off on the run. I put mine in my canvas carrier's bag as the truck headed out Sunset Boulevard for Hollywood. Each of us charged in a different direction to hustle our investments for a profit. It was called "Boot-jacking papers." We all had neighborhoods in mind where we could make sales. At a dogtrot, Sitka and I headed up Glendale Boulevard toward Edendale where we knew a lot of people.

I started yelling, "Extra! Extra! Read all about the big fight. It's all over. Extra! Extra!" As I hustled along calling out, porch lights popped on and doors opened. A guy yelled, "Who won, kid?"

Another voice yelled, "Buy a paper you tightwad!" They laughed.

"Over here, kid. How much tonight?"

"Five cents." A nickel in the pocket here and another over there. Up the street we'd go. A window opened, a woman yelled, "Who won, kid?"

"Buy a paper and read all about it lady." I sang out.

"O.K., over here."

"Five cents please. Thank you."

The guy next door on his porch took one. He gave me a dime. We jogged along. Another light came on. "Who won the fight?"

"Buy a paper to know."

A big laugh, again, from a man walking down the street.

"I'm up on the porch. How much, kid?"

"Five cents."

"Why, it says two cents on the paper."

"This is special delivery, mister. Five cents please."

"Here's your nickel."

"Thanks! . . . Extra! Extra!, the big fight is over. Read all about it."

"Up here, kid. Here's a dime. Keep the change."

"Thank you, mister. Extra! Extra!"

Up and down the streets we trotted. Lights came on. Doors opened. Interested people called to each other about the fight. On Sitka and I went until almost 10 o'clock sometimes. If the fight finished early, we got the papers earlier. A late decision meant the presses rolled late with the headlines. We kept moving, yelling and selling until we sold them all. I only got stuck with three papers once in six nights. I figured I made good money for one night's work.

With Sitka along, my folks never worried about my safety. Mom always said, "I can't see that you make enough for all the effort and time you put into this boot-jacking business." But Dad understood and just smiled. He had sold papers on Los Angeles' streets and told me of the great sales he made during the San Francisco earthquake and fire. We agreed selling papers was fun and exciting.

The people were interesting and I had to laugh. They thought because I had the paper I had read all the facts and knew all about the fight. "How many rounds did it go, kid?" they'd ask, or "Did

In at least five or six pictures I played a Newsboy

they get cut up much?" Each buyer had different, funny and exciting things to say, so I was enthusiastic too.

"It was a great fight," I could truthfully answer. "Read all about it, you'll see."

A man grabbed a paper, handed me a dime and started to read. "That's okay kid, keep the change."

"Thanks, I'll see you after the next fight."

I did like meeting people on my own and boot-jacking to make money. I knew Dad and Mom were pleased to see me earning my spending money.

Dad always said things like, "What a person earns he appreciates more than what's handed him. Everything you do helps you enjoy life a little more. The more you learn about people, the more you'll learn about life. Go by the Golden Rule: Do unto others, as you would have them do unto you. Be friendly, willing to work hard and honestly, and you'll always be happy."

He was right. I am.

How I Lost Sitka

1920

In 1920, when I was eight years old, automobiles were replacing horses and wagons on the Los Angeles streets where I lived. One day, my Dad and I were surprised to see Sitka, my wolf and malamute dog, running and growling at the wheels of a passing Model T Ford. Dad whistled him into the yard, scolded him and hit him a couple of swats on the nose with his hand.

I felt pretty bad to see my pal slapped. Dad explained to me, in very serious words, that it was dangerous for Sitka to chase after cars. I had seen dogs enjoy this fun, but I never understood why. Then Dad assured me that if my dog didn't stop his chasing he could be killed. I thought about that and believed my dad was right. So, whenever a car chanced by, if Sitka started to run for it, I let out a big yell and called him back to my side and scolded him.

One day Mom told me he sometimes chased after cars while I was at school. That really bothered me. I couldn't keep him tied up all the time, though I did a couple of days. He was my best friend, my lifelong buddy. I didn't want him to get killed!

That feeling made me remember something Dad had said a couple of years earlier when I had stood bent over as he was about to apply his razor strap to my upturned fanny. I was about to be punished for breaking the Golden's window with a stone from my slingshot. Sadly, Dad had said, "This is going to hurt me as much as it hurts you. You make me feel bad when you're not a good boy. I promised you this strap if you disobeyed again. You knew you were not to shoot stones across the street. Now I must keep my promise to you so you will believe me when I tell you something."

He kept his promise and it hurt! I learned to believe, and never doubted my dad again. I knew he'd always keep his word.

I kept training Sitka, and after awhile, Dad and I thought he understood us and had quit chasing cars.

About two months later, Sitka and I turned nine years old. Dad said that was old for a dog. I knew my buddy was slowing down. He didn't run with me as much, or as fast anymore, and he wasn't eating as much either. Poor old fellow! He was still a great watch-dog though. Day or night he allowed folks to come just so close to the house. He'd never bark, just stand and look at whoever came near, stranger or friend, and make a low, snarling growl until they'd call out. "Hello! Anybody home?" or "Hey, Coy or Goldie, it's Charlie. Call Sitka." Then Dad or Mom went out and Sitka would lie down and let the folks come in. Sitka had always been a true member of our family.

One evening as we sat around the dinner table, we heard a loud yelp and some sharp whining cries from the street. Oh, no! I knew that yelp. My dog was hurt. I was off of my chair with a jump. My bare feet hit the floor and I was through the screen door on the run. I could see him down at the corner. The car was gone. With his front legs he had pulled himself up over the curb, out of the street and onto the sidewalk. Without a sound he was dragging his help-less rear across the dry grass-covered vacant lot toward me. My playmates, Sonny and Sis, had heard and were running to him. Mrs. Hatchberg, our neighbor, had left her porch chair and was also running to us.

When I reached Sitka, he stopped crawling and lay still looking up at me, breathing hard. He was hurt bad. I fell to the ground beside him and gently patted his head and talked to him. He made a very quiet whining sound as I put my face to his. I didn't know what to do. I couldn't help him. I started to cry. "Oh, Sitka, I'm sorry." I knew he was crying too.

Now my Dad was there kneeling beside us. "Help him, Daddy! That Model T hit him and hurt him. He feels so bad."

Dad nodded. "Yes he does."

My mom and Vivian came and stood beside me. Folks coming

home from work walked over to look, and share our sorrow. One man asked, "What's the matter here?"

Mrs. Hatchberg answered him, "Coy's dog was hit by a car."

"Oh," the man said, "Just a dog. I thought somebody was hurt," and left.

Dad's eyes met mine, and he said, "That man never had a dog. Let's take Sitka up to the house."

Ever so gently we picked him up and started to walk. Sonny and Sis were beside me saying, "We're so sorry, Coy." Mom, Vivian, and Mrs. Hatchberg walked with us as we carried my dog to the front porch. Some blades of dry grass were caught between Dad's hand and Sitka's coat. He moaned a little as we laid him down on his blanket bed. Dad patted his head and knelt down beside him.

"There, old fellow, take it easy." He began to examine Sitka, running his hand over his rear quarters. I patted Sitka and wiped off my tears with the back of my hand so Sonny wouldn't see them.

"Will he be okay, Daddy? What's the matter with him?"

Sitka—My first playmate and friend, from whom I learned so much

"He must have been chasing a car and a wheel hit his left hip. It's not too good." Then he put his hand on my shoulder, leaned close to me and whispered, "Don't cry." He knew how I felt. "Be a big boy. Sitka is a tough dog and we'll do all we can to help him, won't we?" Then he spoke to the kids and neighbors standing around the porch.

"It looks like his left hip is badly hurt. We may have to get him to a vet, or possibly I can fix him."

Sonny and Sis stood watching and nibbling some cookies. Mrs. Hatchberg nodded her head and spoke in her dear old, Jewish accent, "I'm sorry et happened, but I yest knew he vas goeng to get runned over. He vas always chasing da cars."

They all told us how sorry they were and hoped Sitka would be all right. After they left, I thought, "Oh, Sitka, I tried so hard to tell you what could happen." I patted his head and stroked his nose. He always liked that. I knelt there looking into his eyes. They were sad and I knew he was saying, "Oh, Buddy, can't you do something? I feel so bad."

Mom and Vivian went into the house. Dad sat down on the edge of the porch with his feet on the step. He leaned forward, put his elbows on his knees, folded his hands and just looked at Gloria's doll buggy under the apple tree. What was he thinking?

I put my arms around my pal's neck and pressed my cheek to his nose, closed my eyes and whispered, "Oh, God, Sitka is sorry he chased cars. He's hurt now. Help him not to feel bad, and please help Daddy to make him well and strong again. We want to play together some more."

Mom spoke through the screen door. "The sun has gone down. Don't you think you boys should come in?"

I shook my head and continued to stroke Sitka's head. Dad talked and I listened for a long time. I trusted him and left it all to him and God. With a "goodnight" to Sitka, Dad put his hand on my shoulder and we walked into the house. I was feeling my life's first, real sorrow. I didn't finish my dinner. In bed I couldn't go to sleep, even after Dad and Mom's many words of comfort. My tears made wet spots on the pillow. I knew big boys didn't cry, but my pal was in pain. After Dad and Mom went to bed, I got up and found Sitka asleep. Finally, I went to sleep, too.

The next morning Dad said Sitka was better and he hoped he might walk again, but not as good as before. After a couple of weeks, Sitka was able to get up and walk a little but I could see he was in pain. His eyes were sad even when I tried to cheer him up. When he walked it was only on three legs. It was so hard for him that he just laid around. I didn't like leaving him, but I had to go to school. All during class I thought about him. When I came home, he couldn't come to meet me as he usually did, and I missed his eager greeting.

I had fun playing with the kids at school, but when the three o'clock bell rang I hurried home to be with Sitka. I knew he was growing old, but we still talked. Then came the saddest day in my life.

Trotting home from school, I crossed the lot and approached the house calling, "Hello, Sitka old boy, here I am!" I stared at the porch. Sitka and his blanket were gone! I whipped open the screen door and ran into the house calling, "Mom, where is Sitka?" Mom was waiting for me. Her face had a look on it I'd never seen before. It frightened me. I searched her eyes. She stepped toward me and pulled me close, pressing my head against her breast. She hadn't answered me. Where was Sitka? I didn't know what to think or feel. Mom squeezed me hard, and putting her hands on my shoulders, held me at arm's length and looked into my upturned face.

"Where's Sitka?" I whispered, trying to be brave.

She angled a couple of chairs out from under the dining room table and we sat down slowly. The silence in the room was scary as I looked into her tear-filled eyes. I'd seen her cry only once before: the night Dad had two guys deliver a Kimball piano for her birthday. That night she had cried happy tears, but now there were sad tears in her eyes as she spoke softly.

"Daddy has taken Sitka for a ride to the desert. Daddy feels very sorry for Sitka and he knows you don't like to see your dog suffer. Sitka is old now and feels bad because he can't play and run with you anymore."

Her lower lip quivered, and I saw the hurt in her face. She wiped away her tears with a hankie from her apron pocket, took a deep breath and continued, "When Daddy went out to see Sitka this morning, after you'd gone to school, he saw that he was bleeding from inside. There was blood on his blanket. So he picked up Sitka with his blanket and carefully put him on the seat of the Ford and told me he was going to drive out to the desert." She patted my arm, squeezed it, tightened her lips, and stopped talking.

I then remembered a movie I had seen. While on a cattle drive out on the lone prairie, a cowhand's horse had broken its leg. It was a vivid, tragic scene in my memory. The horse lay helpless on the ground, nodding its head. The cowboy took off the saddle and bridle. The organ played some sad music as the cowboy's words were projected onto the silent screen. He told his old pal goodbye and drew his six-shooter from its holster. Then there was a big close-up with a "Please forgive me" look on his face as he shot his horse. The scene had disturbed me deeply. Dad loved horses and so did I. I told him about the picture and we discussed it. He knew how I felt for the horse and took the time to explain as only my Dad could.

"The cowboy loved his horse, so he did what he had to do, because he didn't want his friend to suffer."

Mom didn't have to tell me that Dad had taken his Smith and Wesson revolver from the bottom drawer of his dresser. Mom wiped her nose and put her hankie in her pocket. Then, taking my face in her hands, she said, "Daddy loves you and he knows how much you love Sitka. He asked me to tell you he is doing what must be done and he knows you will understand."

Her arms were around me as she held me close and tight and patted my shoulder. "So be strong. Remember, you and Sitka love each other. Only the people you love make you sad or happy."

That day I learned how it felt to lose someone you loved. Sitka was only a dog, but he had been my lifetime friend. I hurt when I lost him because I cared so much for him. To lose one I loved so much so early in my life was a rough experience for a young boy. The loss left a deep impression. During the years that followed, I affectionately owned many good dogs, but I never allowed myself to care for one as I had cared for Sitka.

MY OWN LITTLE BROTHER

1921

After I lost Sitka, I missed him a lot. I wished and wished hard for a little brother. I had wanted one ever since the arrival of my sister, Vivian. Most of my playmates had brothers. Why couldn't I have one? I asked Dad to get me one. He wouldn't promise. Vivian was fun, but I felt one sister was enough. I needed a brother. However, sister Gloria turned up on the scene and then little Louise showed up. So I almost quit believing I'd ever have a brother. I was becoming suspicious they weren't telling me everything. Nevertheless, I tried once more.

I begged Mom and Dad, "Please tell the doctor not to bring us any more girls in his black bag." They wouldn't promise. Then one hot, summer day, August 31, 1921, at Selig's Zoo, I was acting in some scenes with a big tiger. It was for a kid comedy titled, *A Nick-of-Time Hero.* Dad left for a couple of hours.

Left: A proud big brother and little Harry. Right: Harry and me in Wild Puppies *at Fox Studio.*

Later, he showed up on the set all happy, with a big smile on his face. Between scenes, in a loud voice, he proudly told me and the company that the doctor had been to our house and delivered a little baby brother for me!

"Hooray! I got a brother! Oh, boy!" Was I happy!

When we finally finished shooting, I couldn't get home fast enough. I thanked Dad and let him know I was pleased he and Mom finally put the order in right and I got my brother—Harry. I liked to look at him and be with him. I liked to hold Harry whenever Mom would let me. He was a good little brother. Mom taught me to change his diapers and take care of him. Harry later slept with me, and I changed him in the middle of the night when he wet the bed.

One day, when my friend Bob Moore and I rode our bikes to Echo Park Playground to play basketball, I carried Harry in the front half of my canvas newspaper delivery bag. In the back, I took a few changes of diapers, his toys and some graham crackers. While Bob and I concentrated on shooting baskets, little Harry watched us from the sidelines. Tied with a diaper to a tree, he was happy and stayed put. We waved to him. He'd laugh and wave back. We played and then I ran over and checked his supply of snacks and felt for dampness in his diaper.

I had to call "time out" when he fussed with a wet bottom.

Always proud of my five younger brothers. Left to right: Bobs, Garry, Delmar, Billy, Harry, and "Big Brother."

Both teams laughed as they gathered around to watch and rib me while I changed his diaper. Some of the guys had never seen it done. Others asked me why I was doing it and why I brought him along anyway. I just told them, "He is my own little brother. I take care of him and I like to have him with me."

I took him everywhere I went. When he turned five years old, Mom and I got him all dressed up and I took him to school with me. With much pride, I introduced him to the kindergarten class. He took to the teacher and the kids just fine and I left him. But I wasn't upstairs in my classroom 10 minutes when my teacher answered our room phone.

"Coy, your brother is crying and asking for you in the kindergarten."

When I arrived, Harry was crying and sobbing hard. His face was red, tears were dripping off his chin and his little nose was

running. I picked him up. He put his arms around my neck and held on. He wouldn't let the teacher touch him.

He blubbered, "Toy, you tay here wif me. We tan pway!" I dried his tears, wiped his nose and we talked. Finally, I got him to play on the floor with the same blocks I had pushed around on my first day of school! When he was happy again, I left him.

In 20 minutes, my class phone rang again. Same thing. Harry and I talked some more. He tried to understand. After four trips

An Easter surprise for brother Bobs

that first morning, I took him up to sit with me in my class. He and my class liked that, but I don't think my teacher did. The next day was better, but every time Mrs. Elme's phone rang, the class sang out, "Coy, go talk to Harry!" and I did.

We blew out candles together for 66 years—Bobs got a banana cake, I got walnut

A week passed, Harry cried less each day and came to enjoy the kids without me. The teacher remarked, "You and Harry love each other very much don't you?" The belonging and the love that was born between Harry and me was just there from the beginning and it never stopped growing.

Nine years later, I had four brothers. Then one day I received more than I would have thought to wish for, a fifth brother! Born on my 18th birthday! Dad let me name him Bobby after my pal Bob Moore. When he was about four, Dad changed his name to Bobs.

I'll never forget how pleased and happy I was when little Harry's arrival renewed my confidence in Dad and Mom's ability to deliver what was needed at the right time!

After Bobby arrived, Mom always made two cakes for November 16th birthday parties.

THEY LIKED MY WORK

1921

In the summer of 1921, William S. Campbell was producing some of the first "Kid and Animal Comedies" made in Hollywood at the Fine Arts Studio. I was called to play a "meany" in my first Campbell Comedy, *Assorted Heroes*.

I was seen peeking over a fence shooting arrows at a group of kids having a picnic in the park. My scenes were shot at the studio; the kids were shot at the park. Mr. Campbell, directing, told me to imagine that the kids were there. I played to his directions as he explained the action. I was directed to pull arrows from the quiver on my back, load, and shoot the bow. I did as I was told, with slight variations with each arrow. The comedy bit in the picture came when one of the kids tried to hide behind a tree. I took a prop,

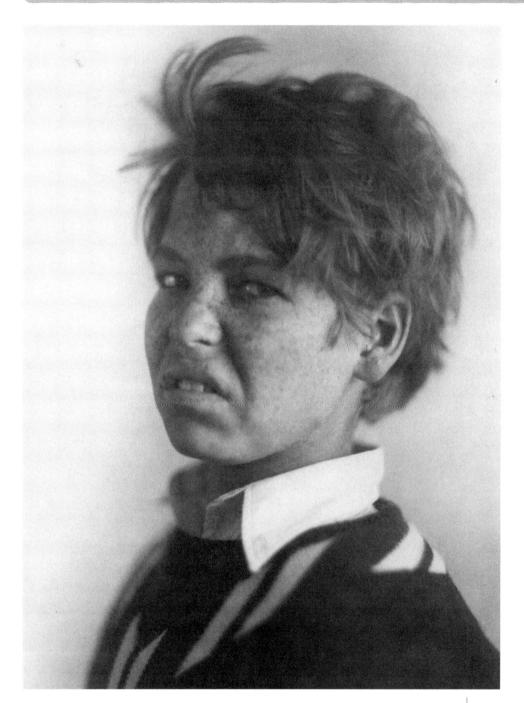

1921—playing the "heavy" in Assorted Heroes

bendable metal arrow from the quiver and bent it into a half circle. This "meany" figured a bent arrow would bend around the tree and hit the hiding boy. But instead, when I loaded and shot the arrow, it made a full circle and flew around behind me and stuck me in the "fanny."

Mr. Campbell must have liked the way I took his directions and played the scene because he wrote the following letter dated August 22, 1921 to Mr. Brooks, an officer of the corporation:

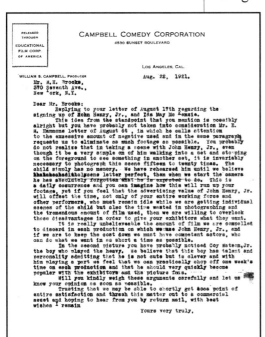

This is the actual letter from Mr. Bill Campbell

Dear Mr. Brooks:

Replying to your letter of August 17th regarding the signing up of John Henry, Jr., and Ida May McKenzie.

This idea from the standpoint that you mention is possibly alright but you have probably not taken into consideration Mr. E.W. Hammons' letter of August 6th, in which he calls attention to the excessive amount of negative used and in the same paragraph requests us to eliminate as much footage as possible. You probably do not realize that in taking a scene with John Henry, Jr., even though it be a very simple one of him walking into a set and stopping on the foreground to see something in another set, it is invariably necessary to photograph this scene fifteen to twenty times. The child simply has no memory. We have rehearsed him until we believe he has learned the scene letter perfect, then when we start the camera he has absolutely forgotten what he is expected to do. This is a daily occurrence and you can imagine how this will run up your footage, yet if you feel that the advertising value of John Henry, Jr. will offset the time, not only of your entire working force and other performers, who must remain idle while we are getting individual scenes of the child but also the time wasted in photographing and the tremendous amount of film used, then we are willing to overlook these disadvantages in order to give your exhibitors what they want.

It is really unbelievable the amount of film we are compelled to discard in each production on which we use John Henry, Jr., and if we are to keep the cost down we must have competent actors, who can do what we want in as short a time as possible.

In the second picture you probably noticed Coy Watson, Jr. the boy who played the heavy. We believe that this boy has talent and personality admitting that he is not cute but is clever and with him playing a part we feel that we can practically chop off one week's time on each production and that he should very quickly become popular with the exhibitors and the picture fans.

Will you kindly weigh these arguments carefully and let us know your opinions as soon as possible.

Trusting that we may be able to shortly get to a point of entire satisfaction and thrash this matter out to a commercial asset and hoping to hear from you by return mail, with best wishes I remain

Yours very truly,

William Campbell

I guess the letter did the trick! A month later, I was nine years old when Bill Campbell signed Doreen Turner, the girl; Pal, the dog; Josephine, the monkey; and me to star in his series of children and animal comedies. Campbell or Frank Griffin directed with a company made up of a cameraman, a prop man, a grip and a couple of all-around hands. In three months we made three pictures. What happy days!

It was all fun except when I had to kiss Doreen at the end of the pictures. She was cute and I liked her a lot, but I never saw

cowboys like Tom Mix, Buck Jones or Hoot Gibson kiss their leading ladies at the end of their pictures, so I couldn't understand why I had to. However, I did as I was told and kissed her and the crew always laughed and kidded me. That's what I didn't like.

Doreen was very clever and played the little rich girl. I was always a poor little boy with my constant companions; a dog and a monkey. The best three of the five films were *A Nick-of-Time Hero*, *Stolen Glory* and *School-Day Love*. *Assorted Heroes* and *The Stork's Mistake* were the other two.

Campbell Comedies were made at Fine Arts Studio, located at Sunset Boulevard and Fountain Avenue. D.W. Griffith had his office here in 1916 when he made Intolerance.

ACTING WITH ANIMALS

1921

I liked animals and worked with them in many pictures: dogs, cats, monkeys, chimps, lions, tigers, horses or donkeys. The man working the animal would usually say to me, "Now don't be afraid and the animal will not hurt you; it will like you. If you are afraid, it will sense your fear of it. That will make it nervous and afraid of you and then it won't obey me."

I learned this truth early and never had any trouble. Often, after doing a scene, the animal owner would thank me for helping his "pride and joy" do what the director wanted. When a dog was directed to enter a scene and lie down at my side, if I stood still and didn't move my legs or arms too much, we got the scene sooner. Many times Josephine, the monkey, was cued to jump onto my head and talk to me. We learned if I stood steady and didn't move or flinch, the director was pleased every time.

My Dad had successfully worked with lions, dogs, bears and horses in many pictures. "Like father, like son," he told me. "Animals have very sensitive feelings. When you work with them you must relax, be calm, quiet, fearless and have a confident attitude."

I didn't have to be told twice to move slowly when working with lions. I knew when kneeling beside a big cat, its eyes were on the trainer. I also knew the cat knew I was there. Any quick movement of my body or hand might attract a little snap or claw in my direction, instead of at the trainer's chair or whip.

Riding along Sunset Boulevard on a tricycle in A Doggone Wedding, *a Fox Studio comedy directed by Eddie Cline. "Josephine" and I become good friends and made many pictures together.*

As a kid, working with dogs and monkeys was very tiring at times, especially when working in the sun. They'd follow me into a scene but run out to get in the shade before the action was finished. So, we'd do it again and again, maybe a dozen times, before I got the girl on the donkey while the monkey riding on the dog stayed in the scene.

One director might say, "Let's be patient, kids, we'll get it."

Another less patient director would only yell and cuss at the dog and the trainer. "All right, let's do it again until we get it. That dog and monkey have to stay in the shot."

At that point an understanding assistant director would come over to me, off-camera, as we prepared to shoot the scene for the 10th time. With his hand on my shoulder, he'd say quietly, "Stay with it, Trooper. Remember you have to look real pleased as you help this girl onto her donkey. Look happy and keep smiling."

I knew the audience wasn't to know that the scene had been shot 10 times before because the animals didn't like working in the hot sun. I knew that Pal, the dog, and Josephine, the monkey, were hot; so was I. I thanked the assistant for his words of concern. He called me a "trooper" and that was a compliment Dad was pleased to hear of me. I truly enjoyed working in pictures! The people too, were great. As I grew older it was still fun, but no easier.

One hot summer day, Jack McHugh (a fellow kid actor) and I were playing a couple of "heavies" in a Smitty comedy. Smitty was a popular newspaper comic strip at the time. The rights were acquired to be made into a series of motion pictures. In this sequence, the

Jack McHugh and me with a friendly cat in a Fox Picture

kid playing Smitty (Donald Haynes) was running home from the grocery store with a dozen eggs in a paper bag. Rounding a fence corner he bumped into us tough guys face to face. Jack was pushed up against the fence but Smitty hit me head on, broke the bag against my front and knocked me down to the sidewalk flat on my back. McHugh and Smitty stood by laughing and making wisecracks. Then the work began.

For over an hour, with the help of the prop man, I laid on the pavement on my back in the sun without moving. The script said my chest was to be covered with a dozen broken eggs that became a batch of newly hatched baby chicks. The prop man had them! The camera took a long shot, then close-up after close-up, trying to get one running scene of my face looking wide-eyed

Playing with an old friend at Selig's zoo in 1936

and surprised at a dozen cute, little balls of fuzz cheeping and walking around in a mess of broken shells on my chest.

I had to lie very still as the prop man knelt beside me trying to keep the happy brood in a group on my chest. One by one they rolled off and one by one the prop man caught them and put them back into the scene. When the cameraman finally said, "O.K. we have enough," the chick trainer and I happily agreed with him. We laughed as we got to our feet, stretching and rubbing tired places.

The prop man remarked, "That scene was for the birds."

"I hope it's all it was hatched up to be," I added.

The director laughed and said he knew it was a tough scene to get and he thanked us for being so patient with the chicks. I felt he was pleased and so was I. When the picture ran, that scene was only on the screen for about five seconds, but it got a big laugh. Five seconds for one hour's shooting! That's what it took and that's the way movies were made.

LEARNING TO TAKE IT

1921

Dad never ever played any team sports like baseball or football, but he knew how to box and wrestle. We were great pals and played together a lot. I was about eight or nine and wanted to learn to box. So, we'd often put on some small-size boxing gloves that Frankie Dolan, Tom Mix's trainer, had given Dad. Dad would get down on his knees in the living room and show me how to box.

"Hold that right hand up, open glove, next to your face for your guard. Left foot forward, on your toes. Lead with your left hand. Keep it out there. Punch, then come across over with a right hook."

I did it all—oh, and did I pay for the lesson, taking punches on

the nose and on the chin. I never let him know how some hurt. When he saw the tears in my eyes, he quickly put his arms around me and pulled me into a big hug. In my ear I heard, "If you want to be a boxer and deliver punches, you'll have to learn to take punches!" Then he put his open gloves on my shoulders, held me at arms' length and looked at me. "There'll always be some guy who wants to fight. Be ready. But Coy, never start a fight. Try to talk out the problem first. Avoid fighting if you can. But when you feel you must fight, be sure it is for a good reason. Then fight to win!" His eyes half closed. "Keep calm and land the first punch—straight and hard to his nose. Don't stop! Keep punching until you win and its over." His eyes opened. "Then tell the loser why you had to fight him." He dropped his arms to his sides. "Be a quiet winner—not a

Our family boxing ring. Garry and Delmar mixing it up as Bobs, with a big cigar, referees. Neighbor kids and Harry cheer them on.

smarty." Then thoughtfully he said slowly, "When you lose a fight, and there will be such times, be a good loser. If possible, give credit to the winner." We were looking into each other's eyes.

"That's the way I hope you'll fight all the contests and problems you'll face during your life." He paused. "You know what I mean do you?" He leaned toward me and held his glove under my chin. I nodded "Yes." He smiled. What a Dad! My life-long trainer.

"Shall we box some more?" he asked. We did. For years. There were times when I finished some rounds with a bloody nose or a cut lip and I learned to take it!

I do admit during

Above: Dad was a husky fellow but smoking shortened his life. None of his sons or daughters ever smoked. Above right: I took a picture of Dad so he took one of me. He taught me to exercise and work out. I'm still in good shape at 88.

World War II, aboard U.S. Coast Guard Patrol Vessel #309, I was out-sparred in a match with shipmate writer and friend, Will Fowler. He was good.

AN EDENDALE MYSTERY

1921

In 1921, before radio, a popular thing to do was play 10-inch, hard-rubber disks or phonograph records as they were called. Old folks called them Gramophone records.

Big Bud, one of my playmates, was two years older and two feet taller than I. Bud's sister bought all the newest records so we three could learn the words of the latest popular song. We'd sit in the living room singing along as the music came out of the big phonograph horn. One of our favorites was "Sweet Little You."

"Sweet Little You,
I'm just crazy about you.
Sweet Little You,

I just can't live without you."

The song never became very popular but we enjoyed learning it and singing it.

One afternoon I came home from school and found Mom and our neighbor, Katie Wilson, in our living room, having coffee together. I listened to their conversation. Katie leaned forward and whispered that the big vacant lot next to her property on Berkeley Avenue, a block south of Mack Sennett's Studio, had been sold.

"Nobody knows who bought it," she said. "There seems to be something odd about the deal and what is to be done on the land." For years the place had had a sort of mystery about it and no one was ever seen checking on it. It was always covered with weeds. A shabby little garage stood on the front of the property near the sidewalk next to the Berkeley Apartments. A hundred feet from the street, at the back of the lot, were two weird-looking, old wooden buildings that looked kind of spooky. Even we kids wouldn't go near them.

"Years ago," my Dad said, "an old man I never met lived there in the house and repaired wagons and wheelbarrows in the shop. He just disappeared."

A view of the lot from my house, a block south of the Keystone Studio where I believe California's first Talking Picture Theater was built, on the south side of Berkeley Avenue in the 2100 block

I thought it all sounded interesting. A week later, on a sunny afternoon, after delivering a prescription for Mr. Proctor, the druggist, I was walking home past the old lot. To my surprise a pathway had been cleared to the back, so I dared to walk slowly toward the old buildings. I was about 30 feet from the shop, when suddenly two men came out of the door with boxes full of rubbish. I stopped. We looked at each other. I waved to them and left in a hurry. The following Thursday afternoon I went out to the street to bring in our garbage pail and across the street I saw a big, light brown, topless Packard touring car pull up and stop next to the lot. A tall man with a nice looking police dog that resembled the movie star "Rin Tin Tin" got out of the car and walked onto the lot. I dropped the pail and followed them.

The dog had stopped and was standing at the door of the shop. He looked at me. I stepped slowly to him, patted his head and knelt down on one knee beside him. He liked me. I asked, "What's your name, fellow?" and rubbed his ears. He was smiling at me when I saw a man's feet step into the doorway. I looked up.

"What do you want here?" the man asked.

"I just wanted to see your dog. What's his name?" He didn't answer me, so I said, "My dog Sitka was my pal. He was kinda like your dog." I was patting the dog's head.

"Where's your dog?" the man asked.

"He's gone."

"Gone where? What happened to him?" He asked as if he cared. I thought a bit, then answered slowly, "He was hit by a Model T Ford."

The man bent down to hear me better, as I continued. "He was hurt badly and was in pain. He couldn't get well, so my dad had to take him to the desert. He shot him and buried him in a nice, deep grave in the shade of some big rocks."

I was patting his dog's head when he asked, "What's your name?"

I looked up at him. "Coy Watson, Jr." Then I asked, "What's your name?" I waited.

"Kellum," he said, "and my dog's name is Chief. I am sorry to hear about your dog. I know dogs are good friends."

"Sitka is all right where he is now, but I still miss him."

"I see Chief likes you," said Mr. Kellum.

"Yes, dogs always like me because they know I like them." We heard an electric motor start. We stood up. "Mr. Kellum, what are the men making in there?"

He looked me in the eye. "Well, Coy, that's sort of a secret right now. I'll tell you sometime later. O.K.?" He smiled and turned away. I talked with Chief for awhile, then went home and put the garbage pail on the back porch. I told Dad and Mom about Chief, Mr. Kellum, and that there was a secret about what was being made in the old shop.

A few days later I went back and visited with the two men working in Mr. Kellum's shop. One's name was Ernie, the other I've forgotten. One was working with pieces of metal at a lathe, while the other worked at a drill press. "Ernie," I asked, "When will you guys finish what you're making?"

"In a couple of months," he answered softly. Mr. Kellum will let everybody know when we're finished. He's having a building put here on the lot." The other man looked up quickly at Ernie, at me, then back to his work. A month later, as Ernie had said, in the center of the lot workmen were putting the finishing touches on a nice looking, red brick building. Mr. Kellum, Chief and I watched as a truckload of things was unloaded into the building.

One warm evening about a week later, as the sun was setting, Dad and Mom and we kids were sitting on our front porch.

"Look over there," Mom said, and pointed toward the lot. A

big, black shiny car had stopped at the curb. A chauffeur opened the door and a well-dressed man and woman in their evening clothes got out, looked around and started toward the brick building. Before they reached it, two more big cars were parking on the street. In minutes more people, also in evening clothes were entering the building. Whooee! Something was going on there! What was it?

I ran and got Bud to come and watch the action with me. From under Katie's jacaranda tree on her front lawn we watched for half-an-hour as cars and folks in fancy dress arrived. It was getting dark when the seventh and last car had parked and four more people went inside. We wanted to get a closer look, so we walked slowly toward the building. We heard talking as we sneaked near an open window. Then the lights went out. We leaned on the windowsill and strained to see inside.

At the other end of the darkened room, over the heads of the seated gathering, I saw a silver movie screen. On the screen was a moving picture of two men made up to look like big black birds sitting in a prop tree. To my surprise, what did I hear? Those birds were talking! Their mouths were moving and I heard their voices. It was scary. I couldn't believe my ears. I was watching a moving picture of characters that were talking!

The audience sat still. They seemed as surprised as Bud and I were. Then a couple of folks clapped their hands. Some leaned toward the screen to hear better. Others chuckled in pleased amazement. I whispered to Bud, "These birds sound like those funny guys we heard talking on Helen's record."

He blinked, "Yes, I think they're the vaudeville stars, The Two Black Crows."

Some viewers were laughing at the jokes they told. It was truly hard to believe the actors in the film could be talking. Then, as I watched closely, something didn't sound right. Now and then the birds' mouths opened, but their voices were heard a little later! Then, in seconds, it was corrected and looked and sounded right. Then again, for just a second, I heard the voices but the mouths didn't open, and yet that too was corrected. After about five amazing minutes the screen suddenly went black. The picture was gone and there was silence. The lights came on. The people applauded and talked excitedly among themselves. Off to one side, I saw Chief lying happily beside Mr. Kellum, who was seated comfortably in a chair. When the clapping stopped, he stood up beside the screen and thanked the people for their approval of his picture. He apologized for the split seconds of time, when the sound went slightly

Big Bud Wilson and me

ahead or behind the picture. He said with a little more time and work he knew he and his men would overcome the problem and make his sound system operate perfectly.

When he asked his viewers if they wanted to hear the birds again, we heard a loud, excited, "Yes!" The lights went out and the talking picture was repeated. The two comedians told the same jokes and the folks watched and laughed in disbelief, shaking their heads in wonder. Even when the birds' mouths opened and the sound of their voices was heard late, it didn't seem to matter to the folks, or to me. We were marvelously entertained watching a talking picture!

When the second showing was over, the lights came on and Mr. Kellum talked again. The people listened carefully. He told them if anybody was interested in talking pictures they could buy shares in his company and help him perfect his sound system and make the first talking pictures for Hollywood. When he finished, everybody stood up, talking and shaking hands. When they started to leave, Bud and I ran to the corner and stood under the streetlight and watched the happy, chatting men and women get into their cars. One by one we heard their car doors slam before they drove away.

Dad and Mom were very surprised when I told them my unbelievable story about hearing a moving picture talk. The next day, I couldn't get to the shop quickly enough so I could tell Ernie about looking in the window. He was working alone at his bench on something he said was to improve their sound system. When I told him how Bud and I had seen and heard the two black birds, he put down his tools, looked at me, and started to laugh.

"What did you think of it?" he asked, when he stopped laughing.

Everything I told him seemed to please him. "Now you know the secret Mr. Kellum didn't want anyone to know. We are going to make talking pictures. Mr. Kellum is selling shares in his company to get money to perfect our sound system."

He talked about the split seconds in the system when the mouths were moving and there was no sound. "We are trying to get the phonograph disk to turn at the exact same speed as the film projector, so the sound and the picture will be together at the same exact split second. Twice Ernie used a word like "sink-row-nize." He said, "That's our big problem. We've got to make the sound work with the picture."

During the next couple of weeks, movie fans kept coming to hear the black birds talk on the silver screen. I watched at the window nearly every night. Then one afternoon came a big disappointment! A six-foot wooden fence, with a locked gate, was built around the

entire property. The next day I watched a sign painter paint "Kellum Talking Picture Company" in big orange, white and black letters along the fifty-foot fence. I knew I'd seen and heard the talking black birds for the last time. For me the sign declared another historical first for little Edendale as the place where Hollywood's first talking picture was both screened and heard.

Sadly, a couple of months later, all was strangely quiet at Kellum's. The gate was locked, the birds were gone and the folks in the big cars came no more. What had happened? I never saw Chief or Mr. Kellum again.

Months later, one Saturday evening as I was standing in the drugstore, I heard something which made me feel really bad. Mr. Kellum was in trouble, maybe in jail! He had taken money from folks for shares in his talking picture business, but he had failed to

This 1928 phonograph record sound machine, like Kellum's 1920 machine, could not be made to successfully synchronize with moving pictures

perfect the sound system as he had promised. What had happened to the money? In court he was found guilty on some charge and sent to prison.

Mom's friend, Katie, laughed when she said she had heard it was because he had bamboozled too many people out of a lot of money when he got them in his little, brick theater showing them moving pictures of two black birds that were supposed to talk in a tree! Dad remarked, "Mr. Kellum isn't the first man to be sent to prison because he couldn't perfect his good idea."

Years later, in 1927, I thought of Chief, Mr. Kellum and Ernie when I saw Al Jolson in *The Jazz Singer*, Hollywood's first talking picture made by Warner Brothers Studio. They called their sound system, "Vitaphone." The Jolson film was a good picture and a good story. But the sound was not "sink-row-nized" too well. The picture had been made using the same kind of "out-of-sink" sound system Mr. Kellum and Ernie couldn't perfect five years earlier.

After making two or three pictures with that system, Warner's found it was impossible to consistently "sync" the phonograph disk sound with the speed of the moving picture camera and gave up. However, Warner's "talkies" gave Americans a taste of the talking picture and Uncle Sam's movie fans wanted more. So Hollywood's camera and sound technicians got together and experimented with putting a soundtrack on the edge of the film. They learned the film had to run through the camera at a faster speed to make the best soundtrack. So, all the longstanding "flicker" silent cameras that had photographed pictures at a speed of 16 picture frames per second were rebuilt or replaced by cameras to photograph at a speed of 24 frames per second. It became the standard, all-time S.O.F. (Sound on Film) camera speed for making talking pictures. By 1930, all Hollywood "Talkies" were made using the S.O.F. sound system. Fox Studio's newsreel, "Movietone News," was the first to show S.O.F. pictures on America's movie screens.

THE CORNER, BOB AND ME

1921

I met my pal, Bob Moore, when we were nine years old. It was a Sunday morning, about 7:00 A.M., before the stores were open. Bob, with his mother, dad, and two brothers, Ben and Bill, were returning from the Edendale Catholic Church service. They lived in an apartment over Proctor's Drug Store on "the corner" of Glendale Boulevard and Berkeley Avenue, where Alvarado intersects, a block south of Sennett's Keystone Studio.

Mr. Moore, a butcher from Boston, had just opened his meat market and grocery store next to Tony's shoe repair shop. I had seen Mr. and Mrs. Moore in their store before, but not Bob. He entered Logan Street School, while I went to Clifford Street School.

I often ran prescriptions for Mr. Proctor, the druggist, when somebody was sick and needed medicine quickly. I later did the same for the Tarlow brothers when they bought the store.

On a particularly memorable Sunday morning, the bundle of the druggist's 20 Sunday newspapers had been delivered and thrown over the locked gate next to Moore's store into the alleyway. The bundle's tie cord had caught on a picket and broken and the papers were scattered all over the alley. I had observed the scene with an interested eye.

When the Moores first saw me, I had climbed over the gate and was putting a couple of papers together for — just maybe — a possible sale. When Mr. Moore questioned me about my interest in the druggist's papers, I quickly dropped them. I wanted the Moores to know I was trying to do a favor for Mr. Proctor. The looks on

Bob Moore when we met in 1921

My brothers built a club house on the lot next door but a week later it burned down

their faces were doubtful. As I climbed back over the gate they were saying what a good boy I was to be so interested in the newspapers. From the day we met, Bob and I began a close, lifelong, wonderful friendship.

The corner of Glendale Boulevard and Berkeley Avenue — our neighborhood's business center — became my second home. Bob and I helped in his dad's market. Sometimes we delivered grocery orders. But most of the time, we just ate his dad's cookies and bananas and played around

Catalina Island — 1935. Bob, me and four newspaper friends on vacation from the Post Record.

Will Rogers — drawn by Bob Moore

on the corner on our bikes or skates, played touch football and talked with passersby. At Christmas time we made tree stands and sold his dad's Christmas trees. We got to keep the profit, which wasn't much, but it drew trade to the store.

On Saturday mornings, I could hear Bob in his apartment above the store, practicing his violin while I earned a few dimes sweeping the wide corner sidewalk that fronted the four stores. On Saturday nights, starting at 6:00 P.M., I sold Sunday's *Times* and *Examiner* newspapers (called "Bulldogs") for 10 cents. I hustled on the corner and sold about 150 papers until 10 o'clock when the route manager came around to pick up the money. I received three cents for each paper sold. That's how I made the money to buy my big $4.50 International Junior Postage Stamp Album.

Bob and I grew up together on that corner. We built a big tree house in a Pepper tree on Mack Sennett's lot. When we were about 12 years old, Bob set up a drawing desk for his artwork. Bob took cartoon lessons and passed them along to me. He became a great artist and worked at the *Post Record* as an artist when I was there as a photographer. He became the Head Artist at the *Daily News* in 1936.

When we were about 15 years old we first dated girls together. The four of us attended movies and dances and always had a good time. Bob and I enjoyed harmonizing together and often sang to our dates.

During World War II we joined the U.S. Coast Guard and served aboard a patrol vessel off the California coast. We even stood up for each other at our weddings.

In 1950, while fighting a case of pneumonia, he coughed violently and died of a heart attack at age 33.

Bob Moore was the closest friend I ever had.

1943 — World War II — Coast Guard. Me with Little Jimmy and Bob with his daughter, Wendy.

HUCK FINN GOES TO THE LIBRARY

1922

In the early 1920s, the city of Los Angeles advertised the grand Saturday opening of its new, big public library. The public school system passed out fliers to the schools inviting children to attend. We were encouraged to wear a costume to look like our favorite book chum. I'd worked in several pictures as a ragamuffin, street kid wearing my own ragged clothes. What could be easier? I decided to go to the big affair as Huckleberry Finn, one of Mark Twain's happy characters.

Saturday morning promised to be a nice warm day. I quickly finished my morning chores and had my lunch. I got into my tattered shirt and pants, the latter held up by a rope over my shoulder. I bade my mom and dad goodbye. On the Edendale streetcar headed for downtown, I met David and Robert, a couple of schoolmates. They were wearing their school clothes — no costumes for them.

We arrived with hundreds of kids from all over the Los Angeles area. What a sight! There was Cinderella, Jack the Giant Killer, Little Toby Tyler the circus kid, Little Red Riding Hood, Daniel Boone and many I didn't recognize, because I hadn't read a lot of books. A lady librarian took a group of us for a walk through the new building and we saw walls of books everywhere. Upstairs and downstairs we went. Even in the cold basement we heard about writers and the stories they wrote. I didn't know there were so many books. It was interesting. I didn't mind that the kids laughed at my bare feet and my ragged outfit. The lady told them they should all read *The Adventures of Tom Sawyer and Huckleberry Finn*. We finished the tour near the exit door. As we left, a librarian reminded us to read if we wanted to be successful and have a happy life.

Outside, the sun was still shining and the cement sidewalk was warm to my feet. We three headed down the street to where we'd catch the little trolley car to take us home. Walking and talking, we agreed the librarians were right — we should read more.

As I neared the stop, a long black limousine pulled up near me and stopped. The chauffeur leaned over toward us, pointed his finger at me and motioned me to come to the car.

David and Robert whispered, "What does he want?" And, "Don't go, Coy!"

I walked over to see what he wanted. As I stepped beside the limo I could see there was somebody in the back seat. The chauffeur put down the window. As quick as a flash a little, old lady, wearing a big, blue hat, stuck her head out. Wide-eyed she looked at me through the bottoms of her glasses. Her wrinkled face was sad and she startled me with a loud, squeaky voice saying, "Hello, little boy."

Surprised, I nodded, smiled and gave her a cheery, "Hello, Ma'am."

Her face lit up with a big smile. She tipped her head to one side, leaned closer and asked, "Are you hungry?" A funny question, I thought.

"No, Ma'am," I replied, politely. She looked at me thoughtfully.

"Do you have a home?" she asked, raising her eyebrows.

I almost laughed, but I knew she wasn't kidding.

"Yes, Ma'am, I do." I felt maybe I should leave. She took a good, long look at me, down and up, ragged clothes and all. Then with the sad look again she asked, "Do you have a mama?"

That was about enough. "Yes, I have a mama and I have a dad, too!"

She slowly shook her head from side to side, then suddenly she pushed her arm out toward me. Here's something for you." Her shaky old hand was holding a crinkled up bill.

Oh, oh, what's this? I stared at her offer and then up at her smiling face. We were looking into each other's eyes. With one eye she winked at me.

"Come on, take it. I want you to have it," she said.

I knew she meant it. I took the bill. We smiled at each other. She gently patted my head and whispered, "God bless you boy!"

I managed a "Thank you, Ma'am" and watched her settle back into the seat. I leaned forward for a last look at her. She nodded to her driver, waved her little fingers to me and said, "Bye-bye." I waved back and watched the chauffeur drive her away. I didn't know what to think. Who was she? I looked down at the wrinkled paper money.

To my surprise it was a five dollar bill! My pals with their eyes popping out couldn't believe it even after they felt it.

"What did she want? What did she say?" they asked.

At home, my story and the five dollar bill put excitement in the air. With a doubting half-smile on their faces, Mom and Dad stood looking at my prize like a couple of flatfoot detectives with a clue in a movie mystery. I told them the whole story just like it happened.

Dad asked, "Are you sure you didn't make some kind of motion or do something that would have made the limo stop?"

Holding back a smile, Mom asked, "You were polite and honest with the lady weren't you? You didn't tell her one of your little jokes, did you?"

"No, Mom, I was really kind of scared all the time."

After I'd answered all their questions and finally convinced them this wasn't another of my practical jokes, we all laughed, yet still wondered.

Then Dad seriously asked, "Why do you think the lady gave you the bill?"

"Dad, I've thought about that. I think she must have thought I was a really poor, street urchin, like the one I played in the Vitagraph Studio picture, *You Never Know*, where Earle Williams picked me up off the street and took me to his home after Gertrude Astor hit me with her car."

Dad and Mom agreed with me. We discussed my story and truly came to appreciate the sincere, loving feelings of kindness felt and shown by the nice, old lady in her big limousine. She would never know how kindly we thought her to be.

That night, in our dimly lighted room, I lay in bed with little brother, Harry, asleep at my side. My eyes were looking at the long stripe of light on the ceiling that came from the lamp on the dining room table. I was thinking about the day.

Dad bent over me with his usual good-night thoughts, "I know you'll sleep well tonight, because honest boys always sleep well. Don't they?" A kiss, and then he was gone.

I was glad when Mom came and sat by me on the bed. "How did you like the new library?" she asked softly and pulled the covers up under my chin.

I told her about everything that had happened at the library. She listened and was glad I'd decided to read more because she knew it was hard for me. Her hands brushed my hair back as she said, "I want to ask you, after you took the money from the lady, if it had suddenly dawned on you and you realized why she had given you the money, what would you have done?"

I thought a while. "I guess I would have told her why I was dressed in my old ragged clothing and that I wasn't as poor as I looked, that I didn't need her money. I would have given the five dollar bill back to her."

Mom asked, "What do you think the lady would have done then?"

I tried to imagine. "I don't know. What do you think would have happened?"

"I think the lady would have had a big laugh at herself, and at her chauffeur. The joke was on her, wasn't it?" I think she would have said, "You are an honest boy for telling me why you're in these clothes. I want you to keep that five dollar bill because I gave it to you."

I was glad Mom told me what she thought. She pinched my cheek, kissed me and said, "God bless you. Goodnight."

My old clothes caused an interesting day

It had been a busy day. I was tired and sleepy, but wondered how many great and small stories there were about people, things and places that would never be written into books.

INTERVIEWS FOR KID ACTORS

1922

Going to interviews for work was the part of the business I liked least. Many times I came home from school and Mom said, "You've got an interview at Fox's right away."

I had to get all spruced up, take an extra bath and even had to wear a suit and sometimes a tie. That day my after-school fun was gone.

I usually arrived at the studio with Dad or Mom. Sometimes there would be dozens of kids, all ages and sizes, with their moms. I think it was thought that half the parents within 50 miles of Hollywood wanted their kids to get into pictures.

I met a lot of good guys and girls and learned some didn't want to work in pictures at all. Some hated it. I never could understand why parents pushed their kids into pictures when the boy or girl didn't like acting. I guess they did it because the pay was good when they worked. Some parents were just sure their kid would become a big "star" if given the chance.

We all sat around in the waiting room of the studio casting office, just waiting.

Harry and Bill off for an interview at RKO with Dad in the old Willys Knight

We played games while the parents asked each other questions.

"What's the picture being cast?"

"Who is the director?"

"How many kids are needed?"

"What's the part?"

"Will it be done on location?"

"How long will it run?"

"What about wardrobe?"

The casting director would finally appear and all the "guess buzzing" stopped and it would become as quiet as a courtroom. He would look around the room and say, "We'll only need three girls and five boys."

There would be groans and grumbles as the parents pulled their kids to their feet. They would start combing their hair, pulling at dresses, straightening ties and tucking shirts into pants. Each one would keep an eye on the director and be ready to push their kid out to the front.

"The picture's director will be here in a few minutes, so relax. He knows what he wants," the casting director would say.

Now it would really get quiet. You could have heard a comb drop, and often did!

The picture director would enter the room. He might say, "Hello, folks." If so, he received a big "Hello" in return. He was already looking around the room at each youngster. Then, as he would move about he'd say things like, "This is a New York street sequence. We need some kids to play on the sidewalk and in the street. You'll do, honey," pointing to a freckle-faced girl. "And you, too, are you her brother?"

"No," answers a boy wearing a cowboy hat.

"And you, and you. How old are you?"

"I'm seven," the boy says, looking at his mother who is shaking like a leaf.

"Have you ever worked in pictures before?"

The kid looks at his mom again.

"I see you haven't. You're okay . . . And you, and you."

He's passing one here and there. If he knew a child from a past picture he'd say, "Hello." He might ask a question referring to something he remembered. When he saw me he said, "Hello, Coy, how's your dad? Do you want to work with me again?"

WANT IT DONE?
"KWICK AND KLEAN"

Coy Watson, Jr.
The Dunce in "Quality Street" M.G.M
TELEPHONE: DRexel 3616
13 Years in Pictures
AGE 14   HEIGHT 5 FEET 1 INCH
WEIGHT 110 LBS
Irish kid in "The Shamrock and The Rose."
See me in

COY as "JIMMIE THE OFFICE BOY
in "RICH BUT HONEST"
FOX PRODUCTION

I was pleased that he'd ask and answered quickly, "Sure, I like doing New York stuff. Dad's fine. He's still working at Universal. My mom's with me today. There she is."

"Okay, I've a bit for you to do."

The room is deep in silence. All eyes are on the "Judge" and hearts beat faster. Around the room he goes, choosing the kids that look the part. Then he moves to the doorway and says, "Those of you I've selected, give the casting director your names and he'll

Dad sent Blotter-Calendars to all the studio casting directors

call you. We'll do the shooting here at the studio on our New York Street. I want you all in shabby clothes like poor New York kids. We may need you for three days. Thank you for coming."

As he turns to leave, he says, "Sorry we can't use you all. Maybe next time. Goodbye."

He's gone, and so is the tension. No more pushing! The selected ones gather around, giving their names. The others, with long faces, move toward the exit saying, "goodbyes."

Some parents shout to the casting director, "Thanks for calling us." Others wave with a "Keep us in mind."

Those picked are told when we will work. Extras' pay will be $5.00 or $7.50 per day. If we do a special piece of business, we can get $10.00 or $12.50. Very often I'd be given a bit to do. By this time the directors knew I didn't work for extras' pay. Dad required $12.50 per day for me. By the week, which could go for seven days, I'd get $50.00 to $75.00. I seldom knew what my pay was.

"Don't discuss your pay with anyone," Dad said. "Your experience and ability is what they pay for, so do a good job and the director will want you again."

As we grew older, some of us teenagers appeared for interviews without parents. Of course, the more we worked in pictures together, the better we came to know each other. Families got together for picnics and overnight visits. The older we became, the more kids quit the business, but friendships had formed between some of us that lasted for years. I met fellows during World War II and afterward that I had worked with during the twenties.

I worked until about 1930 as a teenager. When sound came in, I worked less and became more interested in news photography.

SCHOOL ON THE SET

1922

In 1920, a very early series of kid pictures, "Sunshine Comedies," were made in Hollywood by William Fox Studios. His studio, located south of Sunset Boulevard and on both sides of Western Avenue, was actually two big studios that covered two full city blocks. The dramatic and Western pictures were made on the west side of Western Avenue, while the comedies were filmed on the east side. The studios were completely divided. For four years Dad was casting director for the comedy side. I worked in pictures on both sides of the street.

Standing at the door of Fox Studio's school room on the lot

The gang—all at one time—off to the Board of Education for child's acting permits and quarterly physical check ups. I took the picture and then went along.

By that time, more of the studios were making pictures that used kids.

Some of the studios built school houses on the lots. That made it easier for the teacher and better for us to learn during our three hours of schooling per day as required by the Los Angeles Board of Education. The Board issued permits for kids to work in pictures.

All youngsters hoping or expecting to work in pictures had to apply. Before being issued a permit to work they had to pass a complete physical exam. The studios were required to pay a teacher to teach us our regular schoolwork during school days and to act as a welfare worker on weekends or during school vacations.

It wasn't easy for me to keep up with my regular school studies when I'd miss a day or two now, or a week then, or a month or two when playing a good part in a picture. I never caught up. From my first days in school, I was always behind in my studies. I graduated from high school a year behind the class with which I'd started grammar school.

Brother Delmar and Shirley Temple with their teacher on the set of To the Last Man,*" an early movie for Shirley*

OUR FAMILY SPREAD CHRISTMAS CHEER

1922

We kids started entertaining away from home when there were only eight of us. On several Christmas Eves, after many days of rehearsing, we dressed in our sailor suits.

Dad loaded all of us, with our costumes and props, into the old 1922 Willys Knight modified touring car.

Off we went, singing all the way, to the French Hospital, near old Olvera Street in downtown Los Angeles. For over an hour we entertained, offering our variety show, hoping to bring some Christmas cheer to the poor, bed-ridden patients. There was no radio or TV in those days and entertainment was scarce.

We recited poems, sang songs and acted skits that Mom and Dad had taught us, from the day we were old enough to clap our hands and laugh.

Our very appreciative audience, some sitting in wheelchairs, others lying in beds, nurses standing, responded to our acts with soft smiles, laughs and applause. We and they enjoyed the show. Excitement filled the hall when we finally started to shuffle off for our closing number, waving goodbye and singing words Dad had written to the music of "Smiles." All together we sang it and meant it:

Ready to entertain shut-ins

We did enjoy singing and acting together (Delmar took this photo)

We entertained our newspaper co-workers at the Los Angeles Press Club. We did skits, sang, threw pies and this cake at our laughing news friends. They did continue to ask us back and we never received a cleaning bill for "frosted" suits!

"We are here because we're thankful.
We are here because we're glad.
We are here to spread a little sunshine
To those who are feeling kinda sad.
We sing because we have a tender feeling
And we've tried to bring a little cheer.
So we wish you all a Merry Christmas
And a Happy, bright New Year!"

During one memorable exit, I noticed a very old lady in a wheelchair, with a big smile on her face. She was clapping her bony hands together as tears ran down her cheeks. She did look happy! She liked our show. We had entertained and made a few people feel joyful and that was our family's hope.

Years later, we all continued to drive our cars to carol our friends and shut-ins in our district. Girlfriends and boyfriends came too. The gang always enjoyed entertaining people. In fact, even after Bobs, our youngest, became a minister, the gang got together to rehearse and work up programs to entertain at the Los Angeles Press Club and for many other special occasions.

SHOOTING *THE HUNCHBACK* OF *NOTRE DAME*

1923

I knew I had to go to the studios to interview if I expected any work in pictures. I liked it better when the studio casting director's office called and asked if I was working. If I wasn't, I'd take the job. If a call came about a good part in a big picture, Dad and I would go to the studio and talk salary.

One afternoon when I got home from school, Mom had a big smile on her face and was glad to tell me the casting director at Universal Studio had called.

"They want you to do a bit in Lon Chaney's picture, *The Hunchback of Notre Dame.*" You are to report to the studio wardrobe department tomorrow morning at 8 o'clock. Director Worsley wants you fitted as a French peasant."

"That's good, Mom. Maybe I'll get to work with Lon Chaney. He's one of my favorite stars. Also, I'll get out of school."

"No you won't. There'll be a teacher on the set," assured Mom.

She asked me to sit down and with a grin still on her face she thoughtfully said, "You don't remember, but you worked in the first picture Lon Chaney made in California; here in Edendale at Selig's Studio. It was *The Price of Silence* in 1913."

Lon Chaney as The Hunchback

She told me the story of my first part in pictures when I was nine months old, and of the small part she played in it, also.

The next morning, I don't remember how I got to the studio, but I checked in and was sent to Wardrobe. All studio wardrobes smelled of mothballs and this one especially stunk. The little, stout wardrobe-lady, wearing a black apron asked, "Are you Coy Watson, Jr.?"

"Yes."

She smiled and handed me a coat hanger of clothes. "Here you are," and pointing to a dressing room at one side of the building, "get into these."

I had to laugh at myself as I pulled on an old but clean pair of baggy cotton tights; a shirt with long sleeves and a longer tail that didn't fit any better, a pair of soft leather shoes, and a tam. My costume was complete. When I came out of the dressing room, the lady took a good look at me.

"You look okay," she said. "How do you feel?"

"Loose," I answered.

"Better loose than tight, right?" she said.

I had to agree.

"The assistant director wants you to wait here. He'll send somebody to take you to the set where you'll work."

She seemed a happy woman, humming as she folded and stacked clothes. As we talked and got better acquainted, she told me there had been thousands of extras; men, women and kids working on the picture. Six additional wardrobe people had been on hand to outfit each actor. She was glad the worst was over. All the big, night-scenes had been shot. Proudly she said, *The Hunchback* is expected to be one of Universal's biggest pictures."

Lon Chaney, the "Man of a Thousand Faces," on the wheel of oak with Patsy Ruth Miller

I walked around the huge room between the rows and rows of racks, which held thousands of smelly costumes, hung on hangers. A telephone rang in a corner of the big room and in a few seconds a man's voice yelled, "Sarah! A guy is coming at noon to get into a leather executioner's outfit."

"Okay, it's ready," she screamed back at him.

"Do the actors like wearing these smelly outfits?" I asked.

"No, they don't. The leading actors, once they are assigned their costumes, hang them outside to air."

Just then a young guy, with a big voice and a smile to match, popped in. "Are you Coy, the kid?" As if I didn't look the part!

I answered, "Yes."

"My name's Joe, one of the second assistants," he said, as he looked to the woman behind the counter. "Is he all set, Sarah?"

"Yep," she cracked back at him, as she threw another pair of tights on the pile. "He can leave his clothes here."

"Okay, Coy, come with me," Joe said. As we went out the door Sarah yelled something about tights and laughed. Joe chuckled.

"She's a great old gal!"

I trotted beside him. We got in a Dodge touring car with the engine running and a driver at the wheel.

"To the back ranch, Pete," said Joe as he patted him on the shoulder.

We were off to a part of the studio lot I knew well. Just a couple of months earlier, I'd spent over a month playing Tony, a feature part in a seven-reeler called *The Right of the Strongest*.

It was a mountain story and the U's back ranch, with its open, wild country, was all the location needed. The old log cabin was a real building and the country school house was complete with desks, blackboards and a school bell. We drove past the studio's own western ranch with real corrals and the zoo with cages. In good style, different kinds of animals—from chickens and cats to horses and elephants—were kept ready when needed. We stopped as far back on the ranch as we could go. I got out and was surprised to see a big set over four stories tall. It looked just like pictures of the Notre Dame cathedral.

Joe tapped me on the shoulder, "Come on."

We walked onto a huge, paved courtyard that ran from the front of the church out to an area at least the size of three city blocks. In the center of the vast space was a strange-looking structure about fifteen feet square and ten feet high, made of some fake Hollywood Plaster of Paris rocks. Four rock columns held up a wooden platform, there were rock steps at one side and it was all open underneath. I could see that a heavy, wooden post, about six inches in diameter, ran from the ground up and through a hole in the center of the platform. Attached to the end of the post, just above the platform, was a heavy, thick, wooden wheel about five feet in diameter.

"What's that thing?" I asked Joe.

We stopped and he looked at me. "It's a pillory. In 1831 Victor Hugo wrote a story about a hunchback who lived in the Notre Dame Cathedral. The picture we are shooting is that story. It all took place in Paris, France, in 1480. The law at that time saw to it that people were punished publicly on this kind of pillory for their crimes. Huge mobs standing around this awful thing enjoyed watching the executioner flog offenders. Sometimes ears and hands were cut off, to the joy of the hooting crowd. Such scenes must have been horrible."

He stopped and pointed to the director, sitting in his chair beside the pillory, looking at a script. Next to him was a camera on a tripod in the shade of a big umbrella. Two men were working with the camera.

Three or four people stood nearby chatting. A couple of five-foot square reflectors stood propped up at angles to reflect sunlight into the shaded area under the pillory.

Joe took my arm and led me before the director, who looked up at me with a frown on his face. He quickly eyed my costume. "This is Coy Watson, Jr., Mr. Worsley."

The director stood up slowly with a smile and held out his hand. "Hello, Coy."

We shook hands and he carefully laid the script on his chair. He pointed to a kid standing nearby, about my size, dressed like me.

"Jack, this is Coy. You're going to be working with him."

I said, "Hello, Jack."

Mr. Worsley said, "There's a little piece of business I want you boys and this man to do for me."

He introduced us to Mack, a big guy who looked tough. He was dressed as shabbily as we boys were. We all shook hands as the director called to the prop man, who quickly handed him a big, red apple.

"Now here's the action for this scene."

He was very serious and we listened closely. "You boys are having fun just playing around under this pillory. You're dodging around this pole in the center. Here, Coy." He handed me the apple.

To Jack, he said, "You're trying to get the apple away from Coy. You both keep moving, dodging back and forth. When Coy goes that way, you come around this way. When he goes back that way, you go this way. You really want that apple! You try to grab it! You both keep moving, keep up the action, around and around, around and around. You're playing, laughing, having fun. You won't let him have the apple."

"Now Mack, you're watching this action and your eye is on the apple too. When I cue you, grab Coy by the arm and hold him. Pull him to you and reach for the apple. Coy, look surprised and scared, but don't let him have it. Struggle to get away from him. Mack, you look mean all the time, squeeze and twist his arm, not too hard, of course."

"Coy, I want you to look like he is really hurting you. I want

Putting on make-up was one of my hobbies. Here I am as Peter the Hermit in a high school play, The Seven Keys to Baldpate

you to show pain on your face, but struggle to get free until I cue Mack to reach for and take the apple. Then you let him take it. And he lets you go. Now you're almost crying. You rub your arm. "

"Jack, you're looking scared all this time and don't look at me. When Mack takes the apple, you run out of sight. Now Mack, you look mean at Coy, wave your arms at him, and tell him to go! Look at the apple, then put it in your pocket. Coy, you're still rubbing your arm, looking mean and hurt at Mack as you walk out."

We rehearsed the scene a couple of times. I was impressed with the director's description of how he wanted us to work the scene and the time he took to explain it. He asked us to make it look real. "The timing has to be just right," he said. "Keep it moving."

We shot the scene three times. Each time it moved a little faster, which pleased Mr. Worsley. After the third time, I heard him say, "Cut! O.K." When Jack and I came back under the pillory, he told us, "That was a good scene."

"Thank you."

Jack went back to school across the courtyard behind one of the sets. I stayed and stood to one side watching the cameraman move the camera. They set up for a medium shot on Mack.

In his scene, he stood casually eating my apple as he slowly turned the crank that made the post and then the great wheel of oak turn. After a couple of takes, they got the shot the director wanted.

The director saw I had stayed to watch the action. He walked over to me and pleasantly spoke, "This scene, Coy, will be edited into the picture when hundreds of people will be crowded around this pillory watching the Hunchback as he is flogged with a cat-o'-nine-tails. Your scene, here with Mack, will appear in the picture before the crowd gathers. It's to show what a mean, heartless man he is. First, not caring about you, and later without sympathy for the suffering hunchback above him. Do you get the idea of the scene?" he asked me.

"Yes" I said, and thanked him for explaining the story to me. He thanked me again for a good job of acting.

Then Joe showed me to an area behind one of the big sets where school was in session with eight boys and girls about my age. They were all in costumes like mine. I'd never seen any of them before. They were working as extras and this was their first picture. They all lived in the valley around Universal Studio.

I recognized the teacher, a woman from the Los Angeles Board of Education. After greetings, we recalled the last picture we had worked on together. She asked me what subject I wanted to work on. I quickly told her art, wood shop, baseball or basketball.

I got a laugh from her and the kids and received 10 math problems to work on instead.

Later that afternoon, I heard one of the assistant directors and a prop man talking about the big night scenes that had been shot earlier. Two thousand extras were on the set: women, kids and men, some carrying burning torches. The mob swarmed out from behind the buildings that surrounded the courtyard and ran madly to the steps in front of the cathedral. The two men were discussing how the shooting of such a scene took a lot of

A man of at least seven faces

planning and organizing. It was to be one of the biggest and most exciting scenes in the picture. Five special assistant directors, dressed in costumes to look like the extras, worked and directed—unrecognized to the moviegoer—among the various sections of the crowd.

For the long, wide shot, Director Worsley was seated beside the cameras high on a place at the front of the cathedral. Through his big megaphone, he spoke his directions for the upcoming scenes down to the special directors. They, in turn, relayed his words to the extras waiting out of sight behind the sets. When everyone knew what to do, the director called, "Ready? Cameras! Action!"

Each assistant rushed his section out onto the courtyard. Additional cameras had been set up on the courtyard behind the pillory and in various other locations to get different angles and medium shots of the charging mob. Photographing a vast scene like this was not easy in daylight, and to create such action for a scene at night was a tough undertaking for any director and crew.

The shooting had begun after sundown. There were some waiting periods between scenes. By nine o'clock, and after a couple of takes, some of the extras were tired. The assistants' jobs were to keep the paid actors awake, alert, and on their toes, ready to appear in the next big scene. However, there were some men and women who were really uninterested. They knew their role in the picture would never make them a movie star. As the night became late, they slipped away from this group, found a nice quiet spot in the dark behind a nearby set, laid down on a handy blanket brought for such an occasion and went to sleep, or rested.

Unable to keep a constant count on so many noses, the assistant directors, the keepers of the flocks, with lanterns or flashlights in hand, braved the darkness behind the sets, making routine searches for the missing. They found them, too, looking sheepish in their old, French costumes.

Some searchers surprised wide-eyed couples in the dark and laughingly promised the embarrassed actors leading roles in the studio's next big picture if they would come and finish this night's work.

Most of the cast was excited when the word was passed that the director and the cameramen were ready to shoot the scene again. A loud, "Standby!" was shouted into the quiet night. A hushed undertone of voices filled the air as the mass of bodies moved into place behind the scenes. The five assistants called out their reminder, "Ready?" And then, "Light your torches!"

Two hundred, three-foot, hand-held wooden poles with strips of cloth wrapped around one end, soaked in kerosene, were lit. On the cue from above, the two thousand extras ran into sight and headed for the front of the church.

During the shooting of the first take, a couple of people were burned by torches. Another mishap occurred when the drawstring in the pants of a charging torchbearer broke, allowing his baggy French tights to drop to his knees. The poor dramatic actor tripped and took an instant, unexpected, sliding nosedive to the hard surface of the yard. From close behind, four dashing French peasants hit him and tumbled into a pile. After the shooting of the scene, the pile of actors was untangled.

The stunt got a big, well-enjoyed laugh from fellow actors. A handy nurse standing by with a first-aid kit applied iodine to bruised elbows and skinned knees through holes in torn tights.

The thousands were directed to return to their starting places and stand by, ready for another take. After that humorous, but dangerous piece of business, when the second assistants called the ranks to readiness, they warned, "Light your torches" and laughingly added, "And pull up your tights!" The call got a big laugh from the mob.

Two thousand voices took up the line in a joyful singsong chant, "Light your torches and pull up your tights! Light your torches and pull up your tights!" Some danced and kicked to the rhythm. Even the director and his crew, high on their perch, had to laugh and join in. The night air echoed the silly phrase, which soon became the frequent retort of all who worked on the picture—practically everybody at the studio.

For a long time thereafter, sometimes for no particular reason, perhaps to cover some frustration or just because somebody was happy, you could hear a voice sing out, "Light your torches and pull up your tights!" It was then that I remembered Sarah had joked about tights to Joe when we left the Wardrobe. Even folks that didn't know the story chuckled and laughed when they heard the silly remark. "What's that about?" they would ask.

Months later, having with pride told my family and playmates about my part in Lon Chaney's new picture, I was excited when we all went to see it. However, I was very disappointed when my scene did not appear on the screen. The scene under the pillory I'd played with Jack had been cut out, but the part with mean Mack the apple grabber, was in there.

He was turning the crank and at the same time eating my apple, while Quasimodo, the hunchback, played by Lon Chaney, was publicly disgraced and beaten as Mack turned the wheel of oak.

I never ever again told anybody I could be seen in a picture until I first saw the picture myself. Better to be just another face on the cutting room floor than have to take the jibes of friends. After that, when friends kidded me about my part in *The Hunchback of Notre Dame*, I just said "Ah, light your torches and pull up your tights!"

MY ORANGEADE WAGON

1924

One hot summer I turned my wooden express wagon into an orangeade stand on wheels. I built a counter over the wagon and covered the sides with a piece of canvas. A sunshade above the counter kept my customers cool as they drank my thirst-quenchers. The orangeade, with a big ten-cent piece of ice, was held in one of Dad's five-gallon crocks.

Before leaving home in the heat, I'd wet down the canvas to keep the under-counter area cold. I'd pull my wagon stand anywhere there was action or people. My big sign said, "Ice Cold Orangeade. Made in the shade. Stirred with an old, rusty spade."

The best spot for sales was across the boulevard from Mack Sennett's main studio gate. My friends and good customers were the stars, directors, carpenters and other workers. They crossed the street from one side of the studio to the other during the day. If a company was shooting scenes anywhere in the neighborhood, I was there with the cold drinks. There were no soft drink machines or commissary trucks in those days. I charged five cents or ten cents a glass. Everybody was happy! Sometimes I ran out of product. The customers seemed to be amused and peeked over the counter to watch me dip their drink from the crock into their glasses.

The kids got to drink my watered-down leftovers

Business went great for a couple of weeks. Then Mom, in her own sweet way, let me know she was tired of me squeezing the oranges in her kitchen every day. She didn't mind my using her ten-cents-a-pound sugar, as long as I replaced it. I tried to clean up before I left every morning, but I knew it was hard on her or she wouldn't have mentioned it.

That afternoon, I flagged down the driver of the truck loaded with bottled drinks for soda fountains and stores. I signed a paper and agreed to take at least three cases of pop a week to enjoy a retailer's discount. Now I was really in business!

Once a week, the "Los Angeles Bottling Company" truck stopped in front of our house as the neighborhood kids gathered to watch me receive three or four cases of bottled drinks. The assortment included Coca-Cola, Delaware Punch, Root Beer, and of course, Orange. I paid two-and-a-half cents per bottle and sold them for five or ten cents, depending on how far I pulled my wagon.

Thanks to Mom, business increased and I was out of her kitchen.

I changed my sign to read, "I Don't Know Where Mom is, but I've Got Pop on Ice." It worked and I got lots of laughs. Unlike the orangeade, the pop stayed fresh in the bottle. Previously, after slow days, with my homemade products, I lost profit when all the kids got a drink of my watered-down, leftover orangeade.

I came to feel quite independent. During my profitable trek around Edendale, when I got hungry at noontime, I stopped at a grocery store. A five-cent can of nice sardines and ten-cent box of fresh soda crackers, along with a cold bottle of Delaware Punch made a good lunch for this businessman!

My playmates never did understand how much fun I had making my own spending money.

My cold drink wagon made good money, but not while a newspaper photographer set up this posed picture with neighborhood kids!

THE CRAZIEST PICTURE
I EVER WORKED IN

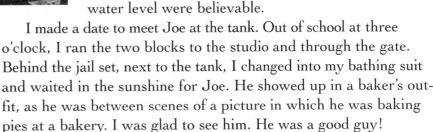

1924

Working in pictures was fun. Some were more laughs than others. In one picture at Sennett's I played a boy in a family that laughed at everything. Directed by Del Lord, the movie was called *Honeymoon Hardships*. Dad was assistant director on the picture. He learned a sequence in the picture called for the cast to ride a Model T Ford into a lake and sink out of sight. I couldn't swim, so he decided I should learn.

Joe Young, a young actor friend of Dad's and mine, was a good swimmer and he offered to teach me to swim at the studio. Joe was the brother of Robert Young, who became a star famous for dramatic roles in movies and later in television. He was Doctor Marcus Welby. He was also Jim Anderson in "Father Knows Best."

On the studio lot there was a concrete pool or tank, 20 feet by 40 feet and 10 feet deep. It was used to shoot scenes for a picture when a room in a house was to fill up with water, or as the interior

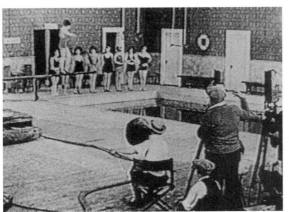

The Tank! Shooting a scene at Keystone's own swimming pool.

of a houseboat sinking at sea. A three-sided set of the room, without a roof, was built in the tank and completely furnished, even to the pictures on the walls. The camera was set up on the floor of the tank to shoot the story action as water from the corner fire hydrant filled the tank. On the screen, in an earlier scene, the audience would see water running from a faucet, water overflowing from a sink onto a kitchen floor, or maybe even a pesky chimpanzee boring a hole in the floor of the family houseboat, allowing the water to rush in. Scenes in the tank of the rising water level were believable.

I made a date to meet Joe at the tank. Out of school at three o'clock, I ran the two blocks to the studio and through the gate. Behind the jail set, next to the tank, I changed into my bathing suit and waited in the sunshine for Joe. He showed up in a baker's outfit, as he was between scenes of a picture in which he was baking pies at a bakery. I was glad to see him. He was a good guy!

"I see you made it," he said and grabbed me and messed up my hair. "It's easy to swim. You're not afraid of the water are you?"

"No, but my Mom is and that's the reason I'm nine years old and can't swim. She doesn't know about this."

Joe started his instructions. "Use your arms. Reach 'em way out on the water ahead and pull 'em back to your sides with your hands cupped. You gotta keep your feet kicking all the time."

After a few minutes we agreed that I had the idea. Then, to my surprise, he tied the end of a rope around my chest below my arms. The other end he tied to the end of a six-foot drapery rod from a window of a nearby set. He was prepared. I was ready.

We laughed as he lowered me, belly down, into the tank of six feet of not-too-clean water. He kept the rope taut as he walked along the side of the tank and pulled me through the water as I stroked and kicked with all my aquatic power.

"Keep your hands cupped," he called. "After each stroke, bring your arms out of the water just enough to clear the surface. You're doin' fine!"

Joe Young

I couldn't see him but I could tell he was laughing and having fun.

"Keep your feet kicking." I felt I was getting the hang of it. "Roll your face back with each right stroke and take a breath."

I almost laughed when I saw Charlie Murray smile down at me and heard him ask, "What are you fishing for, Joe?"

A couple of carpenters looked in and laughed, too. We kept going. After about 20 minutes, Joe asked if I was getting tired. I was.

"Okay, come on out."

He pulled me to the side, laid down the pole, took the rope in his hands and lifted me as I crawled up the side to finish my first lesson.

"At home you can lie with your stomach on a box or chair and practice your stoke and kick." I did!

During the following three lessons, Joe let me float a little more each time until I was able to float and swim on my own without the rope. The fourth time he told me I was swimming well.

"Go to the plunge over at Bimini Baths on Vermont Avenue where you can practice. You'll get better all the time, but remember water can be dangerous."

156-8

A quiet family evening. Left to Right: Billy Bevan as my dad; Raymond McKee, the groom; me and the White triplets; Alice Day, the bride; and Sunshine Hart as my mother. The laughs never stopped!

Three days later, we started shooting *Honeymoon Hardships* on a studio set. The story line was simple. It starred Alice Day and Raymond McKee, a newly married couple. They took the groom's three city nephews with them in their Model T Ford to spend their honeymoon on a farm with the bride's parents and younger brother. The picture showed one disastrous mishap after another.

The family just laughed and took each one in stride while the city folks thought them strange! Billy Bevan and Sunshine Hart played the farm folks and I was the younger brother. The White triplets, real brothers, were the "city kids."

We had as many laughs shooting the picture as it got on the screen. There was a long shot in the farmhouse diningroom of seven of us around the table waiting for dinner. Sunshine entered from the kitchen carrying a big tray with a huge, roast turkey and all the makings of a dinner: Potatoes, gravy, peas and cranberries.

We all cheered her! Oh, oh, she stumbled, fell to the floor, throwing the bird into the air. Her face dropped into the mashed potatoes. The city folks screamed. My movie father and I gave her a big laugh and another cheer. She came up laughing with her mouth full of potatoes and managed to roll over on her back. She rubbed the potatoes from her eyes just in time to catch the falling turkey in her arms amid cheers and laughter. Her husband and son stood up proudly and applauded her entertaining gymnastic stunt! Our guests stood and watched in horror. Without help, mother scrambled up with our turkey as her two rooters led a college "Rah, rah, rah, Mom!"

The director and everybody on the set howled with laughter, except the city folks, who didn't dare break a smile. Then Mom got the turkey on the tray and staggered to the table with the dinner. The father, like a sculptor working in clay, scraped the mashed potatoes from her face with a spoon and flipped them back into the

When the second floor water heater blew up, it got a big laugh

bowl. Still laughing and pleased with Mom's performance, he told us all to sit down and tried to reassure and calm our frightened guests. We settled down and the father looked up to give thanks for the meal. At that point, a close-up of the gauge on the second-floor water heater showed the temperature at two hundred degrees and rising toward "Danger!" The director had warned us that a lot of light rubbish would be dropped on us from above when the boiler exploded.

A subtitle appeared on the screen with father's remark, "We are grateful for all we receive."

The water heater exploded in a puff of smoke, shaking the house! The ceiling came down! Sawdust, talcum powder, wood shavings, plaster of Paris dust, strips of balsa wood, and pieces of cardboard released from a holding bin suspended over the set fell, covering all of us and the table!

Alice and Sunshine screamed! Dust filled the set. We could hardly see one another. The event called for hilarity and more laughs from the slaphappy farmers.

As the dust cleared, the frightened and disgusted honeymooners told us they wanted to return to the quiet life of the city. We talked them all into staying for more laughs.

We were brushing the stuff from our hair, when the director told us he was pleased with the way we had done the scene. We were still laughing. My dad and the prop man had rigged the prop lath and plaster ceiling to fall at the exact second on a cue from the director.

For the last two days of shooting on the picture, we went on location to the San Fernando Valley near Chalk Hill. It didn't always happen, but we were going to shoot the final scenes to be seen in the picture last. The scenes of a picture were seldom, if ever, shot in story continuity, from start to finish. Sometimes the last scenes were taken first.

The company had rented a farm-style house with a big, deep swimming pool surrounded by trees. Dad, George Spear and I arrived early. I watched the crew of workmen placing tree branches and bushes around the edges of the pool to make it look like a natural lake in the woods. Something happened that morning I'll never forget and Dad always laughs when he tells about it.

A studio rule was "Whenever actors were going to be working in water, play it safe." George Spear, a studio stock comedian and a good swimmer, was to be the lifeguard for the day. He had changed into his swimsuit and stood watching the cameramen and their assistants set up the cameras. We were all waiting for the rest of the company to show up. I had worn my bathing suit under my clothes and had taken off my pants and shirt, and stood beside the pool. I wanted to show Dad I could swim.

The director and cast arrived and were getting out of the cars when I got Dad's attention. I gave him a high sign to watch me. I dove in and went down, down, and down. I wasn't coming up. I realized then, I hadn't learned to dive! Stroking and kicking I tried to come up. What should I do? I ran out of air and couldn't breathe, taking on water. I was scared. Somehow I floated up and got my head above the water. I still couldn't get my breath. I was blubbering, gasping and pawing for air with both arms.

Some of Sennett's first bathing beauties (1912)

Lifeguard Spear had welcomed some of the new arrivals and stood with his back to the pool chatting with Jack, the carpenter. Dad said he watched me. He knew I wasn't swimming. When he thought I'd had enough, he called to George, "Get him!"

To everybody's surprise, the carpenter jumped into the pool fully clad in overalls, hat and shoes, and hammer, screwdriver, pliers and pockets full of nails, to save the sputtering, drowning boy actor.

"When he reached for you," Dad laughed and told me to my embarrassment, "You climbed up him like a monkey going up a tree and sat on his shoulders with a good hold onto his hat! Jack could barely stay afloat himself. Everybody stood watching, amused at the action. You were both fished out to a round of applause and laughs and stood dripping beside the pool. You looked like a drowned rat and poor Jack looked like the guy that tried to build a boat under water."

George got a laugh when he dried Jack's hammer with a big towel. Jack stood squeezing water out of his hat.

"You didn't have to jump in," Dad said. "I could have gone in for him."

Jack laughed as water ran from his pockets and he removed his shoes. I felt sorry for him when he let his overloaded overalls slide down his legs to the deck. "Coy, when you said, 'get him,' I thought you meant you couldn't swim." That got a laugh. I laughed along with everybody but I didn't think it was very funny. George told me he was sorry he didn't see me in trouble and took a ribbing the rest of the day. In fun, I suggested the carpenter get the lifeguard's pay for the day, and the carpenter agreed!

The next day's shooting started when my silly, laughing movie father talked the groom into teaching him to drive his nice, new Ford. After a couple of verbal instructions, my eager, slaphappy, over-confident father insisted he drive us out into the woods for a family picnic. Seated at the wheel, he made us all pile into the car. I sat between him and mother in the front with the lunch basket. The worried and frightened honeymooners and the triplets—against their better judgment—settled into the back seat. A big puff of smoke shot out the rear of the car as we rolled out of the scene.

A camera car drove beside us to photograph the laughing, happy faces in the front, and the fearful, frightened expressions in the back, as we wove our way down the road. We took a scary turn off the road into the woods doing some crazy maneuvers, bouncing and ducking through bushes and trees. Then for the big scene, we approached the lake set. The shiny Ford was replaced by one without an engine. Piano wires were tied to the front of it and run to a big Reo truck across the pool, behind the bushes. The director told us when we were in the water not to let any-thing loose float to the surface. Oh boy! Tension filled the Ford. It was to be a scary scene.

On "Camera, action," with a 50-foot running start, we were pulled, with arms waving, to a speed of 15 miles per hour into the water. Kerplunk! Down a wooden, underwater ramp installed by the studio carpenters! We sank quickly out of sight and rested on the bottom of the pool. Without moving, we hung onto the car to stay under for a few seconds. Only Sunshine's straw hat, fitted with a couple of pieces of cork in it, floated on the water. We did it! When we bobbed up, everybody was yelling and laughing.

"Okay, okay, great shot!" said the director.

We were glad to be helped out of the pool. The Ford was then pulled up and out of the pool on the ramp anchored to the bottom.

The next scene audiences saw on the screen was a pan shot across a big lake from left to right—as if following us as we drove along the bottom of the lake! The "Tin Lizzy" was then turned around. With the wire still attached to the front, it was backed down the ramp and into the pool. The cameras were moved and set up to shoot the next scene from the opposite direction, so the car would come out left to right, appearing to have crossed the lake. The scene that followed was the hardest for the unsinkable actors.

Keystone director Hampton Del Ruth poses for a publicity photo with Mr. Sennett's girlfriend, Mabel Normand, at "the tank"

It wasn't until after several attempts that we eight, water-soaked actors managed to duck ourselves underwater all at the same time and stay down in the car. We finally stayed under long enough for the truck, on "Camera. Action!" to pull us up the ramp and out. We didn't have to act to look half-drowned as we rolled up and out onto what was supposed to be the opposite bank of the lake!

Sunshine Hart, weighing 300 pounds, received a well-deserved cheer as she was helped out of our Model T submarine. She was brave, but the poor thing just couldn't make herself sink. Billy Bevan and I had to pull her down under into the seat. Then we got back into the operating Ford, which now carried two 10-gallon tanks of water at the rear doors. For the final scene of the picture, we drove away from the camera, down a road, weaving from side to side. Water ran from the doors of the car as it carried its load of happy and unhappy, accident-prone passengers to their next disaster. It was the craziest picture I ever worked in!

Director Lord told us he knew it would edit into a very funny, fast-moving picture. And it did. Alice Day and Ray McKee went on to star in features. Five years later, I worked with Alice in *The Smart Set*, when she starred with William Haines at M.G.M.

The things I learned early, doing fast-moving comedy at Sennett's, were good training for later when I did slower scenes in dramatic pictures. I heard many men in the business who knew what they were talking about say, "Any director can make a dramatic picture, but it takes a special director to make a good comedy."

By the end of the twenties, a large number of people, in all capacities, making feature pictures at the big studios, were ones who got their start making slapstick comedies at Mack Sennett's studio. Ray Enright, Lloyd Bacon, George Marshall and Frank Capra were some of the directors. Many actors and technical people got their start the same way.

DAD'S MAGIC WIRE WORK

1924

In 1924, Douglas Fairbanks, Sr., the biggest name in the business, hired Dad to produce many of the magic tricks for his mystical Arabian Nights picture, *The Thief of Bagdad*.

It became one of the biggest productions of its time and included many firsts for unbelievable sets and scenes. The entire picture was one bit of movie magic after another. With his years of experience and imagination, Dad and the cameramen created the unreal for the picture.

Dad rigged and directed the operation of the amazing magic rope, made of old witches' hair that uncoiled and rose to stand straight up in the air. For an underwater scene, he suspended a man on wires laced inside a huge spider outfit. Hanging from a carriage rolling on the track overhead, the man gave action to the spider's legs and head. It fought Doug to its death, while attempting to protect the ancient treasure chest at the bottom of the sea. A man with flapping wings was an ugly flying bat. It, too, was swung on wires. As it swooped down on the mysterious, haunted forest, it was also killed by "the Thief."

Another trick Dad performed during the making of *The Thief of Bagdad* was when a horse Doug was riding near the palace garden was frightened by a buzzing bee. The horse started bucking and threw the aspiring prince from the saddle into a significant rose tree. To get this scene, Doug wore one of Dad's wire belts under his costume. Two piano wires were attached, one on each side, and run through a specially designed pulley overhead. While the camera turned, Dad watched closely. When the horse bucked hard enough, he cued the three men holding the wires to pull on them. This lifted Doug off the horse about twelve feet into the air, swung him over and dropped him down into the center of the rose tree.

Douglas Fairbanks as "The Thief of Bagdad"

Dad rigging "the magic rope"

Dad always appreciated the confidence that Doug and he had for each other. A mishap during the taking of such a scene could have meant serious injuries to Doug, a man Dad had come to know and regard as a dear friend. The athlete and gymnast in Doug often came out between scenes when he was hung up on wires. He liked to clown, pretending to fly and do impossible gymnastic tricks as he swung himself through the air. This caused Dad concern and he often had to remind Doug that he was not rigged to do circus stunts and he was playing without a net below!

Dad said, "Doug's trust in my work sometimes worried me. I never knew what he'd do next."

Near the end of the picture, to escape the cheering palace folks with his princess in tow, the newly-crowned prince dons the invisible

Julanne Johnson, "The Princess of Bagdad"

cloak. Photographically he was made invisible, but the princess was seen. Dad had to rig a seat hung on wires to simulate Doug's arms carrying her. She too wore one of his wire belts. Hanging by wires from above, tied to a carriage and rolled along a track, the princess floated up the stairs, as if in Doug's arms.

In a following scene, the princess was lowered to the center of the flying carpet, which was laid out on the floor. The prince removed the invisible cloak and again appeared on the screen. Then, with more wires rigged from the magic carpet to the rolling carriage on a track above, at the waved command of the prince, Dad made the carpet take off from the floor and fly out of the palace and over the city.

The carpet was a three-quarter-inch flat piece of steel, five feet by eight feet in size and covered with a Persian carpet with an eight-inch fringe hanging down around the edges. Flying the magic carpet over the city of Bagdad was the greatest challenge of Dad's career. It was the last scene in the picture, the toughest to set up and the most dangerous to perform.

The thief became a Prince and, with the Princess by his side, he flew over the city of Bagdad on the flying carpet as thousands cheered below

Piano wires, the size of pencil lead, were carefully tied to special fittings in six places on the carpet's steel frame. Then sixteen wires from the frame were tied to the top end of a lowered one-hundred-foot construction crane. With the leading lady, Julanne Johnson, seated and the star, Douglas Fairbanks standing, the crane lifted the carpet and its riders to a height of thirty-five feet above the solid concrete pavement!

Eighteen cameras were placed and ready to shoot long shots and medium shots from all angles as the carpet made its one pass over the city. A special camera platform for a manned camera was mounted on the underside of the crane, about fifteen feet above the carpet. All was ready.

The "Camera, action" cue was signaled and two thousand extras in costume on the streets of the mythical city of Bagdad began to cheer. The crane operator started his 180-degree, half-circle turn to carry the carpet a distance of 400 feet over the heads of the waving throng. All cameras turned to photograph one of the most spectacular scenes ever created for a moving picture.

The camera on the crane, shooting down, got a most convincing medium shot of the prince and princess waving to the crowd, seen below them, calling wishes for happiness ever after. The fade-out on the picture was done in miniature and showed the couple on the carpet flying over a desert scene, across an Arabian Night sky

The Thief of Bagdad *was one of the biggest productions of its time* glittering with stars that spelled out the moral of the story, "Happiness Must Be Earned." Doug told Dad he had surely earned that. By all standards, the picture is a classic for all time!

FAIRBANKS CALLS ON DAD AGAIN

1926

In 1926, Doug called on Dad again to work on one of the first big, early color movies, *The Black Pirate*. Dad helped Doug and 50 sailors swim underwater to capture a pirate ship. The underwater scene was shot on the big studio stage. A hundred-foot, greenish-colored cloth was hung high across the back of the entire set to give underwater color to the vast scene. Loose hay was scattered a foot deep over the entire floor of the set and covered with one large, blue-colored, lightweight cloth. This created an irregular wavy effect.

Douglas Fairbanks as "The Black Pirate"

To rig the big scene, Dad designed a special wire belt, with a heavy John Brown belt across the chest. Then, he alone tied his two wires to the front of each of the 50 belts, one at the waist and one at the chest. The other ends of the wires he tied above, out of camera view, to large, flat carriages that set on a hundred-foot track, which would roll and carry the swimmers across the scene. The men got into their belts and lay on their backs, to the right of the set out of the camera's frame, atop removable scaffolds, 20 feet above the blue-cloth floor.

Doug was the last into his belt. The only water on the set was in a four-foot-by-five-foot aquarium, about six-inches thick. It was stocked with some very small fish and fine bits of seaweed. Two cameras were set up "upside-down," to photograph the scene through this tank, so that when projected on the screen, the blue cloth on the floor would be at the top of the screen and look like the surface of the ocean, as seen from underwater with swimming fish and swaying seaweed. As Dad suggested, each swimmer filled his hands with feathers from a bed pillow. When all was ready and the cameras were set to turn, the scaffolds were quickly rolled from under the sailors, leaving them hanging on their backs in midair.

Dad called, "Ready to go!" The director yelled, "Camera. Turn them!" Then he shouted to Dad, "Start them!" A wave from Dad and the crew started their pull to roll the carriages. "The Black Pirate" and his 50 sailors floated into the scene kicking their legs and stroking with their arms. With each stroke, they released a couple of feathers, which floated down toward the covered hay.

Sailors swimming on their backs in the air

To the inverted cameras, the feathers floated up to the surface as bubbles. The sword-bearing sailors moved across the set in beautiful formation, like marching soldiers. If the audience looked above the swimmers for the wires that supported them, they didn't see any, because they were *below* the swimmers.

The tiny fish in the tank and the swaying bits of seaweed, between the camera and the sailors, added more reality to the underwater scene. The sailors continued to swim. The bubbles floated upward and the filming of a most convincing scene was made with one take. Unexpected applause and praise burst forth on the set from company members and visitors.

The director called "Cut" to the cameramen. "A good scene. Great action!"

Then, as "The Black Pirate" and his men proceeded to capture the rival ship, Doug made his way up to the poop deck. He took a strong hold of and cut the rope holding a three-cornered sail full of wind. The scene looked as if Doug was lifted by the wind-filled sail, up from the poop deck to the top of the mast. In fact, two wires went from the belt of Fairbanks, through pulleys at the top of a 90-foot crane above the mast, and back down to the control of Dad's men off the scene. Doug and the sail were pulled up as the strong wind machines filled the sail, lifting "The Black Pirate" to a spar atop it. There he stuck his sword into the top of the sail, which was full of wind. Using the two wires, Dad controlled Doug's spectacular slide down the sail, splitting it wide open as he slid. This reduced the speed of the ship and allowed his men to capture the prize vessel of the pirate fleet. The battle won, "The Black Pirate's" happy crewmen, again with the help of Dad's two wires, passed their captain, hand-by-hand, from the hold of the ship up three decks to the main deck for victory cheers and rejoicing.

Laughing, Dad said, "Pulling Doug up and down on the ship was the most fun I ever had on a picture."

The Black Pirate premiered at the Hollywood Egyptian Theater. When the underwater scene appeared on the screen that opening night, the audience broke into impressed, appreciative applause. Until now, it has never been told how it was done. It was a big night for Dad. Later he told me he most appreciated the unusual and unexpected cheers from the gang on the set, who understood his work and recognized his ability.

Many stories have been told or written about how these impressive scenes of Doug Fairbanks's were made, but these are the facts. My dad was the first and, at that time, Hollywood's only piano wire technician.

BROADCASTING AN EARLY, CHILDREN'S RADIO PROGRAM

1926

A spring breeze had started to blow, so I was making a tissue paper kite on our front room floor. Mom answered our wall phone.

"Coy," she called, "There's a lady on the phone wants to talk to you."

"Hello," I said, and I heard a sweet, southern accent voice.

"Hello Coy, I hope you have a few minutes to speak with me."

"Yes, I have."

"I'm Mammy Simmons here in Hollywood, with radio station KMTR. I've seen you in some of your movies and I've enjoyed your acting."

"Thank you," I answered. I knew when *School Day Love* was shown for 17 weeks at Miller's big theater in downtown Los Angeles, followed by long runs of four good, dramatic pictures in which I played featured roles, many fans had seen me on the screen and told me they liked my work. I thanked the lady for calling.

She quickly said, "Coy, I've another reason for calling you. I'm starting an all-children's afternoon radio program here on our station and I would like you to be my guest next Wednesday afternoon. I want to talk with you on my program and hear you tell me and all the boys and girls in radio-land about your experiences working in moving pictures. They have seen you on the movie screen and I know they would like to hear you speak to them on the radio."

Silence. What's this . . . me, on the radio?

"Do you have a radio?" she asked. "Do you listen to programs?" Her voice sounded serious and interesting.

"Yes, I do have a radio and I listen to some programs."

"Good, well then do you understand if you come to our studio and we talk, your voice will be transmitted on my program into the air and we will be heard on all the radios tuned to KMTR? Don't you think that would be exciting and fun? Wouldn't your family and friends like to hear your voice on their radios?"

More silence. I did understand and thought what a kick it would be for Mom, Dad and the girls to hear me with our crystal sets. The woman did sound sincere. So I asked, "How much will it cost to do this program thing with you on your radio?"

She laughed a little. "Coy, it won't cost anything. It will be a big favor to me, which I will appreciate very much. Do you sing or play an instrument?"

"I play a few songs on my harmonica."

"Oh! That would be wonderful. Then you are interested, and you would like to be my guest?"

I thought it would be fun. "Yes, where do you do this kind of a program?"

"Well, first you talk it over with mammy and pappy and have them give me a call, and I'll give them the information. I'm so glad you are interested and I know we are going to have a good time together. Don't you feel that way too?"

"Did you say your name is Mammy?"

"Yes, Mammy Simmons."

"Yes, Mammy, it sounds like it would be fun to be on your program. I'll have my dad call you."

"Here, take my phone number." She seemed pleased.

"Goodbye, Mammy."

I told Mom and Dad the story. Dad called the lady and got all the dope on when and how to get to her radio studio. He learned she had conducted a children's program in Atlanta, where she told stories for young people. Miss Georgia Simmons was brought to Hollywood by KMTR Radio Corp. Dad liked the idea. "Do it if you want!" he said.

With smiles, my five boosters just knew this radio business was going to be fun and they spread the word through the neighborhood.

To get to the radio studio in Hollywood, I took the Edendale street car for a dime, and transferred at the Sunset Blvd. bridge to the Santa Monica Blvd. car. Dressed in my Sunday sweater and white shirt, with the time and address flashing in my mind, I got off the big red car at Cahuenga Blvd. and walked to the studio. To my surprise, it was on the upper story of a wooden two family flat. The 1028 address plate was on an outdoor stairway. I took the steps up to the porch and knocked at the screen door. A voice said, "Come in." I did, and there stood Mammy Simmons with her hand out.

"Hello Coy." We shook hands. Her happy eyes sparkled with a big smile from a "no make-up" face. Her hair was shoulder-long, like my Mom's. In fact, she looked like Mom. I felt she was truly glad to see me. Even her handshake was firm and warm and I felt like she meant it when she said, "I'm so glad you've come to be with us," and whispered,"you look just like your pictures on-screen."

"I'm glad to meet you, Mammy, and I like the sound of your southern voice."

We laughed. With her hand on my shoulder we walked across the large, scarcely furnished, heavily carpeted living room, and faced eight or ten seated, nicely dressed folks. Mammy's introductions were charming and funny. I met boys and girls about my age, some older, and three parents. We all chatted to become acquainted. It was a friendly group. The kids, I learned, were from nearby

KMTR

"TOP OF THE DIAL"

HOLLYWOOD—EST. 1924

FREQUENCY: 570 Kc. POWER: 1000 Watts. OWNED BY: KMTR Radio Corp. OPERATED BY: KMTR Radio Corp. BUSINESS ADDRESS: 1000 Cahuenga Blvd. PHONE: Hillside 1161. STUDIO ADDRESS: Same. TRANSMITTER LOCATION: Same. TIME ON THE AIR: 5:00 A.M. to 1:00 P.M.

PERSONNEL

President ....Victor E. Dalton
General Manager ....Victor E. Dalton
Asst. General Manager..Kenneth O. Tinkham
Production Manager ....Rudy Cornell
Musical Director ....Salvatore Santaella
Chief Technician ....Carrol Hauser

POLICIES

Station does not accept patent medicine or medical advertising. Beer and wine advertising accepted; hard liquor advertising accepted only after 10:00 P.M. Station does not accept advertising for stock-selling companies, lotteries, fortune tellers or astrologists. Station accepts foreign language programs.

REPRESENTATIVE

J. J. Devine & Assoc.

Information on radio station KMTR as published in a radio journal of the time schools, chosen by their teachers to entertain on the program with poems, songs and stories. A cute, blond girl was to play the piano for a girl to sing. I sat down with them and felt a little embarrassed when one mentioned she had seen my pictures and asked me a lot of questions.

Mammy took a chair at the end of the room, facing what she called a "mike," short for "microphone," near her on a stand.

A man came in from the adjoining room and was introduced by Mammy as the radio station's chief technician or operator. He was a pleasant, but serious, guy and told us how our voices, and all the sounds we would make in the room, would be transmitted on the airwaves, to be heard in all directions, by radios within a hundred miles of the studio.

As I listened, I knew Mom, the girls and our neighbors were by their radios, wearing earphones, ready to hear me on the new kids' program.

The operator told Mammy, "After I introduce you with the mike in my room, I'll wave you a signal to speak and start your program."

Mammy nodded, "Okay, am I close enough to the mike?"

"Yes, and the two chairs beside you are for those with whom you will want to talk. The mike over at the piano is for the players and the singers. You must all speak and sing with good, strong, clear voices so you will be heard out there in radio-land. Any questions?"

There weren't any, but everybody shifted in their seats.

"No questions? Now Mammy, during the program if I wave a signal to you from my desk in the other room, I'll close down your mike to read some commercials into my mike. That will give you all a couple of minutes to relax and take it easy, but don't speak. Then, Mammy, I'll cue you again when to continue with your program. Okay? Everybody keep your eyes on Mammy."

He walked over and closed the front door, the three windows, and then pulled the drapes over the windows, so we heard very little sound from outside. The room was very quiet. This was becoming weird.

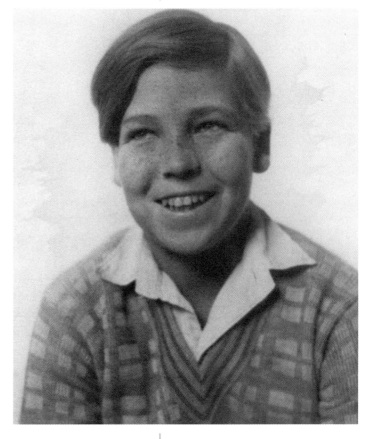

This photograph was taken around the time I did the children's radio programs

"All right folks, now don't be nervous. Relax." He sat down at his desk and pulled his mike to him. The big clock on the wall showed four o'clock. His hand flipped the switches and I heard him say, "It's four o'clock, this is radio KMTR, Top of the Dial, owned and operated by KMTR Corporation, here at 1028 Cahuenga Blvd. in beautiful Hollywood, California. Today, we are pleased to introduce our new weekly 'Mammy Simmons' all-children radio program, by children and for children. And now, here is Mammy Simmons!"

He waved his signal and the voice with a southern accent said, "Good afternoon boys and girls and all you parents and good friends at home here in Southern California. Mammy is so glad to have you talented boys and girls here with us in our studio to entertain on our first program. Are you all pleased to be here today?"

She smiled when we all yelled a big, "Yes, Mammy Simmons."

Glancing at a card in her hand, she introduced the girls to do their number at the piano. They were good and when they finished we gave them a little hand. A boy sat beside Mammy and read from a book a good, short story about a mountain man and his dog. Each kid, in turn, was introduced to do his thing, and we gave them all a hand. Mammy kept the program moving by talking about each kid, and it was going well. A boy was good as he recited some poetry for us. Then Mammy seemed pleased to introduce me as a movie star. As we sat at her mike, I felt something different about radio when she talked about my pictures she had seen, and asked questions about everything. I had to wonder how many phones were pressed against ears. Strange!

"How long have you played in pictures? Do you like working in pictures? Were you hurt when the fire engine hit you in *While the Devil Laughs*?" She made it fun. I enjoyed the talk with her. Then she asked, "Did you bring your harmonica to play for us?" I took it out of my pocket. She smiled when a couple of kids clapped. So I played, "Swanee River." After a little hand, they asked for another tune. When I finished "Stars and Stripes Forever," I got a big hand. I didn't think it was that good but I thanked them all. Then Mammy remarked, "Our time is up and that's a good song to finish this program; thank you all for being here today. We hope all of you out there in radio-land have enjoyed our program as much as we have enjoyed giving it. I hope you all tune in again next Wednesday, at the same time here on KMTR. This is Mammy Simmons saying goodbye for now. God Bless you all."

She waved to the engineer, stood and said to us, "That was wonderful folks. Thank you each one."

Everybody, including the radioman, was pleased with the program. I was invited back four more weeks to talk with Mammy, play my harmonica and sing with my ukulele.

When I got home, the whole neighborhood came out to say how much they liked the program. Little did we kids know that that day in the living room of that house made early Hollywood radio history.

BITTEN BY THE PHOTO BUG

1928

With Dad's box camera, I started taking pictures when I was nine years old. For a couple of years I tried hard and folks said I took some good snapshots. I never took my camera to the studios, but I wish I had. I could have made some interesting shots when I worked with some of the big stars of the early, silent movies.

After I had mastered Dad's box camera, he allowed me to use his 120 Eastman folding camera. That was encouraging. I took pictures of the family dressed for Easter, at the Fourth of July picnic in Echo Park, at the beach, and time exposures of evening traffic on Alvarado Street. Just taking the pictures wasn't enough for me. I wanted to learn to develop my films and make my own prints.

One day, I learned that Mr. Barker, my Sunday School teacher and scoutmaster of Troop 75, was going to teach a class for boys interested in earning the "Photography" merit badge. I showed up and, in a small darkroom set up in the basement of the Echo Park Methodist Church, I learned to develop and print my own pictures. I shall never forget how I stood in the dark at a table under a little red light, rocking a tray of developer. A small piece of photo paper that I had exposed to one of my negatives was moving back and forth in the solution. I watched intently, then saw a faint image grow stronger and stronger until there was a picture of my sisters and Harry standing in Echo Park with ice cream cones in their hands. I was amazed and inspired! The photo bug had bitten me! I wanted to learn more!

Working with the red light and the chemicals reminded me of how I had sat years before in that little pantry watching my Grandpa Watson as he stood in the dark by his red light developing glass photo plates.

Dad helped me turn the little storage house in our backyard

Dad plays his "squeeze box"

into a darkroom. We made it lightproof by covering all the cracks. We installed an old kitchen sink, ran a garden hose from a tap beside the house around the darkroom house through the wall to a faucet over the sink. A quarter section of old bicycle tire was fitted to the sink's drainpipe to run out through the wall to the outside. As I washed my pictures, the grass got watered and I was the happiest, if not the youngest, photographer in town.

I took my camera almost everywhere I went. Parties, hikes, church picnics and all scouting events became subjects of my picture-taking abilities. Everybody seemed to like my pictures and gave me orders and paid for prints. With their nickels and dimes I was able to buy darkroom equipment, more paper and chemicals.

Oh boy! I was having more fun and learning all the time. I took my camera to Thomas Starr King Jr. High School. I asked the teachers of each of my classes if they would please stand with the class on the school's front steps for a picture. They were delighted to do so. Even teachers liked to be photographed! I got them all to smile and I didn't shoot until I could see every face. I photographed all of my six classes, the stage crew and a few special groups of guys and gals. I quickly developed the film and made a print for every

Below left: Money makers — Class photo (1928)

Below center: Drama class photo. That's me, front, second from left

Below right: My rubber stamp

face. A day or two later, I took the prints to each class. They sold like hot cakes at five cents each!

I felt it was good publicity to have each teacher accept a free print. After all, they were my agents and they, too, had stood for class pictures. Taking pictures of the kids at school proved to pay well. They loved them. Shooting groups and singles in their costumes, when our dramatics class presented a school play, proved to be big business for me. *The Man Without a Country* and *The Big Race* were the two biggest moneymakers. I had a part in each play: I was a sailor and Lt. Morris in one and I shared the male lead with my lifelong friend, Jim Boles, in our graduation presentation, *The Big Race*.

Acting in moving pictures was fun, yet I was finding that still photography was enjoyable, interesting and a new challenge. I liked everything about it and wanted to learn more. At that time I didn't realize it was later to change my future, from acting in motion pictures to becoming a news photographer/reporter, later called a "photojournalist."

One evening, my interesting little enterprise got a big boost. Dad's brother, my Uncle Rally, also known as George, and his wife, my Aunt Mamie, came to visit us. In the course of conversation, Dad mentioned my interest in photography and showed them some of my prints. I knew Uncle Rally was a news photographer, but I never thought he'd be interested in my little business. Instead, he was very pleased to see what I was doing. Even my darkroom surprised him and made him laugh. He said it was great! This made me feel good.

"Why don't you come down to my office in *The Los Angeles Times'* building at First and Broadway and see our darkrooms," he invited. "I'll show you how news pictures are made and how, with our photos, we service newspapers all over the world."

Coming from him, that invitation blasted my imagination. He was manager of the Los Angeles Bureau of Pacific and Atlantic Photos, one of the four, big international syndicates in America. The photo bug bit me in new places with new ideas. I didn't need a second invitation. The next day after school, I was all eyes and ears in the P&A darkroom.

From that day on and all through my junior high school years, when not working in a motion picture or playing my position on a basketball or football team, I drove my Model T Ford to downtown L.A. At first, to avoid parking fees, I parked at the top of Court Flight and walked down more than one hundred concrete steps to Broadway. From there, it was only a couple of blocks to the side door of the Times Building and then up to the second floor. There, I swept and cleaned the darkrooms and learned to

My Uncle Rally autographed this photo "To Coy Watson, my favorite photographer, From Uncle George." I asked for a steady job and got it!

28   Mid-Week Pictorial   December 20, 1930

Winners of Cash Awards in the Amateur Photographic Competition

ON THE LONG TRAIL WESTWARD.
Sent by Coy Watson Jr., of Los Angeles, Cal. (Cash Award, $3.)

My first cash reward was for this photo. Left to right: Delmar, Billy, Garry, Blackie and Snibs.

Dad and Mom. My first flash powder picture.

mix developer and hypo. I washed prints and put them on ferrotype tins to give a glossy finish. I pasted captions on the pictures and helped put the day's service into the clients' forty-one, pre-addressed, eight-inch-by-ten-inch envelopes and applied the proper postage.

I made my first flash powder picture on a glass plate at home one evening, just before the family sat down to dinner. I had explained the dangers of the highly explosive magnesium powder to my younger brothers and sisters and they could hardly wait to see my demonstration. I set up and focused for a shot of Dad sitting in a rocking chair holding Mom on his lap. I shall never forget the scene. As I raised the loaded flash gun to shoot, the kids were excited and waiting. They were crouched around the room behind me, giggling and watching with their eyes half-closed and their hands cupped over their ears. I looked at Dad and Mom, who were posed and laughing, so I said "Hold it," and fired. The booming flare of light and smoke bounced to the ceiling and filled the room. The tribe war-whooped and started laughing and jumping up and down with excitement. Little Garry stood clapping his hands. I had my shot! Mom jumped to her feet waving her hands at the smoke.

"Oh Coy, must you make that much noise and smoke every time you take a picture?"

I was laughing too, as I rubbed the burned hair on my hand.

"No, Mom, I won't use that much powder next time."

Dad nodded and grinned.

"I'll have to try different amounts of power, until I know how much to use for each shot," I admitted. "It depends on how far I am from the subject."

The kids crowded around for a close look at the hot and smoking gun. Dad opened the front door to help clear out the smoke. I took my camera off the tripod, as Dad stood beside me. He brushed his hand over the side of my head and whispered, "That was some flash! You burned your hair."

"Yeah, I guess I should hold the gun up a little higher."

He grabbed a handful of my mop and shook my head. "You'd better. A few more shots like that and you won't have any hair!"

The following night, I came home proudly with a photograph I shall always treasure. It wasn't just my first flash powder exposure, it was a great picture of Mom and Dad laughing and looking very happy.

Learning to shoot pictures with light from burning flash powder was fun but a bit scary. Practicing shots on the kids at home was like covering a news assignment. There was always action, noise, confusion, and ready subjects. A shot of the family around the dinner table was my first wide-angle effort.

I got a lot of practice at making portraits, and Dad could always use a recent picture of the boys to run in the Motion Picture Casting Director's monthly directory.

Our family at dinner. Mom was absent by choice, she'd had enough flash powder.

Ad for the Watson clan from the Motion Picture Casting Director's monthly directory

THE BUCKING RIDE

1928

One Friday evening after a touch football game at my junior high school, I drove my Ford into the yard. Little brother, Harry, came to meet me with some news. Studio carpenters had left some lumber on Mack Sennett's lot next to ours. Here were fifteen or twenty four-inch-thick-by-twelve-inch-wide planks about ten feet long.

"We could make something good with these boards, couldn't we, Coy?"

"Yes," I said. "I wonder why they left them here and when they will be down to pick 'em up."

"Mom said they've been here since this morning," Harry urged.

"Then they're here for Saturday and Sunday, that's for sure. Maybe for Monday," I said.

"Let's do somethin' with 'em," Harry said, trying to pick one up.

"I've got an idea, Harry. They're good, heavy timbers. Let's make some roller coaster tracks. We'll run two planks side-by-side just far enough apart so the kids can ride their wagons down them."

"That sounds good, let's do it!" was Harry's reply. "We can make the tracks run up and down when we put some wooden packing boxes under the ends of the planks. They'll go up on one side and then down the other. It'll be like a bucking horse." Harry laughed.

The story of "The Bucking Ride," with photos, appeared in the Los Angeles Times *and was syndicated to newspapers across the country via Pacific-Atlantic Photos*

"We can call it 'The Bucking Ride,'" I said.

Harry yelled, "Yeah, and we can charge two cents a ride!"

"We'll start it tomorrow," I concluded.

When we later presented the idea to our family, the kids all accepted it with much excitement. The next morning everybody was up early to watch the bucking runway take form. After a couple of hours of lifting, pushing, shifting and fitting the 50-pound timbers into place, the attraction began to draw the neighbor kids. By noon, we had a ticket office with the big sign, "BUCKING

RIDE—2-Cents," and a lineup of wagons of all sizes waiting to take the bumps.

Dad's wheelbarrow stood by to serve as the "emergency vehicle" in case of an accident. Harry was the "starter" and kept the wagons rolling down the track. Softhearted sister, Louise, was a good ticket girl, but sister Gloria said she let too many kids ride free. The kids were having so much fun it made a happy scene for all.

I brought out the four-inch-by-five-inch Graflex news camera and took some pictures. The following Monday, I developed the film and made prints in the P&A darkroom and showed them to Uncle Rally and Dele Tack. They liked 'em.

"Leave the prints on my desk and I'll show them to the *Times* picture editor," Uncle Rally said.

The next day, to the surprise of this aspiring young photographer, I saw my first published feature picture story appear in the *Los Angeles Times* with a "P&A Photo" credit line.

I was not only pleased, but encouraged. I knew then, if I could make feature pictures good enough for the *Times*, I could make news pictures!

From P&A I received $3.00, the going rate paid by news picture syndicates for photos used. The kids were delighted to see their pictures in the paper, along with the following article, with information from Uncle Rally:

Cash customers with 2 cents are doing handsomely by Coy Watson, Jr., 15-year-old Los Angeles promoter, who is doing a brisk business with what he calls "The Bucking Ride" and which he has established in the backyard of his home. Tree sitting is quite pale in comparison.

Patrons are expected to walk away after enjoying the thrills of a ride, but if temporarily unable, a wheelbarrow capably managed by Mr. Watson's sisters and brothers is at their disposal. Of course, you've got to be young to enjoy it.

The ride consists of a runway, something like that of the roller coasters, only different.

There are bumps on the runway. This adds to the excitement. There are signs along the runway, cautioning the patrons to hold tightly on to their hats.

Oh yes, it's for children mostly, although Mr. Watson will take 2 cents from an adult as readily as from an adolescent.

"The Bucking Ride," Mr. Watson predicts, will prove much more popular than midget golf, for the youthful element of his neighborhood, at least. Whee! Let's go!

About a month later, the ride disappeared. Mom told how it happened. The two carpenters from the studio came with a truck to pick up the lumber. Through the kitchen window, Mom heard

The bucking ride in action

them grumbling about the planks being moved and that they had to carry them so far to load them onto the truck. She went outside and asked the men to stop a moment and told them how the whole neighborhood had enjoyed the use of the lumber.

MY FIRST NEWS ASSIGNMENT

1929

I received my first news photo assignment on a Friday afternoon, about 5:30 P.M., entirely without warning.

Uncle Rally, the manager, and his secretary, Dele Tack, were in the office after the company's two regular photographers had left for the day. I had just finished making up 10 gallons of fixing bath for the hypo tank in the printing darkroom and was about to leave for home when my uncle came in.

"Do you have your gear together?"

"Yes," I said, surprised.

"Do you want to take an assignment?" he asked.

Oh boy, did I! This was it; this was what I'd been waiting for! "Yes, sure, I'm ready," I said, a little excited.

"The *Times* City Editor just called. The *Times* photographers are all out and our two guys have gone. He wants us to make a head shot of a suspect at the police station for the next edition."

The police station and jail were just across from the *Times* Building, up First Street a half block. Here was my chance to make a news picture.

"I'd like to do it! What's the dope?" I asked.

He explained the suspect figured in a murder case and was being held because he had a record. My uncle handed me my first news photo assignment. Written on a piece of newsprint paper was the man's name and some info on the case.

"Check with the desk sergeant; he knows you're coming over."

"O.K.," I said.

Gear in hand, I was off. I headed out through the buzzing City Room. I didn't even feel the weight of the tripod and case, with over ten pounds of camera and two magazines each loaded with twelve glass plates. I took the elevator to the street and started to hustle up the hill. Everything I knew about how to make a picture was going through my mind. There may have been people on the sidewalk, but I didn't see them. I might have been talking to myself. I was confident and concentrating on the job ahead.

I took a deep breath as I walked through the station door. I could see the cell bars down the hall. The place smelled like floor oil. Stepping up to the desk sergeant I said, "My name's Coy Watson, photographer from the *Times*. The City Editor called. You've a suspect here he wants me to photograph."

He looked at me and smiled a question. "You're the photographer from the *Times*?"

I knew what he was thinking: "Is this 16-year-old kid, just out of Knickerbocker pants, going to make a picture of this hardened criminal?" Sliding off his high seat behind the desk, he came around to me.

"O.K. I'll go back and get him. You get ready."

"Where will I set up?"

"Over there." He pointed to a space in the corner. "You can use that chair."

I put down my gear on the old wooden floor as he walked

toward the cells. After placing the chair a couple of feet from the wall, I unfolded each tripod leg, attached them to the head and set them up. I took out the Graflex and set it on its side for a vertical shot. There was no "revolving back" on the Graflex. (With a later model, a horizontal or vertical picture could be made by just twisting the back.) With the camera set, I slipped a cap into the flash gun making it ready for the flash powder. I was all set. I looked up. Golly! Here came the sergeant with one of the meanest, scrubbiest-looking, unshaven men I had ever seen. He was wearing handcuffs! I was a bit tense anyway and seeing this guy, I was one shaky kid!

The sergeant told him to sit down. He settled into the chair looking at me.

"Is this kid gonna take my picture?"

"Yes, he's from the *Times*."

"He's a photographer?"

"He's going to take your picture. Now be quiet."

"Then hurry up and do it," growled my subject.

The sergeant smiled. I liked that, but I could tell this tough guy didn't want his picture taken and he smelled awful. He had been drinking and he needed a bath!

"Okay Mister, if you will just sit still a minute and let me focus, then I'll make the shot."

"Hurry up!" He actually snarled, but sat still watching me.

I felt he was amused, showing a half-smile. Focused and with the lens stopped down, I reached for my flashgun. When he saw me start to pour the powder into it, the prisoner stood up yapping at the sarge.

"That stuff's dangerous."

"Sit down!" snapped the sergeant. "He's gonna make your picture. So shut up and sit down!"

He sat down, grunting to himself.

I had the gun loaded and ready to shoot, but now he was leaning back in the chair and out of focus. I had to tell him, "Sit up straight.

Old press passes

This won't hurt you. I'm only using a small amount of powder, just enough to light your face."

He leaned forward looking at my flashgun, watching, afraid!

I had to laugh to myself. This mean toughie was scared of my flash. To me it was funny. With the slide covering the lens, I tripped the mirror. It made a little thump sound.

"What's that?" he grunted.

"The mirror opening," I told him.

"C'mon, for God's sake, shoot this thing and get it over with."

"Hold still," I said, holding the gun in my hand well above the camera.

He faced the lens, but his eyes were rolled up, staring at the flashgun. Then in quick, close order, I took away the slide, fired the flash, replaced the slide over the lens and closed the mirror. I had my shot, but when the powder blew, my subject was looking at the flash and I guess it blinded him. He jumped up yelling and kicked the leg of my tripod. The camera started to go over. He fell back against the wall. With the hot gun still smoking in my hand, I threw my arms around the camera and caught it.

Rubbing his eyes, the man yelled, "That's enough. That's enough!" and started toward the cells. I guessed he was just putting on an act. The sergeant barked "Come back here!"

"Okay Watson, have you got it?"

I could hardly keep from laughing. "I would like to take another one just for safety."

"Safety, my butt, you got my picture, that's enough. If this kid knows what the heck he's doing, he should have my picture NOW!" he squawked to the sergeant, throwing in a few nasty words.

The guy was right. "Okay, Sarge, let that do it."

"You're dang right that'll do it!" snapped Toughie.

The sergeant was laughing as he struck a fast pace behind my subject going down the hall. I pulled the plate from the magazine into the pouch, then slipped it to the back; took the camera off the tripod, put it into the case; brushed the burnt powder off the gun and stowed it; broke down the tripod and was leaving when the sergeant returned.

"How long have you been doing this?"

I knew what he meant, but I asked, "Doing what?"

"Taking pictures."

"I've been taking pictures for four years,"

"News pictures?"

In 1946, the Los Angeles Press Photographers Association helped Twentieth Century Fox promote the opening of The Adventures of Casanova *at the Westwood Theater, near the UCLA Campus. I performed as a 1920's-era newspaper photographer making "flash powder" photos for the sidewalk movie fans.*

He was interested. "No, this is my first news assignment," I admitted with a smile.

"That guy didn't make it easy for you. I hope you got a good picture of him."

"I think I did."

"You made this a 'first' for me, too," he said with a big grin. "This was the first time I ever saw a prisoner rush to get back into his cage!"

We both laughed. I thanked him for his help.

"So long, I hope to see you again," the sergeant said.

Hurrying down the hill, I couldn't walk fast enough. It was getting dark. All that happened during the past 20 minutes was thumping in my brain. Did I do everything right? Did I forget anything? I hoped the sergeant approved of me. I liked him, but, oh boy, that mean guy's picture has got to appear in the paper so the ornery so-and-so will see it and know that I knew what I was doing.

Back in the *Times* Building, I crossed the lobby and took the elevator to the Editorial Department on the second floor and passed the City Desk. I headed for the darkroom. "There's got to be an exposure on this plate," I'm thinking.

I took the magazine from the camera in the negative darkroom.

"Now I gotta do this right. Take your time, Watson" I said to myself.

I turned on the water, checked the solutions in the tanks and yanked the light cord, dumping the room into darkness. Dark, no light; just like in Grandpa's little pantry, I recalled.

Having taken the back off the magazine, I took the glass plate in my hand, held it by its edges and, very carefully, with a little prayer, dropped it into the developer and covered the tank. I turned on the light just long enough to set the timer for five minutes and then off again. My eyes had to get used to the dark so I could see by the safe-light. Then I stood waiting, tapping my fingers on the edge of the big wooden sink. It would be the longest five minutes I'd ever known. The smell of the chemicals in the air, the gurgling of the running water in the sink, and the ticking of the time clock were all a part of that impatient wait.

Standing in the dark, I thought of many things. Could I be a news photographer? I felt that this was all like a final test that I was putting myself through to prove that I had what it took. Then, rocking the tank, I breathed another little prayer. I thought of my family, Dad, Mom, and the kids, the guys at school and my girlfriend Anna. They all knew how much I was trying, and how much this meant to me.

Clang! Ding! Ding! Ding! I jumped! It seemed like the whole room shook. The alarm had gone off! I switched on the red inspection light, took the cover off the tank, got a gentle hold on the plate and lifted it slowly out of the "soup" to hold it up to the safe-light. I could see an image! A closer look. It had developed long enough. It looked alright!

"So far so good. Now a dip into the water then into the hypo fixing bath." The exposure looked okay, but now it had to clear

In 1929, I asked my pal Bob to create my first "Newsman's" Christmas card

before I would see if the "dirty guy" was in focus, and if his eyes were open.

I waited another four minutes before sliding the red glass aside, off the safety light. The white light flooded the room and down into the sink. I felt the hardened emulsion on the plate. Then, lifting it up to the light, he was in focus; he hadn't moved and his eyes were open. And how they were open! They were rolled up staring pop-eyed at my flash as if he saw a ghost holding the hangman's noose!

I laughed out loud with relief and joy. The negative was good! However, he looked peculiar, not at all like a possible suspect; more like a confessed murderer afraid to die.

I relaxed, laughing triumphantly over my first news negative! Uncle George came in and laughed with me. He liked the shot. With a bit of self-assured pride, I made a good five-inch-by-seven-inch print, three inches between the ears, and wrote the name of the "not-so-tough" subject on the back. When I proudly approached the City Desk, the sound of a hundred typewriters with tinkling bells and shifting carriages filled the huge room. The whole place smelled like the newspapers I had once sold on the streets.

I laid my print on the editor's desk. He was seated with his face at an old black self-standing telephone, with the receiver to his ear.

"Yes, alright, go ahead," he was saying. He glanced up at me and nodded. Out of the side of his mouth, he whispered a "thanks" as if I had been laying pictures on his desk for years. His head was bobbing "yes" to the phone as his hand, holding a heavy, black lead pencil, reached out for my print. He looked at it, flipped it over, read the name, then wrote "1 COL" on it. That was it! I breathed an "okay" to myself. Smiling, I walked away, striding eight feet tall. He had marked my picture as "art" to run one column in the morning *L.A. Times*.

I had passed my own prescribed test. I had covered a news story. I'd shot my first assignment. Now I knew I could be a newspaper photographer.

A few minutes later, I was rolling down Sunset Boulevard for home. I was quietly satisfied that I had done something good on my own this day. I felt like a winner. It was a different win than I'd ever felt before. I thought how glad Dad and Mom and the gang would be to hear about my big break. A very different kind of break than those we had enjoyed during the many years before. As far back as I could remember, I was a little boy working in motion pictures. How many times had we all been pleased when I got a break and was chosen by a studio director to play or star in a silent picture? It was a big thing in those days. I had always liked acting in pictures in front of the cameras. It always pleased Dad and Mom when I got a good part. It had been my whole life.

"Now my life isn't just a movie anymore. I'm not a little boy any more. The movie business is changing and I feel that I want to change, too. I like taking pictures and I want to be a newspaper photographer." All this was said aloud to the crisp night air.

I turned off Sunset onto Echo Park Avenue. I continued my resolve: "From behind my camera, I want to make news pictures of real people, doing real things, in real life, for newspapers and magazines."

Something had happened to me today! Why was I thinking differently than I'd ever thought before?

At home, the detailed story of my first endeavor as a news photographer was received with deep interest and lots of laughs. I answered many questions from my always-supportive team. During a few quiet moments, I told Dad what I'd thought about on my way home.

DAD HELPED ME CHANGE DIRECTION

1929

The feelings, thoughts and excitement of my first news assignment stayed with me. After dinner a couple of evenings later, Dad and I sat together on the front porch. The neighborhood was calm and peaceful. The kids were playing a quiet game for a change. Smoke from his brier pipe—a pipe I had given him for his birthday—floated around above his head in the still air as he sat in his rocking chair.

The sun had slipped down beyond the Silver Lake hill. Above us, its rays still shown brightly on a few big, white clouds that hung high in the cool, blue autumn sky. From around the dishpan in the kitchen, we could hear the harmonizing voices of my three sisters, Vivian, Gloria and Louise.

"Oh, tell me why the ivy twines . . ." Their song floated softly out into the peaceful evening. Dad cupped his hand over and around his pipe as he took it from his mouth and rested his hand on the arm of the chair. Slowly, he lowered his gaze from the clouds to my face.

In a soft tone, he said, "I've thought about what

Dad and his pipe

After fourteen years, my old Graflex camera and I were still together serving in the U.S. Coast Guard during World War II. Following a year of duty at sea as a boatswain mate, to my surprise, I was transferred to the District Office. My rating was changed to Chief Photographer. I was ordered to build darkrooms, establish a Photographic Section and take charge of photography for the Coast Guard Eleventh Naval District. The photographer in this photo knew he had come a long way from his own little darkroom in his Dad's storage shed.

you said the other night." He paused, with his lips slightly parted. "You're not a boy anymore, but you're not a man yet either. You are in-between: a teenager. You are an adolescent. You are becoming an adult. Every boy goes through it to become a man."

We talked of the past 16 years and agreed any change would be a big one for both of us. We laughed as we recalled some of the parts I had played in pictures, during my very early days. Some were so early only he remembered them! We had to admit the "big break" we had hoped for in motion pictures had not come for me. A lot of good ones had, but not the "one" big one. It had all been great fun and wonderful for all of us from that very first day with Mom in Glendale.

Under our laughs, I knew how disappointed he was, but I was sure he knew how hard I had tried and I knew how hard he had worked to have me ready. I believed I had never let him down at any time. With his fingertip black from the burnt ashes, he packed the half-burned tobacco down into his pipe and put the stem back into his mouth. His thumb rolled the flint spark that lit his lighter. Then, holding the flame to the tilted pipe, he took a few long draws so that the smoke puffed out around his face.

"Sound is going to make a big difference in the way moving pictures are made from now on." He told me. "Making silent pictures was fun and easy. Making sound pictures is going to be all work and little fun. It will be more exacting, more precise, causing actors to be tense as they concentrate to read their lines. Talkies will be more interesting to see and will tell stories in more detail, with sounds and music in the background. I believe we have seen the happiest days of the making of motion pictures."

He paused as he heard the sounds from a pair of motorcycles putting up the hill. "If we were shooting a scene right now, those motors would have ruined the shot."

I received this Bronze medal for covering the Olympic Games in 1932

I nodded.

Dad continued, "There have never been a lot of good parts for adolescent teenagers in pictures. You haven't had many calls lately and I'd guess, until the studios learn more about making sound pictures, there won't be much work for anybody but stage stars from New York or Chicago."

He paused, looked over the edge of the porch, turned in the chair and looked at me. "Maybe you've outgrown the business." He leaned back, rocked slowly, and took a couple of puffs on his pipe. "I think it's good you've found another interesting business where you can apply your talents and enthusiasm. You've always worked hard to do a good job at whatever you did."

He stopped rocking. "If you want to be a news photographer, I know you'll make up your mind to be a good one. Be the best."

He leaned forward, tapped the ashes from his pipe onto his hand and tossed them off the porch. He put the stem in his mouth, blew through it a couple of times, then held it cupped between his hands. I just listened as I always had. I knew he wanted me to be a writer.

The year before, he had bought me a typewriter to encourage me. I took typing at school, but didn't do very well. I had to smile.

"Dad, that's what I want to do," I said.

He knew it. He pointed his pipe stem in my direction. "Remember, life is all about people. Always look for the best in them and they'll see the best in you. People will like you unless you give them reason to feel otherwise."

By 1955, the six Watson brothers had all become photographers. Left to right: Me, Harry, Billy, Delmar, Garry and Bobs

We looked into each other's eyes. I nodded and whispered: "Right." He sat back in his chair. I tried to think of something to say to him, but what? What could I say? How could I thank my dad for his indescribable love, for his patience and understanding, which I had never been without in all our lives together? He was a part of me. He was and always had been my idol, my hero. I looked up to him. He was my example. I loved my dad. I had always tried to be like him. Why not? My entire life had been wonderful, nothing but happiness and fun. Why or what would I change? I knew I could never be as good a man as he, but I had made up my mind to try to be. I didn't speak; only thought. A cool night had settled around us. The song about the ivy twining had stopped in the kitchen. We looked up at the blue sky, which had turned dark. The clouds were gone. Stars were twinkling and from under the apple tree, I could hear the crickets cricketing (or whatever they did to make their sound). From in the house, we heard Mom's voice, "Harry, give that book to him or you're going to bed this minute!"

Dad and I took her cue and stood up for a stretch. In the distance, from somewhere up the canyon, we could hear the turning wheels of the day's last "big red" electric streetcar coming from Glendale, headed for Los Angeles. It approached Effie Street echoing its familiar rolling sound as it swayed its way down the tracks to Berkeley Avenue. The motorman rang the bell and the car made its way toward the underpass at Sunset Boulevard. We turned to the door as the rolling sound grew faint. The clear, peaceful night air smothered the familiar hum when the car passed under the bridge to roll on to the car barn downtown. I closed the door behind us and left another good day outside our "Watson's World."

I received this Lifetime Achievement Award from the Press Photographers Association of Greater Los Angeles instead of an "Oscar," but Dad didn't live to see it

My First Talking Picture

1930

By 1930, I had worked much of my life for most of the studios, playing a variety of bit and feature parts in over 60 silent moving pictures.

In 1927 and 1928 I had seen *The Jazz Singer* and *The Singing Fool*, Warner Bros. first sound pictures, called "talkies." Their "Vitaphone" phonograph-with-film system was not good, but I was impressed. I wondered how it would be to work and speak in a talking picture. Then came the day I knew I was going to learn. Director Ed Sloman wanted me to pick up a script at Fox Studio and learn lines to speak in a sound picture.

Puttin' on the Ritz was to be one of the first, high quality, musical talking pictures produced using the new Sound on Film (SOF) system. It was called "Fox Movietone."

The script called for me to be a tough, fast-talking, New York office boy. This was gonna be fun! I knew I could play the part— but I had only two days to learn a dozen lines. I would be working with six or eight other actors in the opening two-minute scene of the picture. Dad, Mom, Vivian, Gloria, Louise and Harry offered to stand around our dinner table and in fast order throw me my cues. It took a while, but it was fun and it worked. I got the lines down pat.

On the day of the "shoot" I was ready. I'd made at least 15 pictures at Fox Studio and it had always been fun acting, but today it would be different. My voice would be recorded! I parked my Ford and, wearing my blue serge suit, a white shirt and a tie, with script in hand, I headed for the stage.

Wow! What had happened? The old silent stage was now a sound stage. A thick layer of soundproof padding had been nailed to cover every square inch of the high walls and ceiling of the old stage. Even a new, heavy, lockable door was soundproofed to keep outside noises from the stage. The lights were set up and the camera crew had a thick padded cover around the camera. Wires ran from the camera to a portable, five-foot square, padded sound booth off to one side of the stage.

After "hellos" to old friends on the set, I shook hands with Mr. Sloman and met the stars of the picture, the lovely Joan Bennett, Harry Richman and fast-talking Jimmy Gleason.

Rehearsing a long, running scene that involved dollying the camera and moving 20 actors with many speaking lines, took a lot of time and patience. A sound level had to be taken on each voice. We rehearsed the "take" four times and just before noon the director said, "All right now, any questions? None? Then let's shoot it." I felt a little nervous. They hit the lights. The camera rolled. The scene was shot. It was okay. They killed the lights. Mr. Sloman said, "Not bad but we can do it better. Let's do it again and faster." Everything was ready again. "Hit the lights."

Three voices yelled, "Quiet on the set." "Camera rolling." "Action." In a trick shot the camera came up in a quiet, crowded elevator shooting from the back, over the riders' heads. The doors slid open, the sound of a piano playing was heard. The camera followed as the passengers moved out into the large office-set and dollied to a medium shot of me standing behind my desk sorting mail. Lined up to the front of the desk were folks waiting to speak to me.

A man says, "I want to see Mr. Wagner."

I snap, "Mr. Wagner is busy."

Another man, "Do you need a good piano player here?"

"No piano players needed."

A couple, "We want to use 'Come on Mama' in our act."

"See Jim Farrin."

Another man, "I want to have an orchestration made."

"See Harry Raymond," I say.

A stately lady says, "I have an appointment with Mr. Wagner."

I snarl, "Can't you see he's busy?"

"But I've got an appointment!"

"You've got a lot of crust too, but that don't get you by me. Sit down!" I point to a chair.

Joan Bennett steps slowly to my desk and leans forward.

I look up. "And what do you want?"

"I'd like to see someone to publish my song."

After a big laugh, "So would I." And sorted the mail.

"How about Mr. Wagner?" Joan asks.

I frown at her. "Didn't you hear me say Mr. Wagner is busy?"

"Of course, all of Manhattan heard you!" Now I'm surprised and miffed. "Are you trying to make a clown out of me?"

Joan: "Certainly not. Your parents did that!"

I fume and raise my finger at her, "Now you wait—."

Joan shakes her finger at me, "That's just what I'm going to do," and backs off and sits down.

I growl to myself, glare at her, pick up the mail from the desk and walk to the end of the hall. I hand a letter to Jimmy and Harry standing at a piano and exit the scene.

I waited, then heard the director yell, "Cut! Okay! Good scene." I joined the two men at the piano and saw the director standing by my desk with his hands in the air. He thanked everybody and signaled a big "Okay" to Harry, Jimmy and me.

Most of us silent picture actors had delivered our first lines in a talking picture! When the scene was over, we relaxed and realized that the tension created when recording a sound scene had replaced the ease and fun we had enjoyed while shooting silent pictures. There would be no more mood music on the set from the portable organ

*Now I'm surprised and miffed.
"Are you trying to make a clown
out of me?"
I fume and raise my finger at her,
"Now you wait—."*

and the violin. The director could no longer call directions and we knew making moving pictures would never be the same!

Making sound pictures was stressful and more expensive. When actors blew their lines three or four times, everybody on the set became disturbed. Many of the silent stars had no experience in reading lines. The voices of several were not suitable for recording and their careers were ended. Hollywood producers brought stage stars from New York and Chicago to make them movie stars. I guess I'd had too much fun making silent pictures to endure the new stressful way of making moving pictures talk.

I had never seen *Puttin' on the Ritz"* until 1993—63 years after it was released. One night I saw the picture listed in the *TV Guide* as an early classic sound movie. At 11:00 P.M., a little sleepy but ready, I sat waiting to see and hear myself on the "glass screen." My thoughts went back over 60 years to my junior high school days. I was going to see and hear myself as I was then. The titles came on to Irving Berlin's music. The black and white picture popped on with a silent scene of people in an elevator. The doors opened, a piano was playing and then I heard a voice—yes, it was my voice. And there, standing at my desk, I was snapping lines to actors as they approached. I had to chuckle, I didn't know why, I did not understand how I felt, so I can't explain it. I just watched and listened as I know many old actors must do.

I still like old movies best—sound and, of course, silent!

I made six more talking pictures during the early thirties:

MGM—*So This is College* with Johnny Mack Brown and Marion Davies.

FOX—*The Czar of Broadway*.

MGM—*Prosperity* with Marie Dressler.

RKO—*States Attorney* with John Barrymore.

RKO—*I'm No Angel* with Mae West.

RKO—*Wings in the Dark* with Cary Grant.

A FINAL BLOW

1932

In 1932, some twenty years after Mack Sennett built the first three-walled, open-ceiling stages on the west side of Glendale Boulevard in Edendale, a heavy windstorm hit the Los Angeles area. I took a walk to see how the neighborhood had fared. When I reached the corner of Effie Street and Glendale

Mack Sennett Studio in 1917

Boulevard, I was surprised and saddened to see the entire lot of the old studio sets had been blown down.

As I thoughtfully viewed the wreckage, I had to smile when memories came to mind of funny scenes that friends and I had played out within those now-fallen walls. The *Los Angeles Times*

In 1932, twenty years after Mack Sennett built the first three-walled, open-ceiling stages to make silent pictures in the Edendale sunlight, Hollywood was making sound pictures. That year "a strange wind of fate" blew down the first old stages. Sorrowfully, but with some early, happy memories, I took this photograph.

In 1993, I stood by the Mack Sennett studio monument. The plaque reads:

"THIS IS THE BIRTHPLACE OF MOTION PICTURE COMEDY. HERE THE GENIUS OF MACK SENNETT TOOK ROOT AND GREW TO LAUGHTER HEARD AROUND THE WORLD. HERE MOVIE HISTORY WAS MADE — HERE STARS WERE BORN — HERE REIGNED, AND STILL REIGNS, 'THE KING OF COMEDY' MACK SENNETT."

published the photo I took of the destruction along with a story about the almost-forgotten studio. Sennett had left the studio sets years earlier and the roofless structures had been left to the mercy of the weather. It was not surprising that a strong wind had knocked the flimsy, old structures to the ground.

Years later, in 1954, in Edendale, Mack Sennett, "The King of Comedy," was honored with a monument commemorating him, his studio and his creation of the world-famous Keystone Cops. I was saddened again when I saw the marker was placed on the wrong corner — at Clifford Street and Glendale Boulevard. This was actually the site of the Selig studio (the first studio built in the west) which was three blocks north of the Sennett studio location at Effie Street and Glendale Boulevard. The movie industry was never an exact science and the studio's publicity people often stretched the truth, but I thought a three-block stretch was a long one!

A STUDIO FAMILY TIE

1941

Thirty years after Gloria Swanson, the lovable, little star of early "flickers," had pressed her skirt in Coy and Goldie's kitchen, an incidental event occurred, reassuring "The Old Mack Sennett Studio Family Spirit" was real and still alive.

The incident would have gone unrecorded had it not been closely observed by Harry Evans, whose account of the scene appeared in the November 1941 issue of the *Family Circle* magazine:

At lunch, incidents in the unrehearsed drama of "The Return of Gloria Swanson" continued to pile up. On the way to the commissary (studio language for dining room) we were joined by Gloria's daughter, Gloria, and Little Gloria's husband. Her features are strikingly like her mother's, particularly her eyes. She is a charming girl and very pretty.

Our foursome was hardly seated when the visitors started coming over.

First Cary Grant. He and Gloria are old pals. Then Harold Lloyd—and that was really a reunion. But the next visitor created the most interesting moment of drama. He was a man of about 50—tall, angular, with sparse gray hair. He wore working clothes; a sweater, no tie. I saw him start to approach, then walk over to the counter. Finally he started again, reached the table in back of Miss Swanson, tapped her on the shoulder, and said "I don't suppose you remember me."

Gloria looked up, then held out both hands. "Remember you!" she cried. "Do you think I'd ever forget you? I'm so happy to see you again, and how is Gloria?"

"She's fine," the gent replied. "Married, you know."

Miss Swanson explained to us, "Mr. Watson named his first child after me." And then said to him, "How old is she now?"

"Twenty-four," said Mr. Watson, "And I think it worked—naming her after you. She's right good-looking."

When Gloria asked him if the daughter had wanted to become a movie actress, he said, "Well sort of, but I put my foot down and I did the same thing with my second one."

Gloria smiled up at him and said, "And were there any more?"

Mr. Watson looked down at something he was carrying in his hand. "Yes— seven," he said with a grin. "I was going to mention my youngest child—a boy. I - I've got a picture of him here. Thought maybe you might know about him." He slipped a photograph out of a large envelope and handed it to Gloria.

She took one look and gasped, "You mean to say he's your boy?"

Mr. Watson made no effort to hide his pride and pleasure. "So you do know him!" he said.

"Know him!" Little Gloria yelled. "Who doesn't? Why, he's wonderful!"

The little fellow in the photograph was Bobs Watson.

When we all got through telling Mr. Watson what we thought of his youngster's performance as Pee Wee in Men of Boys Town, his grin was a grand thing to see. But he did not let us get his mind off saying the piece he had come over to the table to say.

"Yes," he said, "Bobs is a good kid and I guess he's got a knack for screen acting. But let me tell you something." He turned seriously to Little Gloria. "There never was and never will be a finer person in the picture business than your mother. I was a prop-man on the Mack Sennett lot the first day she came there to work. From that day to the day she became a star, I worked on her pictures. And the bigger she became, the nicer she became. There wasn't a man on our crew who wouldn't have given her his shirt, and it still goes!"

He stopped, confused by his own sincere intensity. "Well," he said more quietly, as he turned to Gloria with a little laugh. "I just wanted to tell you how we feel about you, Miss Swanson." He held out his huge paw. "And I just want to try to let you know how much luck I'm wishing you."

Silent star Gloria Swanson during her "comeback"

He gave Gloria's hand a quick squeeze and walked away.

For a few moments none of us said a word as we watched Bobs Watson's dad stride out of the room. Then Gloria Swanson looked at me and said, "If you want to do a story about my return to the screen, there it is. To come back anywhere and find old friends who remember—I don't think there is a more wonderful experience."

It is not my object to try to sell Miss Swanson's point of view. There are, no doubt, a lot of honest people who do not believe any experience is as wonderful as gaining success and the applause that goes with it. But in the case of this woman, we must remember that she has had all the trimmings that go with the spotlight. She found them good. They brought her fame, fortune, and experience. She sat at the top of the ladder for years. Then at the height

Gloria's chair on the set

of her career she formed her own producing company and lost a lot of money—with it, a lot of so-called friends. More experience.

Now, without any warning, the business that gave her so much and took away so much has called her again. But she is no longer deceived by the siren song; she has learned to make up her own lyrics.

THAT LOVE WILL NEVER DIE

1968

One afternoon, just after Dad died in 1968, I took Mom for a ride.

"Let's ride up Morton Avenue," she asked. She wanted to see her "honeymoon cottage," the little house where she and Dad had first lived. It had been redone, but it was still there. We stopped on the hill and she pointed it out to me as she had done a couple of times before.

"It has all changed," she said. "In 1911 the neighborhood was a clean, popular, upper middle-class area."

It had changed, but Mom's memories had not.

Long after Mom died and I was 70 years old, our old home

The Watson clan on Father's Day, 1967. Back Row: Delmar, Floyd, Joe, Bill, Colleen, Denny, Susie, Gloria, Bobs, Margo, Marilyn, Peggy, Linda, and Harry. Second Row: Jim, Laura Lee, Pattie, my wife "Willie," Jill, Louise, Robb and Dan. On the wall: Vivian, Chris, Jimmy, Rod, Dad, Mom, and Priscilla holding Kimberly, Kathy and Mary. Front: Me and Garry. Photo by Billy.

The Watson Family's second home at 2217 Berkeley Avenue, Los Angeles, California

Mom and Dad looked for the good in everybody and everything and usually found it!

property was sold. I felt a strange loss. Our old house was gone. Could I live without it? Was my place of serene peace gone? I thought: the place, yes; the peace, no. Then I realized it was not the old house that had given me the sense of security, peace and hope. It was the love in the house of Dad and Mom, of my brothers and sisters. The building was nothing. Mom and Dad had made that humble dwelling into a haven with love, for love. The old buildings are still there today, but the Watsons have gone and the kids, each one, have taken that love of Coy and Goldie with them for their kids, and that love will never die.

HOLLYWOOD HONORS ONE OF THEIR OWN

1999

On April 22, 1999, a sunny Friday morning, the Watson family was given one of Hollywood's ultimate honors—a star on the "Hollywood Walk of Fame." It had been over eighty years since Dad and his horses had first appeared in early movies made in the hills surrounding Edendale, and during that time the Watsons had appeared in more than one thousand movies. And yet, over three hundred people turned out to help celebrate our Watson legacy.

Truth told, it was a bittersweet occasion for we seven surviving

Watsons. Mom and Dad, who were truly responsible for all of our accomplishments in the film industry, had passed away years earlier. My sisters, Vivian and Gloria, were also gone. My youngest brother Bobs, certainly the best known of our family, was unable to attend the event because he was bedridden and suffering from cancer. A letter writing campaign led by Hollywood columnist James Bacon and "This is Your Life" host Ralph Edwards had snowballed into a clamor for recognition, eventually convincing the committee in charge of the stars on the walk that it was time to honor the Watson Family. Many people felt that this tribute was long overdue.

A photo of the Watson family with their "Star" on the Hollywood Walk of Fame—April 23, 1999. Photo by Pattie Watson Price.

I arrived near the southeast corner of Las Palmas and Hollywood Boulevard (6674 Hollywood Blvd. to be exact) and was surprised at the number of people who had come out to share in the tribute. A riser had been set up for us and we looked into the smiling, familiar faces of friends from the many years and days of our lives. We were deeply moved when they waved to us and called our names. I didn't think so many folks would remember us; it was an emotional day to say the least. There were those with whom we had attended school and those with whom we had worked in pictures. I knew the Keystone Cops wouldn't be there so I wore my old derby hat in a tribute to those happy, fun-loving guys.

Johnny Grant, the Honorary Mayor of Hollywood, introduced the family. We were very proud when our star was unveiled. There was sincere excitement and cheering. Brother Delmar made an acceptance speech on behalf of the eleven Watsons. The most emotional moment of the day

Los Angeles Times

FRIDAY, APRIL 23, 1999

Star Shines Brightly for Hollywood's 1st Family

■ **Movies:** The Watson clan, former child actors, receives recognition for pioneering contribution to films. Four of the brothers still live in the Valley.

By BOB POOL
TIMES STAFF WRITER

Eighty-eight years and 1,000 movies later, the first family of Hollywood got some overdue credit Thursday.

The film-pioneering Watson family received its star on the Hollywood Walk of Fame as friends and fans recalled family members' contributions on both sides of the camera.

Coy, Harry, Delmar, Garry, Louise and Billy Watson unveiled their star at 6674 Hollywood Blvd. as their ailing brother Bobs listened in from home by cellular phone.

As child actors, the seven had scene-stealing roles with such stars as James Stewart, Lionel Barrymore, Fred Astaire, Shirley Temple, Katharine Hepburn and Henry Fonda.

As adults, the six Watson brothers worked as press, newsreel and television photographers during Hollywood's most colorful and freewheeling period.

There were nine Watson children in all—born 300 yards from the Mack Sennett Studio in Hollywood's Edendale area.

Their father, Coy Watson Sr., broke into show business in 1911 by breaking horses for silent cowboy star Buck Jones and then renting mounts to Hoot Gibson and Tom Mix. Eventually, he performed in two-reel pictures himself and became one of the original Keystone Kops.

Please see WATSONS, B6

RICK MEYER / Los Angeles Times

Watson family members, photo of ailing Bobs; Coy, on ground; Louise, Billy, with beard; Harry, standing; Delmar, and Garry, holding cloth, at unveiling of their Hollywood Boulevard star.

came when Delmar called Bobs on a cell phone and the entire crowd, in unison, happily shouted, "Hello Bobs."

At the conclusion of the ceremony everyone was invited to attend a buffet reception at the old "Hollywood Barn," the building in which Cecil B. DeMille made his first Hollywood moving pictures. Exhibits of early Hollywood memorabilia and a display of old still pictures, from movies in which our family had appeared, were happy reminders as we reminisced with old friends.

Mom and Dad never envisioned the big movie palaces and stars in the sidewalks along the boulevard that would become one of the world's most famous thoroughfares. They just raised one big, happy family having fun growing up, making moving pictures, in a pleasant, little place known as Edendale. Now that the Watson Family star is on the Walk of Fame, the Keystone Kid realized this was "The End". . . or perhaps a new beginning.

MORE MOVIE MEMORIES

A NICK-OF-TIME HERO

1921 • Director: Frank Griffin
Stars: Coy Watson, Jr. and Doreen Turner

ANick-of-Time Hero opens with me and
my dog as I saw and chop wood in an
orphanage yard. The superintendent and
the guards at the orphanage are mean
to the kids. I am the champion of the
orphans and get even with the guards
(one guard was played by my dad) for
the horrible things they do to the kids.
In a chase with lots of action, I play
many tricks on the guards. I pull them
up on ropes, trip them and finally throw
them all into a lake. I escape the home,
steal a locomotive and make my getaway.

In the next town, while riding a
funny, little bicycle made from a tricycle,
I meet a sweet little girl. We go to a
fireworks factory, where an accident
causes us to be carried high into the air
in a box propelled by an aerial torpedo!

After a safe landing in a wooded
area, all seems well until the girl sees a
tiger which escaped from a zoo. In fear,

Main title and cast

she runs into a cave. I go to the rescue
with a long rope, and with the help of
my pals lower myself into the cave.
They then pull both of us up to safety.

1921 • A NICK-OF-TIME HERO

My dog and I saw firewood to warm the orphanage

The girl's mother and father arrive in time to witness the feat and I proudly deliver their daughter. The folks adopt the dog, the monkey, and me—all heroes.

Now with a home, I remember my friends at the orphanage and get my new father to give all of them a party with ice cream and cake. In the last scene, the children are overjoyed. They happily mob the father in a big pile-up. Everybody is laughing. Fade out!

1921 • A NICK-OF-TIME HERO

I'm about to give a guard (my dad) a lift!

A rocket rescue saves my leading lady

1921 • A NICK-OF-TIME HERO

The guards were using their heads, but we got away!

1921 • A NICK-OF-TIME HERO

Josephine and Pal show their feelings for the guard

Doreen's dad adopts me — and she feeds me

STOLEN GLORY

1921 • Director: Frank Griffin
Stars: Coy Watson, Jr. and Doreen Turner

Fun on the banks of the L.A. River

When *Stolen Glory* begins, my pals and I have escaped from an orphanage and are living a life of ease on the banks of the Los Angeles River. I enjoy reading, and lying in a crude, self-made hammock. My dog gently swings me as it fishes the river with a pole tied to its tail and my monkey happily fans me with a homemade fan.

The scene changes. Doreen is seen bidding her wealthy parents goodbye as she

1921 • STOLEN GLORY

Stealing the glory

rides off for a drive along the river in her fancy little pony cart. A duck lands on the pony's back just as the cart nears my camp. The pony is startled and starts to run away. My dog and monkey and I see the runaway and hurry off to stop the pony, unaware we are being watched by a newsreel camera crew. I am about to catch the cart when the pony pulls it through a mud puddle. The girl faints and I fall into the puddle. The dog and monkey continue the running chase with the monkey riding on the dog's back. When the runaway passes under a bridge, the monkey drops onto the pony's back. The dog runs alongside, catching the dragging reins in his mouth and helps the monkey pull the runaway to a stop!

As I approach the cart, I realize the girl has fainted. I chase my dog and monkey—the true heroes—out of the scene. The girl revives, she sees me posed beside the pony, and assumes I am the hero of the rescue.

1921 • Stolen Glory

Doreen saves me from my sister's wrath

The next day, I pass a theater and am surprised to see a life-sized photo of myself on display standing beside the rescued pony cart. At that moment the little girl and her parents arrive to see the show and invite me to be their guest. As we walk down the aisle, the crowd cheers, recognizing me as the boy in the picture.

The lights go out and the newsreel comes on the screen. More cheers as I chase the pony cart. I stand and bow as my dog and monkey come down the theater aisle unnoticed. The film then shows me in the mud hole and the real heroes doing the rescue. The crowd hisses and boos. The father is disgusted with me.

"I still like him," Doreen says, and to my surprise she gives me a big kiss on the cheek!

1921 • STOLEN GLORY

Between scenes me, my dog, and my monkey invite Doreen for a fish dinner

We four share two sticks of candy

SCHOOL DAY LOVE

1921 • Director: Ade Linkoff
Stars: Coy Watson, Jr. and Doreen Turner

I can't get Ella onto the donkey

School-Day Love was shot at Comport's dairy ranch near Mixville, over the hill from Edendale. In the movie, my "sister" Ella and I had just a half-hour to go five miles to the little, red schoolhouse in Shady Lane. There was no school bus service.

Ella's newly acquired transportation to school is a little donkey named Hector but, because of her extremely large size, Ella has a problem getting on the donkey. I try with all my strength to put her aboard but it is "no go." Then I have a good idea!

1921 • SCHOOL DAY LOVE

But I use some quick-thinking and hoist her up!

The poor donkey collapses under Ella's weight

With the willingness and the full cooperation of her little Hector, I get Ella into the air with the help of a rope and a windlass. She is grateful and encouraging as she hangs aloft and expresses her thanks for my sincere efforts. Now she is hopeful she will make it to school on time. I carefully let the squeaky windlass unwind and

1921 • SCHOOL DAY LOVE

The Schoolmaster catches my girl, my pals and me playing hooky from school in an old storage cabin loaded with high explosives

lowers my dear sister to the back of her brave little Hector. Unfortunately, he grunts and lays down on the ground. Ella is just plain too heavy for him!

Ella cries real tears until I convince her Hector can pull her to school in a cart.

1921 • SCHOOL DAY LOVE

We survive the blast, but need a bath! Making this picture was a lot of fun!

WHILE THE DEVIL LAUGHS

1921 • Director: George W. Hill
Stars: Louise Lovely, William Scott and Coy Watson, Jr.

My family didn't appreciate my theft of an apple

My first dramatic role in a silent feature picture starred Australian actress Louise Lovely and William Scott. I played Louise's little brother. At the beginning of the picture, I steal an apple from a street vendor and bring it home to my sickly mother as big sister Mary and little sister Helen look on. I remember how much fun it was doing the scene

1921 • WHILE THE DEVIL LAUGHS

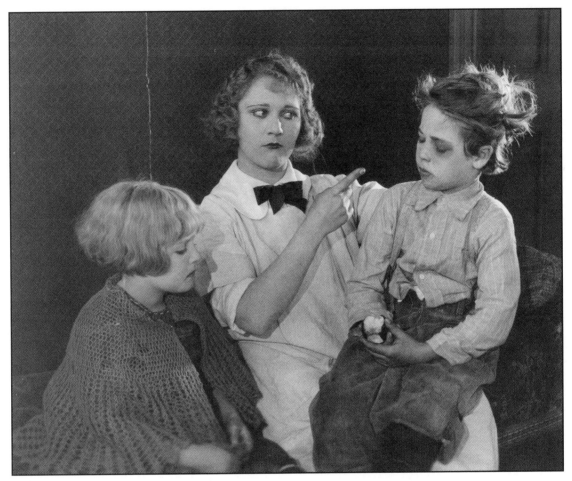

I get a stern lecture from my "sister"

where I stole the apple from a fruit wagon set up on the studio's New York Street. I liked to play a New York street kid because I didn't have to dress up—I wore ragged clothes and usually went barefoot.

My big sister and I were very close. She tried to make me into a good boy even though she herself was a thief, living a shady life working in an underworld speakeasy. Our father liked his booze and was making his own when his still blows up and sets fire to our tenement building.

1921 • WHILE THE DEVIL LAUGHS

My "sister" prays for my recovery

The fire scenes were scary—I run down the corridors of our apartment house yelling "Fire" to warn our neighbors of the danger. Smoke and flames bellow out from the rooms into the hall as I run by. Prop men were blowing "Lacapodium" (which made the flames) at me from the doorways to simulate fire burning in the rooms. I run outside and stand in the middle of the street in order to stop and direct

1921 • WHILE THE DEVIL LAUGHS

A miracle!

Me and my dummy

the approaching fire engine to our building. The fire truck strikes me and throws me to the pavement. When the fire crew attends to the fire, excited bystanders carry me to a safe room in the building.

When Mary learns I'd been seriously injured, she quickly leaves the speakeasy and hurries home to be with her little brother. She vows to "go straight" if her prayers for my recovery are answered. Her lover Billy joins her at my bedside and her prayers are answered. I come to, smile, and the picture ends happily.

Shooting the accident scene was interesting. When I ran out into the street waving my arms, the fire truck came around the corner, but before it hit me, the camera stopped turning. I was replaced by a dummy. The camera turned again and saw the truck hit the dummy. The dummy fell. After the truck hit the dummy and the camera cut, I lay in the street in the exact same position the dummy had fallen. The camera was turned on again and the people from the sidewalk picked me up and carried me out of scene.

The dummy with my papier-mâché head that stood in for the accident scene was created by the studio. I sat for a sculptor who modeled my head in clay. A plaster of Paris mold was made from the clay, and papier-mâché heads were formed in the mold. Three extra heads were ready on the set but weren't needed. The scene was made with one take!

YOU NEVER KNOW

1922 • Director: Robert Ensminger
Stars: Earle Williams, Gertrude Astor and Coy Watson, Jr.

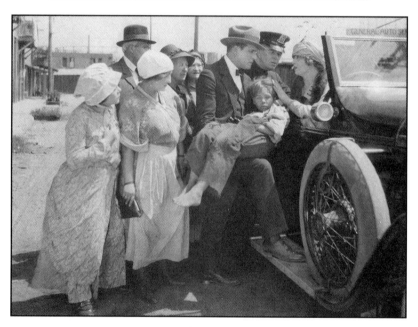

I'm hit by a car

My second feature role in a dramatic picture was a mystery story. Earle Williams is a Secret Service Agent. I am a New York street urchin living in the slums. Gertrude Astor knocks me down in the street with her car. Williams sees the accident, picks me up and carries me to the stopped car. He meets Astor. The two and a policeman realize I am okay, just shaken up a bit.

1922 • YOU NEVER KNOW

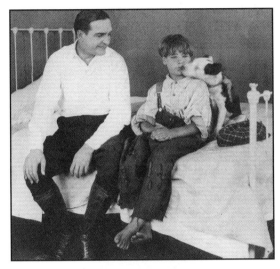

Recovering in the chauffeur's room

Williams takes me and my dog to his room where we become good friends. Williams then becomes Astor's chauffeur.

Gangsters capture Williams and hold him gagged and tied with rope in a room below the street. He has information on a big South American gunrunning plot. My dog and I see him through a small window. I climb down and untie him just as a thug comes in to get him. Williams socks the thug and we get away.

An interesting part for me with a lot of good "business" to do.

The big escape

NO LUCK

1922 • Director: Unknown
Stars: Lloyd Hamilton and Coy Watson, Jr.

Fishing the L.A. River

This movie featured star comedian Lloyd Hamilton and me fishing in the Los Angeles River. Today this beautiful spot and the entire river is a concrete storm basin.

Some kids saw us shooting the scene and snickered at me, "There's no fish in the

1922 • NO LUCK

Waiting for my big catch

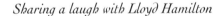
Sharing a laugh with Lloyd Hamilton

river." They were surprised when they saw the catch the prop man had put beside me. Then they ran home and got their fishing tackle!

Right after I worked on *No Luck* I caught scarlet fever from my next door playmate, Sonny Holmgren, and was quarantined for over a month. Each of my brothers and sisters came down with the fever and the house was under quarantine for six months. Not a good time for Mom. Dad was the "breadwinner" and was allowed to come in and go out of the house as long as he changed clothes each time.

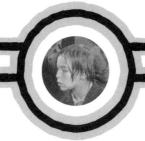

THE RIGHT OF THE STRONGEST

1923 • Director: Edgar Lewis
Stars: E.K. Lincoln, Helen Ferguson and Coy Watson, Jr.

E.K. Lincoln, me and Helen Ferguson

This film is a vivid story of life in the Alabama hills where a group of squatters are trying to drive out E.K. Lincoln, a newcomer, from their region. Helen Ferguson introduces me to Lincoln, who hires me to be his cabin keeper.

The town's mean bullies don't like Lincoln and don't want me working for him. I

1923 • THE RIGHT OF THE STRONGEST

In trouble once again

Getting pushed around by the town bullies

learn of a plot to kill my boss, so I run 10 miles through a fierce wind-and-rain storm to the camp of his company to tell his men of his plight. There is a big fistfight and a shooting death. Lincoln becomes a friend of the town folks and everybody is happy.

I enjoyed playing a good feature role in this picture.

1923 • THE RIGHT OF THE STRONGEST

Protecting Lincoln's cabin

Here I am telling Lincoln's men about the plot to kill our boss

DOROTHY VERNON OF HADDEN HALL

1924 • Director: Marshall Neilan
Stars: Mary Pickford and Estelle Taylor

My ragged costume at the beginning of the picture. At the end . . . fancy velvet duds, and a feather in my hat, when Dorothy wins Hadden Hall.

Dressed like an "Old English" street kid and later as a castle page boy, I worked for three months on Mary Pickford's *Dorothy Vernon of Hadden Hall*, while Dad worked on Doug Fairbanks' *Thief of Bagdad*. The two married stars shared one big studio on Santa Monica Boulevard. Between scenes, when I knew I wasn't needed, I would slip away from Mary's set to watch Dad do some of his piano wirework for Doug. An interesting note: In the film, I shared a scene with Miss Pickford's sister, Lottie Pickford.

IN JAIL

1924 • Director: Unknown
Stars: Charles Puffy and the Watson Kids

Charles Puffy and the Watson gang

In this film, comedian Charles Puffy and his wife are in jail long enough to have six kids. This was the first time all of the Watson kids appeared in a movie together. In our scene, we each had a hammer to match our size, and we were trying to break up the rocks.

THE GOLDEN STRAIN

1925 • Director: Victor Schertzinger
Stars: Kenneth Harlan, Madge Bellamy and Hobart Bosworth

Showing Hobart Bosworth my muscles

I play an orphan kid who applies for work at a Southern Mansion. Hobart Bosworth asks, "Are you a hard worker?" I assure him I am.

The colonel introduces me to his "spoiled" son. I accidentally knock over some of his toy soldiers and he yells unkind words at me, so I square off at him. The father

1925 • THE GOLDEN STRAIN

About to fight my future "brother"

sees his son is not manly but unreasonable and needs to learn about living and getting along, so he adopts me to be his son's brother.

The movie sees us boys grow up to become the stars of the picture and go to war. The love between the two men proves to be "The Golden Strain" that finally sees them through.

STELLA DALLAS

1925 • Director: Henry King
Stars: Belle Bennett, Jean Hersholt, Ronald Colman,
Douglas Fairbanks, Jr. and Lois Moran

Kid actor, Buck Black, and I played Belle Bennett's brothers. Scenes in her lower-class home were funny as Buck and I chased each other around the kitchen and bedroom. The funniest sequence was in the bedroom. The camera was shooting through the window. I took off my shirt and pants and stood naked with my back to the camera. Then I jumped into bed as directed. When the scene was shot, the crew and director were laughing. Mr. King said, "Good scene Coy. I hope you won't be embarrassed when this runs on the screen." I was not.

I didn't see the picture until 1994 at a summer showing of old silent pictures at a college campus amphitheater in North San Diego County. The crowd laughed and looked my way because I had been introduced before the picture was shown. It was an unusual evening. Also in attendance was Belle Bennett's grandson, Ted Bruner, of Carlsbad, California.

1925 • STELLA DALLAS

Belle Bennett surrounded by children that had worked with her in pictures. We had all gotten together at a
party at her home in Beverly Hills one summer Sunday afternoon. She sent an autographed photo to each
of the children stating: "In this world is darkness. So we must shine: You in your corner. I in mine. Belle."
That's me next to the arrow. Buck Black is to my left.

QUALITY STREET

1927 • Director: Sidney Franklin
Stars: Marion Davies, Conrad Nagel and Helen Eddy

Left to right: Helen Eddy, me, Mickey McBan, Marion Davies

The movie features an 1815 school room scene in England. During a fight between Mickey McBan and me, I'm supposed to receive a bloody nose. Helen consoles me, the "bully," while Marion is in Mickey's corner. The class of boys like the fight. I thought it was better than studying. The blood under my nose, a thick mixture of cranberry juice, was from a bottle out of the prop box. I didn't mind letting Mickey beat me in the scene. He was a good, little kid and, after all, I was playing the "bully."

LOVE MAKES 'EM WILD

1927 • Director: Albert Ray
Stars: John Harron, Lois Wilson and Arthur Housman

Me, Arthur Housman, Lois Wilson and John Harron

This was the first office comedy in which I played the part of an office boy. I enjoyed working for Al Ray. The Assistant Director told me, "Mr. Ray likes you because you behave and do as he directs you." I guess it was true. I made three pictures for him and went to school in the studio school room on the lot. Mr. Farrell, a nice guy, was the teacher. Between scenes I did wood-working in the room.

RICH BUT HONEST

1927 • Director: Albert Ray
Stars: Charles Morton, Nancy Nash and Ben Bard

Charles Morton, Ben Bard and lady employees look on as I clown around with a bolt of fabric

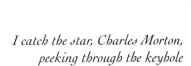

I catch the star, Charles Morton, peeking through the keyhole

I'd spend a week to ten days on a picture like this. Attending Thomas Starr King Junior High School at the time, I had to get in three hours of study each day.

BARE KNEES

1927 • Director: Clyde Carruth
Stars: Fox Gang Comedy Kids

Left to right: Jimmy VanHorn, me, A.J., Chang, Wayne LaFever and Harry Watson (my little brother). We were brought together for this particular picture, the second of a series of "Kid Comedies." In 1917–18 Fox had made a series of kid comedies and these 1927 pictures were the first Fox made since that time.

This movie was shot on Fox Hill Ranch, where cowboy star Buck Jones's horse, Silver Dollar, was kept, as were all the studio's horses, cattle, wagons, buckboards and farm equipment. The ranch covered over 40 acres and is now a part of Century City.

1927 • BARE KNEES

FOX FILM CORPORATION
HOLLYWOOD, CALIFORNIA
PHONE: HOLLY 3000

THIS

Engagement Agreement

MADE UNDER THE FOLLOWING CONDITIONS:

1. *A week under this agreement consists of seven actual working days.*

2. *When an artist or employee is engaged for one picture only, salary does not begin to accrue until the artist or employee actually starts working in the picture and ceases the day artist or employee finishes part in picture.*

3. *The employer, in its discretion, reserves the right to make alterations, changes, substitutions, additions and eliminations in the scenario or picture, or any part thereof, and the term of employment hereunder is subject to the exercise of such right.*

4. *The services hereunder shall be under the direction and control and to the satisfaction of the employer.*

5. *When an artist or employee is sent away from Los Angeles, salary is not paid for time consumed in travel unless artist or employee has actually started work on the picture before leaving.*

6. *The employee will return to work at same salary rate for such retakes or additional scenes as may be necessary.*

7. *Wardrobe, except for costume parts, to be furnished by employee.*

8. *If, prior to or during production, work shall be postponed by causes outside of the employer's control, the employment may be terminated or postponed at the employer's option. This right shall be in addition to, independent of, and not in limitation of any other right of the employer hereunder.*

Name __Coy Watson, Jr.__ Production No. __Carruth #__

Address __2211 Berkely Ave.__ Character __Gang__

Phone __Dr. 3616__

SALARY ARRANGEMENTS

$ __100.00__ per __week__

__One hundred and no-100- - - - - - - - -__ Dollars per __week__

Accepted as the entire Contract of Employment.

FOX FILM CORPORATION

Date __December 24th, 1927.__

FORM 37

A Fox Studio Engagement Agreement—Dad went with me on interviews and together we would decide if I wanted to take the part. Dad signed the contracts as I was under age.

WILD PUPPIES

1927 • Director: Clyde Carruth
Stars: Fox Gang Comedy Kids

That's me in the white shirt

An on-going fight between the bully-boys and the sissy-smart boys caused most of the action in this movie. To get behind a fence, unaware of what was on the other side, we "toughies" dug a tunnel. We wanted to come up from behind and attack the "sissies" from the rear. Very surprised, we came up in a lion's enclosure!

When I had my back to the lion, I wasn't worried. Charlie Gay (the lion trainer) told us not to make any fast moves with our arms or legs and the lion wouldn't bother us. We moved very, very slowly. I could feel the lion's whiskers on my face and his breath on my neck. When I turned to look at him, he was looking at me! That was a little scary. It was the only time Jack and I worked in a scene and didn't kid around.

Much time was spent getting the lion to remain between us and to look at us. Charlie

1927 • WILD PUPPIES

Lined up for a publicity photo. We kids made a good "gang" and enjoyed working together. Left to right: Jimmy Van Horn, Annabell Magness, Jack McHugh, Wayne LaFever, me, Chang, Leon and A.J.

was cueing the lion off-camera and we waited for the cue to do our action. The crew was particularly quiet. The only movement was the cameraman's hand turning the crank. Reflectors were used to put sunlight in the shadows on our faces.

It took a special team to work with kids and lions. This crew was great and everybody worked well, even though there were a dozen kids on the set. Director Clyde

1927 • WILD PUPPIES

Seated: Director Clyde Carruth. Right of camera: Ray Wise

Carruth had been a tough kid in his youth and I felt he enjoyed talking with Jack and me. We joked a lot and it made the work fun.

It took us more than an hour to drive to Gays Lion Farm from Fox Studio at Sunset Boulevard and Western Avenue. A truck hauled all the shooting equipment. The crew, we kids and our folks followed in cars.

The closing scene in the picture got a lot of laughs because it showed McHugh and me, the "toughies," trapped in a small lion cage with the smart "sissy" kids happily throwing rotten fruits and vegetables at us. The bars of the cage broke the flying produce into small pieces and covered us with a thick layer of sticky, stinking garbage. The crew nearly died laughing at us.

Jack and I never forgot that scene and 53 years later, over lunch in Stockton, California, we relived the entire picture.

TAXI 13

1927 • Director: Marshall Neilan
Stars: Martha Sleeper, Chester Conklin, Louise Fazenda,
Louise Carver and the Watson childern

Seven of the ten kids that appeared in the pictures as Chester Conklin's family were Watson family members. Left to right: Me, my friend Godfrey "Duffy" Craig, Vivian Watson, Gloria Watson, George Dunning, Louise Watson, Harry Watson, Jackie Sturnberg, Billy Watson, Delmar Watson. The photo was taken on a New York Street set at FBO Studio. "Duffy" Craig and I became good friends and spent weekends together.

Dad was working for Mack Sennett when all the kids were born and the "Sennett Studio Family" was always interested when another Watson arrived. When Gloria was born, Dad named her after Gloria Swanson. Two years later, when little Louise

1927 • TAXI 13

Left to right: Louise Carver, the Watson kids — Billy, Louise, Delmar, Garry and Gloria — Chester Conklin and Louise Fazenda. In background: Tom Kennedy.

arrived, Dad named her after another Mack Sennett movie veteran, Louise Fazenda.

After many years of not seeing each other, it was a great reunion for our family to get together and work in a picture with family friends from our Edendale neighborhood. Louise Carver, Louise Fazenda, Tom Kennedy and Chester Conklin were "Sennett Studio Family" that hadn't seen or worked with the Watson family for many years. Thanks to *Taxi 13* for bringing us together again.

1927 • TAXI 13

A 1932 publicity photo at Warner Bros. Studio. The gang clowning for Mom and Dad, as Delmar grinds the camera. Delmar had just finished good parts in two pictures: We Three *with Ben Lyon and Rose Hobart, and* Outside the Law *with Edward G. Robinson. That's Mom holding Bobs.*

BUTTONS

1927 • Director: George W. Hill
Stars: Jackie Coogan, Lars Hansen, Gertrude Olmsted,
Paul Hurst and Polly Moran

In the script, Jackie Coogan and I start off as friends

This was a vivid story of life aboard a modern Atlantic ocean liner. Fifty boys played seagoing bellhops. It was the third of eight pictures I made at MGM.

1927 • BUTTONS

I was Brutus, the Captain's "Tiger."
Jackie wanted to be the "Tiger" so
he cut the seat out of my pants.
When I couldn't report for duty,
he took my job.

Side gate to "The Big Lion's Studio" (MGM).

    While working on the picture, I was pleased to become friends with Captain Burton, formerly of the Royal Air Force, WW I, and an official of a British Steamship Line. He was the technical advisor on the picture to assure the accuracy of the actions regarding the life and duties of the bellhops. He had been one of the first Boy Scouts when Sir Baden Powell started the movement in England. He was proud to tell me stories about some of the men who were the first scouts and how they fought and died in the First World War.

1927 • BUTTONS

We weren't friends anymore and I got tough

A fight was stopped by Paul Hurst. He was the Yankee soldier in Gone With the Wind *who Scarlet O'Hara shot in the face. He was a good guy to work with.*

THE SMART SET

1928 • Director: Jack Conway
Stars: William Haines, Alice Day, Jack Holt,
Hobart Bosworth and Coy Watson, Jr.

Me and William Haines share a sad moment

This is a picture about polo with actual footage of the big game between England and America as the climax. It is the heart-warming story of a horse and groom involved in winning the big match.

Billy Haines is Tommy, a wealthy, conceited polo player. Alice is Polly, Tommy's girlfriend. Arriving at Midwich Polo Field for work at 7:00 A.M. dressed, made-up, and ready to work wasn't easy. Putting on make-up for all of my pictures was the part of the "game" I didn't particularly like.

1928 • THE SMART SET

William Haines and me in happier circumstances

William Haines and Alice Day celebrate Billy's polo victory while I look on

At home on a cold morning, rubbing on flesh-colored make-up from a hard stick of M. Stein's Theatrical Stage Grease Paint was tough. Then I lined my eyebrows with a black liner pencil. To make my small eyes look larger, I applied green eye shadow to my eyelids and a thin, black line just above and below my eyelashes. With a big power puff, I applied enough powder to keep the grease paint from shining. After lunch, with a mirror, I checked my make-up for smears and powdered again.

At home, before dinner, I had to take off the make-up with lots of cold cream and a towel and then scrub with plenty of hot water and soap. If I was working a picture barefooted, I had to stand in the bathtub with hot water and scrub some more.

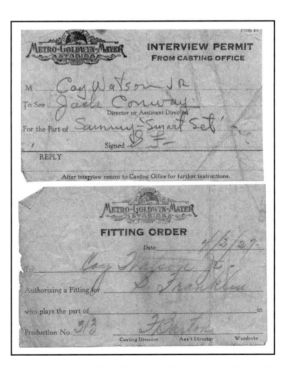

Interview pass and fitting order for the groom's outfit

SHOW PEOPLE

1928 • Director: King Vidor
Stars: Marion Davies and William Haines

Director Harry Gribbon (with the cap) stands with Marion Davies and William Haines (with the mustache) and Kalla Pasha (in the chef's hat) and discusses a pie-throwing sequence

Douglas Fairbanks, me, and Marion Davies

Show People was one of the last feature-length silent comedies made, showing the fun early movie-makers had producing slap-stick comedies. Director-Producer King Vidor knew that with the help of some of Mack Sennett's original Keystone comedians, he could produce a classic, silent feature comedy, and he did!

The story is about a young girl, Peggy Pepper, from a small town who comes to Hollywood hoping to be a movie star. She is discovered and makes a name for herself as a comedienne in comedies, but she wants to be a dramatic star. The public doesn't like her as a dramatic actress—they preferred her in comedies—and it becomes the

1928 • SHOW PEOPLE

The boss blows up at me and starts yelling

I listen scared—wide-eyed with open mouth

duty of the studio manager to tell Peggy the news. Her pictures are losing money at the box office, and she must go back to making comedies. At noon, the manager sends his office boy (me) to the commissary to tell her to come to his office.

In the commissary, at a long table, sitting side-by-side, 16 of Hollywood's biggest stars are seen enjoying lunch in a long pan-shot: Polly Moran, Dorothy Sebastian, Estelle Taylor, Claire Windsor, Aileen Pringle, Karl Dane, George K. Arthur, Leatrice Joy, Renee Adoree, Rod La Rocque, Mae Murray, John Gilbert, Norma Talmadge, and at the end of the table, Douglas Fairbanks, Marion Davies (as "Peggy") and Wm. S. Hart.

Acting very sophisticated (in a sub-title) she answers, "Tell him I am having lunch." A bit surprised at her reply, I go to a nearby phone to give the boss my report. "She's eatin'." The boss blows up at me and starts yelling. Boy is he angry. I listen, scared and wide-eyed with open mouth in fear of losing my job and my life! He wants "Peggy" in his office right now. I hang up the phone.

Visibly shaken, I return to the table and quickly tell her, "The boss says you'll have plenty of time to eat when he gets through talking to you." Disgusted, "Peggy" excuses herself. I pull out her chair, and she leaves to go see the boss.

When we shot my telephone scene, Mr. Vidor sat off-camera directing and feeding me the lines the boss could have been saying to me. I hear "The boss didn't like your report from "Peggy" and he's mad at you. 'Can't you do as you're told?' He wants you to get her to his office NOW! Do you hear that? Nod your head, Yes! Yes! Yes! You're scared—look scared—with big eyes and open mouth. Ham it up! Take it big! You're gonna get fired. Is that what you want! Good! All right, hang up and go back to 'Peggy'—out of the scene. CUT." When we finished, Mr. Vidor was smiling at me and said, "O.K. that was good, Coy."

Other Keystone alumni appearing in the movie were Polly Moran, Charles Chaplin, and Lew Cody. King Vidor even acted in the last scene. Dad and I felt complimented that Mr. Vidor had selected me to work in the scene with Marion at the end of the long, one-take-pan with the sixteen stars and the bit at the phone.

WHITE EAGLE

1933 • Director: Orville Dull
Stars: Buck Jones, Gladys McConnell, Vester Pegg and eight tough boys

Buck and his new, young friends salute each other in the woods as his horse, Silver Dollar, looks on. That's me, second from left.

Cowboy Buck Jones encounters a man living a meager life with his eight sons in a rundown shack. Buck and the boys become good friends and he buys them Boy Scout uniforms.

A group of bad men plot to disrupt and take over Buck's stagecoach business. The boys learn of the plot and set out to bring about justice in their own way.

1933 • WHITE EAGLE

One night, we discovered the leading bad guy was pretending to be a friend of Buck's girlfriend. With Gladys' help we overpowered him and held him for the sheriff. In back are Jack McHugh, Leon Holmes and Rusty Tolbert. On the floor: little Harry Spear, me, Billy Butts, George Dunning and Monty O'Grady with the villain.

We boys in the "Tin Lizzy" chased a bad guy two miles outside of Bishop where I roped him. Vester Pegg played the bad guy. In his younger days he was one of the cowboys who toured Europe with the world-famous "Buffalo Bill Show." I had practiced roping and caught him the first try. That's me in car with lasso.

1933 • WHITE EAGLE

We hog-tied the bad guy, threw him into the Ford and took him to the sheriff. This was an ideal picture for a group of boys to work on. We had a lot of running gags and ribbed each other all the time. During serious scenes we sometimes made wise cracks to try to make each other laugh.

The "company" at lunch around the chuck wagon. Judd Steven, the owner, with a helper prepared our lunches. The wagon was a mobile kitchen with hot plates, chopping boards and storage space for food. Judd lived up the street from us on Berkeley Avenue and drove his chuck wagon to various location shoots for all the studios. Left to right: At the end of the table, Director "Bunny" Dull; Gladys McConnell seated in a white dress; Buck Jones, standing in white shirt; Jack McHugh and Rusty Tolbert, in front of car; me and my Dad front right. I'm sorry I don't remember more names of the people I knew while working on the picture.

COY'S PICTURES

Year	Title (Studio)	Stars	Director
1913	*The Price of Silence* (Selig)	Dorothy Phillips, Lon Chaney Sr., Jack Mulhall	Joseph De Grasse
1914	*Fatty's Gift* (Keystone)	Roscoe "Fatty" Arbuckle, Minta Arbuckle	Roscoe "Fatty" Arbuckle
1915	*The Mailman* (LKO)	Mack Swain	Henry Lehrman
1916	*The Show* (Vitagraph)	Larry Semon	Unknown
1920	*Kid Gang Pictures* (Fox)	Fox Kids	Unknown
1920	*Pals & Petticoats* (Fox)	Unknown	Harry Williams
1921	*The Lady of Quality* (Universal)	Virginia Valli, Lionel Belmore	Hobart Henley
1921	*Assorted Heroes* (Fine Arts)	Kids and Animals	William S. Campbell
1921	*A Nick-of-Time Hero* (Fine Arts)	Coy Watson, Jr., Doreen Turner	Frank Griffin
1921	*Stolen Glory* (Fine Arts)	Coy Watson, Jr., Doreen Turner	Frank Griffin
1921	*School Day Love* (Fine Arts)	Coy Watson, Jr., Doreen Turner	Ade Linkoff
1921	*While the Devil Laughs* (Fox)	Louise Lovely, William Scott, Coy Watson, Jr.	George W. Hill
1921	*Partners in Fate* (Fox)	Louise Lovely	Bernard Durning
1922	*You Never Know* (Vitagraph)	Earle Williams, Gertrude Astor, Coy Watson, Jr.	Robert Ensminger
1922	*No Luck* (Arrow)	Lloyd Hamilton, Coy Watson, Jr.	Unknown
1922	*Bull and Sand* (Keystone)	Bull Montana	Del Lord
1923	*The Hunchback of Notre Dame* (Universal)	Lon Chaney, Patsy Ruth Miller	Wallace Worsley
1923	*The Right of the Strongest* (Universal)	E.K. Lincoln, Helen Ferguson, Coy Watson, Jr.	Edgar Lewis
1923	*Doggone Wedding* (Fox)	Unknown	Eddie Cline
1923	*Little Johnny Jones* (First National)	Johnny Hines, Margaret Seddon, Molly Malone	Arthur Rosson
1924	*Dorothy Vernon of Hadden Hall* (Mary Pickford)	Mary Pickford, Estelle Taylor	Marshall Neilan
1924	*Honeymoon Hardships* (Keystone)	Ray McKee, Alice Day, Billy Bevan, Sunshine Hart	Del Lord
1924	*In Jail* (Universal)	Charles Puffy, Watson Kids	Unknown
1924	*On the Threshold* (Paramount)	Ronald Colman, Vilma Bankey	Unknown
1925	*Savages of the Sea* (Universal)	Frank Merrill, Marguerite Snow	Bruce Mitchell
1925	*Stella Dallas* (Paramount)	Belle Bennett, Jean Hersholt, Ronald Colman, Douglas Fairbanks, Jr., Lois Moran	Henry King
1925	*His Majesty Bunker Bean* (Warner Bros.)	Matt Moore, Dorothy Devore, David Butler	Harry Beaumont
1925	*The Golden Strain* (Fox)	Kenneth Harlan, Madge Bellamy, Hobart Bosworth	Victor Shertzinger

Year	Title (Studio)	Stars	Director
1925	*The Dark Angel* (Goldwyn)	Ronald Colman, Vilma Bankey	George Fitzmaurice
1925	*Some Pun'kins* (Charles Ray)	Charles Ray, Watson Family	Jerome Storn
1926	*Fig Leaves* (Fox)	George O'Brien; Olive Borden	Howard Hawks
1926	*A Regular Scout* (R.K.O.)	Fred Thomson, Olive Hasbrouck	David Kirkland
1927	*Willie the Worm* (Fox)	John Harron	Albert Ray
1927	*Love Makes 'em Wild* (Fox)	John Harron, Lois Wilson, Arthur Housman	Albert Ray
1927	*Rich but Honest* (Fox)	Charles Morton, Nancy Nash, Ben Bard	Albert Ray
1927	*High School Hero* (Fox)	Nick Stuart, Sally Phipps	David Butler
1927	*The Fair Co-ed* (MGM)	Marion Davies, John Mack Brown	Sam Wood
1927	*Quality Street* (MGM)	Marion Davies, Conrad Nagel, Helen Eddy	Sidney Franklin
1927	*One Woman Idea* (Fox)	Marceline Day, Rod La Rocque	Berthold Viertel
1927	*Publicity Madness* (Fox)	Lois Moran, Edmund Lowe	Albert Ray
1927	*Wild Puppies* (Fox)	Fox Gang Comedy Kids	Clyde Carruth
1927	*Taxi 13* (F.B.O.)	Martha Sleeper, Chester Conklin, Louise Fazenda, Louise Carver, Watson Kids	Marshall Neilan
1927	*The Shamrock and the Rose* (Chadwick)	Mack Swain, Dot Farley, Maurice Costello	Jack Nelson
1927	*The Callahans and the Murphys* (MGM)	Marie Dressler, Polly Moran, Watson Kids	George W. Hill
1927	*Buttons* (MGM)	Jackie Coogan, Lars Hansen, Gertrude Olmsted, Paul Hurst, Polly Moran	George W. Hill
1928	*Blue Skies* (Fox)	Frank Albertson, Helen Twelvetrees	Alfred Werker
1928	*Restless Youth* (Columbia)	Marceline Day, Ralph Forbes	Christy Cabanne
1928	*The Smart Set* (MGM)	William Haines, Alice Day, Hobart Bosworth, Coy Watson, Jr., Jack Holt	Jack Conway
1928	*No Camping* (Columbia)	Donald Haines	George Marshal
1928	*Bare Knees* (Fox)	Fox Gang Comedy Kids	Clyde Carruth
1928	*Telling the World* (MGM)	William Haines	Sam Wood
1928	*Show People* (MGM)	Marion Davies, William Haines	King Vidor
1929	*A Song of Kentucky* (Fox)	Lois Moran, Joseph Wagstaff	Lewis Seiler
1929	*Her Private Life* (First National)	Billie Dove, Walter Pidgeon, Thelma Todd, Zasu Pitts	Alexander Korda
1929	*Nix on Dames* (Fox)	Mae Clarke, Robert Ames	Donald Gallagher
1929	*So This is College* (MGM)*	Elliott Nugent	Robert Montgomery
1930	*The Czar of Broadway* (Fox)*	John Wray, Betty Compson	William James Craft
1930	*Puttin' On the Ritz** (United Artists)	Harry Richman, Joan Bennett, Jimmy Gleason	Ed Sloman
1932	*Prosperity* (MGM)*	Marie Dressler, Polly Moran, Anita Page	Sam Wood
1932	*State's Attorney* (R.K.O.)*	John Barrymore, Helen Twelvetrees, William Boyd	George Archainbaud
1933	*White Eagle* (Fox)	Buck Jones, Gladys McConnell, Vester Pegg	Orville Dull
1933	*I'm No Angel* (RKO)*	Mae West, Cary Grant	Wesley Ruggles
1935	*Wings in the Dark* (RKO)*	Cary Grant, Myrna Loy	James Flood

*Sound on Film

INDEX

OF MOVIES & MOVIE PERSONALITIES

Books Available From Santa Monica Press